James Solomon

James Solomon Russell

*Former Slave, Pioneering Educator
and Episcopal Evangelist*

WORTH EARLWOOD NORMAN, JR.

McFarland & Company, Inc., Publishers
Jefferson, North Carolina, and London

ISBN 0-7864-6789-1 (softcover : 50# alkaline paper)

LIBRARY OF CONGRESS CATALOGUING-IN-PUBLICATION DATA ARE AVAILABLE

BRITISH LIBRARY CATALOGUING DATA ARE AVAILABLE

On the cover: *inset* James Solomon Russell (courtesy of Russell
Memorial Library, Saint Paul's College, Lawrenceville, Virginia);
background © 2012 Shutterstock

Manufactured in the United States of America

*McFarland & Company, Inc., Publishers
Box 611, Jefferson, North Carolina 28640
www.mcfarlandpub.com*

To my wife Patricia,
to our children
Michael, Curtis, and Cynthia,
and in memory of my parents
Curtis "Kurkee" Lee Jones Norman,
a native of Lawrenceville, Virginia,
and Worth E. "Doc" Norman

Acknowledgments

Ms. Deborah Price, archivist at the Russell Memorial Library, Saint Paul's College in Lawrenceville, Virginia, and Mr. Christopher Pote, archivist for the African American Episcopal Historical Collection at the Bishop Payne Library of the Virginia Theological Seminary in Alexandria, Virginia, deserve initial recognition and high praise for the assistance they provided me. Both schools' archives are rich in historical documentation and both archivists were instrumental in providing me with much of the core material used in this book. Both Price and Pote are professionals of the highest order.

Dr. Benjamin King, my advisor and assistant professor of theology at the School of Theology at the University of the South in Sewanee, Tennessee, provided the appropriate guidance in my pursuit of the life of James Solomon Russell when working on the Master of Sacred Theology degree. A stickler for detail, and insistent on accuracy on content and language, Dr. King encouraged his senior (meaning my old age of 66 at the time) student to continue his studies after graduation. And so I have.

My wife Patricia not only supported my wish over the years to write a book, but contributed to the content of this book with her astute criticism and as my "first editor."

Table of Contents

Preface

O N JUNE 14, 1962, A THURSDAY NIGHT, I graduated from Norview High School in Norfolk, Virginia. It was, of course, a happy event. But it was also an historical event. When I was about to enter my high school freshman class in 1958, the governor of the Commonwealth of Virginia closed all of the state's schools that had been ordered by the federal government to be racially integrated. That was the period of Virginia's "Massive Resistance." With our public school doors chained — not just Norview but Granby and Maury high schools— the white community set up schools around the city. In my neighborhood, three churches allowed the use of their buildings for temporary schools. In the Five Points section of the Norview community there were three large churches: Norview Presbyterian Church, Norview Baptist Church, and Norview Methodist Church. All of these churches became temporary schools in the fall of 1958. Not all of the students attended these church schools. Some moved away to live with family members in the western part of Virginia which was not affected by the closures. Many went out of state. But I settled into my new high school, Norview Methodist Church. Many of our regular high school teachers taught in those temporary church schools as if the high school had never closed. So we didn't miss a beat, academically. The Norview High School Band still rehearsed in the afternoons for football games, and the football team practiced each week for their upcoming games. And despite the interruptions, the Norview HS football team became the best team in the state of Virginia over the four years until graduation in 1962.

My class studies in the church school were the same as if I had entered the official high school. The "colored" students (as they were called then) who were selected by the school board to attend the previously all-white schools were tutored at the First Baptist Church on Bute Street in downtown Norfolk. We all waited on the outcome of the huge political battle between the governor of Virginia and the United States Department of Justice. Eventually Virginia complied with the Federal court order and the city's schools opened in January 1959. That first day — that first day of integration — presented itself as a mass of humanity converging on almost every square foot of Norview's campus. Of the seventeen colored students selected, seven were assigned to Norview.

I lived on Sewells Point Road directly across from the high school. Never did I have to ride buses to schools during my twelve years of public education — I walked. But the colored students near our neighborhood, who, ironically, lived behind the high school in a section named Oakwood, had to ride school system–chartered commercial buses across town to attend Booker T. Washington High School or Ruffner Junior High. Those buses passed by my house every school morning and afternoon. But on the day of reckoning — in January 1959 — seven African American students entered Norview High School, and so did I.

Of the new students, the one who was most memorable to me was Andrew Heidelberg. My personal history with colored people made them somewhat familiar to me, but attending school with them was simply expected to be different, and I didn't know what to make of it. I remember Andrew fairly well because the two of us were in many classes together and in our senior year we were in the same homeroom. He was athletic, but that is not the attribute I remember most. He had personality and was not shy. Or so it seemed. He was certainly assertive in spirit but allowed himself no aggressiveness, which, according to our expectations, would have been natural for a Negro in a strange place, or so I thought at the time. It was only later in life that I learned that Andrew was mortified at attending the previously all-white school; he was scared to death. From my point of view, he was successful in his high school career despite the many obstacles placed before him. He and the other African-American students had to have been brave. I know, because I recall hearing ferocious verbal attacks thrown at them. But Andrew appeared to brush them off. Such was the image I have held for all these years in the back of my mind. Why do I write about this experience now in 2012?

In the spring of 1965 or 1966, I cannot remember precisely, while stationed at Marine Corps Schools in Quantico, Virginia, I thought I saw Andrew. A regional college sporting event was taking place at the base. I was a military musician returning, in formation, to my barracks from the opening ceremonies at the football field. Out of the corner of my eye I thought I saw Andrew, so I cocked my head slightly to the left and looked directly. It *was* Andrew. So I yelled "Heidelberg" as loud as I could. He looked up to find who bellowed his name, but with seventy military musicians in uniform marching past him, it would have been difficult to pick out a single voice. And after the band was dismissed I walked to the athletic field to find him. I never did.

For more than forty years afterward I forgot about Massive Resistance and all that went on during my high school days. As I began studying James Solomon Russell, and through the rigors of that process of research and learning, my youthful and adult experiences with matters racial returned to my mind. One day last year I connected with friends (from high school days) on one of the Internet-based social media websites, some of whom were connected with Andrew Heidelberg. Well, you know what I had to do. I made the connection with Andrew and we exchanged several Internet-based chats. Although he recalled that particular Quantico sporting event, he did not remember my yell. This, however, was sufficient verification for me.

Andrew told me that he had written a book* about his experiences from 1958 to 1962. Naturally, his experiences were totally different from mine. There was so much that I did not know; so much that escaped my attention; so much activity that I thought would never have happened. It was an awakening for me. For those days in the late '50s and early '60s were dark for many. Hopefully Andrew and I will meet again before our times come to an end. In the meantime, I struggle with my own thoughts. My high school experience was one factor in my research on James Solomon Russell.

Although now mostly unknown, James Solomon Russell was a key person in the post–Reconstruction educational movement with former slaves in Virginia. Russell was a double-sided entrepreneur: his educational venture produced what is now Saint Paul's College in Lawrenceville, Virginia; and in his spiritual and religious life he was at the center of developing the largest convocation of African-American churches in the Episcopal Church. Why study Russell?

Russell's life was, seemingly, lived mostly "under the radar" as we would say in the twenty-first century. Although he wrote his *Autobiography*,† other people wrote three academic theses (one Ph.D. dissertation and two masters' theses) about either Russell himself or Saint Paul's College. Several articles have been written about the man and his work. Russell is remembered mostly in a small quarter of the African-American community, the Episcopal Church, and the Southside Virginia region. Why was Russell important to me, important enough to write about?

In the year 2000 I began my serious investigation of Russell. There were two reasons motivating my research. The initial reason, and at the time the only reason, that I began my study was due to my mother. During my child-

---

*Andrew I. Heidelberg, The Norfolk 17: A Personal Narrative on Desegregation in Norfolk, Virginia in 1958–1962 (Pittsburgh: Rose Dog Press, 2006).

†The single word Autobiography, in italics, is used in this book as a substitute label for the book Adventure in Faith: An Autobiographic Story of St. Paul Normal and Industrial School, Lawrenceville, Virginia (New York: Morehouse, 1936).

hood she would talk about Dr. Russell, off and on. But her talk was frequent enough and so consistent in its content over the years that it must have made an indelible impression in the back of my mind. My mother was born and reared in Lawrenceville, Virginia, and to her Lawrenceville was idyllic and the perfect place to grow up. She did not stay there for long after her high school graduation and eventually moved to Norfolk, where I was born in 1944. For eighteen years of my life mother would talk of Lawrenceville and Russell and, of course, we traveled the short ninety miles to visit family over the years. So when I began my investigation of Russell it was a project taken up in my own old age. My initial output was a thesis for a master's degree in sacred theology from the School of Theology at Sewanee, the University of the South. I was awarded that degree at age sixty-six, and I knew that I could not stop with just the thesis; I had to study more because something happened to me during the project.

As I wrote above, my mother provided the initial motivation for my study of Dr. Russell. But it was my engagement with that study that brought to light my second motivation — my high school experience and its attending race problem. Why do we have race problems in the United States? In 2011, 150 years following the start of the American Civil War, our nation is recalling those years when we were divided. Did the North and the South really reconcile? Have we as a nation learned anything over these years? Am I learning anything which might shed light on our continuing national predicament? It came to me that if I could attempt to fix James Solomon Russell within the context of his circumstances, his history, then perhaps I could identify the parameters of my own experience. Little things that my mother told me about Lawrenceville and Russell have stayed with me. For example, Russell was really white in complexion, but he lived as a black man. He was the nicest man in town. My mother and one of her sisters were telephone operators. In those days there were no push-button or rotary-dial telephones. The caller had to speak with a telephone company operator in order to place a call. On more than one occasion, my mother and her sister Willie would tell stories about directing calls to the "Archdeacon." (Many, if not most, of the Lawrenceville locals referred to Russell as the Archdeacon.) Almost without fail the Archdeacon, after finishing his telephone conversation, would reconnect with the dispatching operator (my mother or one of my aunts) to thank them for placing the earlier, usually long-distance, connection. My grandfather, Fredrick Lewis Jones, owned and operated the grocery store in Lawrenceville. He conducted business with the St. Paul School and Dr. Russell. My grandfather died in 1952 and whenever we visited him he always had a nice story to tell about the Archdeacon.

Russell's *Autobiography* is just one resource that I have studied to understand his life. His addresses, sermons, and work logs also provide clues to his approach to living. He cites four situations where he is mistaken for a white man, yet he pleads no interest in nor has available time for ancestor worship or genealogy search. He was a man about tasks and projects, both secular and ecclesiastical. He was often presented with many vexing situations during his lifetime, many situations filled with manifestations of racism. He successfully dealt with black and white alike. He argued with and challenged both. Of concern in this book is Russell's statement that the mass exodus of former slaves from the Episcopal Church was a mistake. Though it was understandable, why did Russell deem it a mistake? He exhibited the patience of Job in some of his judgments which may have led some to call him an "accomodationist," a term some would link with "compromised" as it was applied to Booker T. Washington. But how Russell handled his situations is instructive.

James Solomon Russell certainly was a pioneer in post–Reconstruction education for former slaves and their families, and he was a principled leader in the reconstruction or reordering of ecclesiastical attitudes of racism played out in canonical manipulations and justifications. The simple fact that Russell was born and reared in Virginia is also significant. Virginia, the colony and then the state that produced Washington, Jefferson, and Madison, generated the new American republic and its ideas of freedom. Virginia also produced Booker T. Washington, Robert Russa Moton, and James Solomon Russell. How Virginia as a state worked through its racial situations, and how the Episcopal Church in Virginia did the same, formed Russell. He lived his entire life as a Christian evangelical. In this book I attempt to situate Russell in the history he inherited and in the milieu he experienced. How I present the Archdeacon to the reader necessarily filters through my own life experience. I remain faithful to the facts found in Russell's writings and in third-party documentation, but in no way can I avoid interpreting his life. He was a man who understood who he was, accepted what life gave him, and made something of it.

Introduction

THE SUBJECT OF THIS BOOK is James Solomon Russell, a former slave and founder of Saint Paul's College in Lawrenceville, Virginia. Russell served as Archdeacon for Colored Work in the Episcopal Diocese of Southern Virginia from 1893 to 1929. This book covers not only the time from Russell's birth in 1857 to his death in 1935, it provides colonial and early American historical background in support of a broad perspective of Russell's environment in the late nineteenth and early twentieth centuries. It takes into account the nonstop efforts of Russell toward reconciliation within the Episcopal Church among whites and African-Americans. This book is an attempt to answer the question: "Who was Russell and why did he work the way he did?"

In the context of post–Reconstruction education, Russell's entrepreneurial achievements at Saint Paul's College were overshadowed by the seemingly greater achievements and the much wider notoriety of Hampton Institute in Virginia and Tuskegee Institute in Alabama. The linkages among these three schools are intimate, however. Both Russell and Booker T. Washington were students of Samuel Chapman Armstrong at Hampton in the mid–1870s, and their two schools were modeled after that of Hampton. In ecclesiastical life it will be argued, using established historical facts, that James Solomon Russell was not only a leader, but possibly the major player in the development of educational access for former slaves in the South and within the Episcopal Church in the period from the end of Radical Reconstruction (1877) to the early years of the 20th century. In ecclesiastical affairs he was the human linchpin holding in dialogue and debate rival positions concerning the full and equal participation of African-Americans in the governance of the Episcopal Church in general and within in the Diocese of Southern Virginia in particular. That long-term exchange of dialogue and debate was a microcosm of the secular struggle to accept African-Americans not only as equal and participating citizens under American law, but as human beings. In this regard Russell is seen as pivotal in the eventual reform of not only the canons (laws) of the Episcopal Church but the reform of prevalent and negative racial attitudes toward colored people.

When the Diocese of Southern Virginia was created out of the undivided Diocese of Virginia in 1892, Russell was appointed Archdeacon for Colored Work, a charge that lasted — off and on — until 1929. In this work as Archdeacon, as well as that of principal of Saint Paul's, Russell had the perfect secular/religious platform for working for full acceptance of African-Americans not only within the Diocese of Southern Virginia but in the Episcopal Church as a whole. Perhaps Russell's most aggressive educational challenge came from the American Church Institute for Negroes (ACIN) and its first executive director, Samuel Bishop. The ACIN, formed in 1906, was the Episcopal Church's successor organization to previous church agencies chartered to fund colored schools in the South after the end of the Civil War. But the ACIN and Samuel Bishop had problems with Russell and the manner in which he operated his school. Bishop, frustrated with Russell's opposition, actually underwrote the cost of a trip to Europe for Russell to get him out of the country while he and the ACIN tried to assume full operational control of the school.

In 1999 the book *Dangerous Donations: Northern Philanthropy and Southern Black Education, 1902–1930* was published by Eric Anderson and Alfred Moss, Jr. The book documents efforts of wealthy Northern philanthropists attempting not only to fund but to control the funding mechanisms of all similar philanthropic agencies assisting Southern black schools and colleges. The leading agency funding southern black schools in the nation was a private organization known as the General Education Board (GEB). The GEB was established by the Rockefeller Foundation in 1902. As a case study, Anderson and Moss use two of their seven chapters examining the character and the operations of ACIN. In those chapters they track its beginnings (modeled on the GEB) and ACIN's ongoing operational and financial problems with James Solomon Russell. The present book examines, in part, the skirmish between Russell and the ACIN and places it in the context of the career of this educator, fund-raiser, and archdeacon. Russell unavoidably was a participant in the national debate between liberal arts and industrial education for the former slaves. Though not of the national notoriety of Booker T. Washington, Russell had his own battles with educators, parents, and the church over industrial education. Russell was able to satisfy most of the requirements of his students' parental demands and outside funding agencies regarding liberal arts and industrial training. But there was spill-over from the heated debates between the visions of W.E.B. Du Bois and Booker T. Washington. For many years no black educational institution was unaffected by the debates' content and public rhetoric. In a sense, Russell's life work is linked with other more famous

African-American pillars: W.E.B. Du Bois, Booker T. Washington, R.R. Moton, William Sanders Scarborough and Alexander Crummell. Not a stranger to white industrialists, from whom he requested funding for his school, Russell approached with confidence such moguls as J.P. Morgan. Russell had no choice but to participate in the national debate over the approach to black education, but his parallel responsibility as a clergyman placed him in a position of leadership countering the "Jim Crowism" which enveloped his church. Russell emerged as a man of long-suffering patience, strong convictions, and a protagonist of racial reconciliation, both in the secular and ecclesiastical realms.

Given that former slaves flocked to the all–African churches and avoided the Episcopal Church at the end of the Civil War, why did Russell join the Episcopal Church? Russell thought it a mistake that blacks rushed to all-black Methodist and Baptist denominations instead of participating in the successor to the Church of England. An examination of colonial America and colonial Virginia particularly provides background for Russell's actions. The Virginia colony had the largest number of slaves of any of the colonies. The Church of England was Virginia's "established" and legal church, although other denominations were tolerated over time. The current-day notion of the separation of church and state was an unknown if not initially unthinkable concept in colonial days. The established church and the state (colony) were virtually one in purpose and governance.

The gradual transition of an indentured servitude system of labor into a total reliance on racially-based (black) slave labor was coupled, oddly enough, with the emergence of a sense of freedom among second- and third-generation colonials. The colony was becoming prosperous and landowners did not wish to return to England nor to continue to pay taxes to their mother country. Originally, young English entrepreneurs wanted to make their big money in the colonies, then return home to live in comfort the remaining days of their lives. But the spirit of freedom and the emergence of republican ideas began to take on an irreversible force. Of course, it was the white landowner and not the black slave who was experiencing these encounters with freedom away from his mother country. African slaves simply wanted their freedom.

The large landowners, who were also the politicians, began to recognize more and more their need for electoral support from the small yeoman landowners. Big landowners needed small landowners to maintain control of the proprietary then royal colonial governments. Likewise, the small landowners sensed their power, collectively, in getting what they wanted from the elected. Both sets of landowners believed in their eventual independence from England. The events involving the appearance of racially-based slavery instead of indentured servitude, the maturing of white colonials into sensing their own freedoms outside of England, the Great Awakenings of spiritual consciousness, and a popular aversion to the potential presence of Anglican bishops — no Anglican bishop ever set foot on colonial soil — all had an impact, it is suggested, on the actions of James Solomon Russell and other American evangelicals more than one hundred years later. The virtual demise of and the actual disestablishment of the Anglican Church in Virginia within a decade of the Revolution forced the newly-formed Episcopal Church to identify itself with the new nation. Not untouched by the republican sentiments responsible for the creation of the new nation, Episcopalians and all of the new Christian denominations had to deal with the issue of freedom while clinging to slavery.

There were periods in both colonial and post–Revolutionary times when black Christians worshipped with white Christians. But this did not mean that there were necessarily close ties between the two. The introduction of the ideas of freedom and independence to the colonials caused a change in social relations among whites themselves as well as among Africans. It was the first Great Awakening beginning in the 1740s that was significant in developing a new American mindset — it affected slave and free alike. It legitimated Anglican Church dissenters. The group or social class way of life was giving way to individualism and privacy. At the same time, blacks, who saw and knew what was happening to whites, became more and more social and less individual. The mere existence of slavery meant that privacy, individualism, and freedom were impossible for slaves. But the slave efforts to maintain family, a sense of their own pride during the social transformation of the colonials, made the slave family and group bond stronger.

To those white Christians who clearly understood the contradiction of slavery within a free society, a dilemma raised its ugly head. The colonials (or the new Americans) had to deal with the dilemma sooner or later, and they knew it. Slaves knew it too. How they dealt it with was painful, difficult and slow. How they dealt it with affected later American generations, both white people and former slaves. These issues are explored and analyzed. Another phenomenon occurred in the early decades of the new republic: free African-Americans in the North broke away from their white Methodist and Episcopal Churches and formed all–African churches, while Southern evangelical churches became biracial, imperfect as they were. This sociological irony is addressed herein.

In 1996 the Diocese of Southern Virginia honored the memory of James Solomon Russell by making him a "local saint." The diocese later submitted a memorial to (triennial) General Convention 2009 of the Episcopal Church to make a Commemoration in the church calendar for Russell. That memorial failed in committee. Another attempt to submit the proposed memorial is planned, as of this writing, for the 2012 General Convention. This book analyzes and then interprets Russell's probable thinking behind his actions. It is based on available documentation — the results of his efforts through history. This is simply a story. The book's chapters focus on certain aspects of Russell's history and development as well as conditions, attitudes, and laws preceding and concurrent with his life. In this book James Solomon Russell is introduced as a young man (perhaps in his late teens) who was elected secretary of a local Methodist-like church of mostly former slaves in Boydton, Virginia, near the North Carolina line. It is clear that his election as secretary of his church's annual conference, and his insistence on a literate and trained clergy, exposed him as a clear thinker and leader early on.

CHAPTER ONE

Beginnings

O N A THURSDAY MORNING in Richmond, Virginia — July 11, 1878, to be precise — the Rev. Mr. Grayson Dashiell left his office to travel the seventy-five miles south-southwest to the town of Lawrenceville, the seat of Brunswick County. He arrived at the home of Mr. and Mrs. Francis Emmet Buford. Mr. Buford was the commonwealth attorney for that area of Virginia and Mrs. Buford, also known as Miss Pattie Buford, was a self-styled evangelist to former slaves in the area, a planter of several Sunday schools, and the owner and operator of a hospital[1] for the indigent. All three were white Episcopalians. Miss Pattie was an active member of St. Andrew's Church and the statewide Episcopal Diocese of Virginia. For at least four years she had been requesting funds to aid her in supporting the Sunday schools for local African-Americans. Her method of financial solicitation involved writing letters to the editor. Most of her appeals were directed at church-based newspapers and to secular journals in the North. The North was where the money was. Some of those journals included *The Churchman* and the *Spirit of Missions*. The acquisition of funds from local and regional sources was next to impossible because, only twelve years since the end of the Civil War, the people of the State of Virginia were virtually bereft of capital, property and morale. It was because of Miss Pattie's work that Dashiell made the trip.[2]

The Zion Union Apostolic Church

Over time a small African-American religious group, known as Zion Unions, began to build small structures to use as worship centers in and around the Southside of Virginia and bordering North Carolina. By 1877 one of those structures was built near Miss Pattie's farm. It was a church with a Sunday school for former slaves and their children. Miss Pattie heard about the Sunday school and its fairly large attendance which meant, to her, that

Above: Overseer's House. *Left:* The writing on the back of the above picture: *"Larry Jackson—Overseer's House on an Old Virginia plantation. This photo was taken in 1930. I am standing in the doorway. Rose Creek Plantation was a slave breeding farm that supplied the deep south slave trade after importation was outlawed. It operated up to the Civil War. When this photo was taken the remnants of nine dirt houses for slaves remained. Around 1900 the property was acquired by St. Paul's College and it was used as a produce farm until around 1940"* (Russell Memorial Library, Saint Paul's College, Lawrenceville, Virginia).

fewer and fewer black children attended her school on Sunday afternoons. The mere existence of that Zion Union school was somewhat of a disappointment for Miss Pattie because since her childhood she had had slave children come to her house to learn the Gospel and to learn about her. It was common practice among plantation owners or slave masters to maintain supervised Sunday schools on their property for the purpose of "Christianizing" slaves. Buford learned that the Zion Union leader, Bishop James R. Howell, was teaching a gospel of hatred toward whites and that his church members were involved in "wild superstitions and practices, and strange doctrines." She became convinced that true heathens were at her gate and so she decided to do something about it.[3] She approached the church's leadership and offered her services as a teacher in their school. To her surprise, she was received with open arms. But what she soon found was not good.

The Sunday school had no Bibles and no books. Resources were virtually nonexistent, making it difficult for effective learning. So she began asking for Bibles, books, and money. Her classes were attended not just by little children; there were also gray-haired adults who were mostly illiterate. About twenty or so could read and write. Over time, as the books arrived, she taught her students the Bible, the Creed, the Commandments and the Calvary Catechism. Her own local church had been without a minister for some time, so she had no one to help her, except for the students themselves. As more and more colored people heard about the classes, her Sunday school grew larger. Adequate space became a problem. She continued her requests for books, Bibles, and money, and she received them. The school grew to over one hundred students and measureable progress was evident. The more her students learned, the more they desired. Their thirst for knowledge was voracious. In her letters to contributors in the North, she let them know that all that she received was distributed to her students and that demand for more seemed unending.

While her work continued, a reversal in beliefs was taking place within the Zion Union leadership. Howell, the doctrinaire anti-white preacher and leader, was beginning to make changes in his belief system, according to Miss Pattie's observation. His hostility to whites had lessened and his separateness and isolationist philosophy turned into one of friendship and helpfulness. Miss Pattie reported in her letters that Howell had become a friend and a helper, a person totally transformed. He, among others, still exercised the greatest influence over the former slaves in the Southside of Virginia. The relationships between Pattie Buford and her students blossomed; her relationship with Bishop Howell evolved into one of trust and mutual support. None of the work conducted by Mrs. Buford went unnoticed by her Episcopal Church leadership, either. After all, she was an active church member both locally and within the greater church diocese. In addition to the contributions from church and non-church organizations in the North, the Episcopal Diocese of Virginia, through its Commission on Missions, was also a contributor to her work. The growth of Miss Pattie's work, coupled with the turnaround of the leader and one of the founders of the Zion Unions, presented an evangelical opportunity taken seriously at the Episcopal Church bishop's office in Richmond.

The bishop of the Episcopal Diocese of Virginia and its Diocesan Missionary Society were interested in the work going on in Brunswick County. The Bishop of Virginia, Francis M. Whittle, directed the Rev. Mr. T. Grayson Dashiell to conduct an investigative visit to Brunswick and then upon its completion to report his findings. Mr. Dashiell was for many years the secretary of the council of the diocese, and he had made an earlier visit to Miss Pattie's school in August of 1877. Prior to his planned trip in 1878, a circular letter was sent to all of the interested Zion Union churches stating that a representative from the Episcopal Church would visit with them between July 11 and July 14, 1878. Once there, he discovered something amazing.

The Zion Union Apostolic Church (ZUAC) had more than two thousand members spread across the Southside of Virginia and the bordering counties of North Carolina. Serving with its one bishop were seventeen ordained ministers who led twenty-five to thirty churches and Sunday schools. The ZUAC bishop and his ministers, on behalf of their church members, expressed to Mr. Dashiell their indebtedness to Mrs. Buford for her work with them, and as such, Bishop Howell proposed placing all of the Sunday schools and church congregations under the charge of the Episcopal Church. In a report weeks later to the Missionary Society, Dashiell noted that the Zion Union people, their leader and the citizens of Brunswick all "set forth that a great, a marvelous, change for the better has taken place in the colored* population since Mrs. Buford broke down the barriers that kept these people to themselves." Dashiell observed that these people talked as if they had just found the Gospel and that they hungered for more. The ministers of the church wanted more, and Bishop Howell now required the ministers to know the Bible, the Creed, and the Commandments before ordination. But there was more to come.

In a meeting held on Saturday morning, July 13, 1878, Howell and three of his Zion Union ministers met with Dashiell for more than one hour. The details of that meeting would be made known later. Dashiell had a second meeting on that Saturday afternoon with another Zion Union minister and his nephew, a young man about twenty or twenty-one years old. But it was on the next day, a Sunday morning, that Howell, three of his ministers, Mrs. Buford, and that young man, met with Dashiell. Howell proposed, without any reservation, placing not only his Sunday schools but himself, his ministers

---

*The term "colored" most likely had a double meaning: former slaves of pure African heritage or half African/half white. Literature of the post–Civil War era includes both "colored" and "Negro."

and their people under the direction of the Episcopal Church, not unlike John Wesley and the Methodists within the Church of England a century earlier. Although Dashiell thought the proposal wise, he reminded Howell and his ministers that he was not in authority to accept such a proposal and that he was there only to make observations and report to the Bishop of Virginia and the Missionary Society. He let Howell know, however, that he personally had an interest in, and was in sympathy with, the proposal and asked that Howell and his ministers continue to confer with one another and not to commit to any path of action until he had done so. After the meetings, since it was Sunday morning, Bishop Howell and his ministers departed for a special place of worship, which on that day was to be in an open field with an arbor set up as a pulpit.

The circular letter that was mailed earlier was of great interest to Zion Union members, and many walked miles from the rural Virginia countryside to the outside worship service that morning. It was reported that no fewer than five hundred people attended the morning service. Mr. Dashiell left the meeting for the service with the Buford family and J. Ravenscroft Jones. Once at the worship site, Jones, along with the Rev. George Taylor, conducted the service. By the time Dashiell and his party reached the place of worship a choir was singing "From Greenland's Icy Mountain." Dashiell delivered the sermon. After the sermon, Howell, excited about the possibility of union with the Episcopalians, could hardly contain himself when he rose to speak. "Thank God, the day is breaking. For nine long years I have been praying to see it, and now I do see that the light is coming. I sha'n't [sic] say any more right now, but wait until August [next month] at the [Zion Union Annual] Conference, and you'll understand me." After the service was an intermission until the three o'clock afternoon service of Sunday school catechesis, which no fewer than 700 Zion Union people attended. Dashiell opened with his usual Sunday school service and then began the question-and-answer examination. He took them through the Calvary Catechism and the Church Catechism, followed by the singing of a hymn. The examination and the questions lasted until five o'clock. Knowing that most of the people had another ten miles of walking to return home, Dashiell then closed the service with prayer and the benediction.

The activities of that long weekend were reported to the bishop and the Missionary Society, with the added assurances of Mr. and Mrs. Buford, Mr. Jones, and the Rev. Mr. Robb White that they had all honor, respect, and confidence in the colored people in Brunswick County. Knowing that a great responsibility now rested on the Society and the Diocese of Virginia, Mr. Dashiell noted that there was only a moment's hesitation about the thought of the diocese coming into formal relations with the Zion Unions. On

Wednesday, April 30, 1879, the committee, at the invitation of the Zion Union leadership, Grayson Dashiell and A.W. Weddell, both representing the Missionary Society and Committee on Colored Congregations of the Episcopal Diocese of Virginia, met at the Chapel of the Good Shepherd, two miles east of Lawrenceville.

When Dashiell and Weddell arrived there were one thousand to twelve hundred people and ministers from the various Zion Union congregations standing in the field. The pre-planned arrangement directed that Dashiell would meet with the ministers and as many lay persons who could be accommodated inside the chapel. There was a worship service followed by the conference. The result of the conference was that the entire organization voted without dissent to place itself under the care of, and thereby give consent to the doctrine, discipline and worship of, the Protestant Episcopal Church within the Diocese of Virginia. In his report to the 1879 Annual Council less than a month later, Dashiell reported that "this society of colored people are not under the influence and convictions which usually bring other denominations into our fold," and that it "ought to be understood by all in our diocese, and especially by friends in the North, that these ministers and their congregations desire to be with us— not because of any change in their opinions as to Episcopacy, not because they have any trouble in their minds concerning the validity of their [ministerial] orders.... They have been led to desire such a union for reasons which in our judgment are more to the glory of God and to the credit of our church." Dashiell also brought to the attention of the Council the innovative and creative evangelism toward the Zion Unions by Mrs. Buford.

Saturday, July 13, 1878: it was in the morning that Dashiell met with Howell and his ministers, but in the afternoon he met with two men who had requested an audience. After traveling forty-five miles, the Rev. Macklin Russell and his nephew, Mr. James Solomon Russell, met with the bishop's representative. Later, in a report to the Episcopal Bishop of Virginia, Dashiell wrote about meeting the young Russell and described him as "a man of about twenty or twenty-one, a bright mulatto, of very prepossessing appearance and manners." Many people, both white and colored, who had spoken to Dashiell of the young Russell said that his "record is without blemish, and he seems to have their entire confidence as to his honesty and piety." The Rev. Robb White had been dispatched months earlier to Hampton Institute to meet with Russell. Since Russell was absent from the school that session, White met with Hampton's founder and principal, General Samuel Chapman Armstrong, who testified to Russell's high character. Sunday morning, July 14, 1878, James Solomon Russell and Howell, according to Dashiell, had a "frank and pleasant interview" with him and Mrs. Buford. It had been rumored that Russell intended to seek Holy Orders (ordination) in the Episcopal Church, but it was not until this Sunday morning that it was confirmed and blessed by the Zion Union bishop, Howell. Howell's perspective was that Russell would do a great work within the Episcopal Church for the Zion Union organization. Coupled with the concept of Zion Union's participation as Wesley's Methodists did with the Church of England, much work was placed on the table. But where and when would this aspirant for Holy Orders begin his studies?

The New Seminary in Petersburg

In Alexandria, the Board of Trustees of the Theological Seminary and High School of Virginia met on June 25, 1878, to vote on a plan to expand its theological education program to African-Americans. On a motion put forward by Dr. Daniel Francis Sprigg, rector of Grace Church–Alexandria and editor of the *Southern Churchman* at that time, the board resolved to create a separate school to be located in Petersburg and charged the Rev. Dr. Churchill Jones Gibson, rector of Grace Church–Petersburg, with the responsibility to begin collecting funds for instructors' salaries. The announcement of this decision was published in *The Churchman* weekly journal on August 31, 1878. Quickly, opposition to the plan arose. Why a separate school? Why in Petersburg? In his letter to the editor of *The Churchman*, the Rev. F.B. Chetwood of New Jersey in the September 1, 1878, issue — only one week later — objected not only to the "unnecessary" expense of creating a new department in a different city, but to the reported news that African-American aspirants had already been rejected by the Alexandria campus. Calling this decision "arbitrary and impolitic," he questioned the wisdom of training black students separately as fatal to the progress of the Episcopal Church. Respondents arose.[4]

Thomas Spencer, who would become one of the instructors in the new Branch Divinity School in Petersburg, responded to Mr. Chetwood's charges by saying that no colored applicant was ever rejected at the Alexandria campus because of his race. Those applications received from African-American aspirants asked for a separate training facility in Petersburg at St. Stephen's Church. At that time there was no training program in Petersburg, but apparently word had spread that such a possibility was in the making. The seminary trustees in Alexandria never "rejected" a colored applicant because there had been none for the Alexandria campus. The reason Petersburg was selected was that it was the geographical and demographic center of African-American citizens in Virginia. It made sense to the trustees to place the new branch seminary in Petersburg.

If that were not enough of a reply, a Mr. H.M. Jackson of Richmond (H. Melville Jackson, a member of the clergy in the Diocese of Virginia and rector of Grace Church), in the same September issue, linked Mr. Chetwood's argument with the editor of *The Independent* magazine, whose criticism of the new seminary plan was the hope that the trustees would fail in any attempt to raise money from the North. Revealing regional North/South suspicion still active only one year following the end of Reconstruction, Jackson thought it "too much to expect that our northern friends will ever adequately understand the problems which grow out of our new and altered state of affairs, and which determine our actions." He also asserted that "we [in the South] who have been brought up among this people, who know them in the mass and not in isolated instances, who have had a large experience with them under the old regime, and are rapidly acquiring it under the new, are in better position to judge than those who sit afar and speculate and criticize." He also brought to light that the 2,000-member colored church organization Zion Union had recently voted at their annual conference to place themselves under the jurisdiction of the Protestant Episcopal Church in the Diocese of Virginia. Jackson closed his letter with a charge to the Rev. Mr. Chetwood that because "of his good will toward us, and of [any] real interest in the race whose cause he deemed himself called upon to champion, we shall expect an early contribution from our reverend brother in New Jersey." Without any further objections, the new seminary opened its doors.

It appears that things neatly fell into place for James Solomon Russell. In his *Autobiography*, he wrote that he entered the new seminary in Petersburg on October 1, 1878. Although he was the seminary's original student, he would not be its first graduate and would not be the diocese's first ordained African-American. The board of trustees of Virginia Theological Seminary had acted quickly in opening the new Petersburg seminary, probably without knowing who the first student(s) would be. But it was Grayson Dashiell who used his understanding of the situation not only of the Zion Unions but the person of James Solomon Russell, and who championed Russell's education and development. He wanted the Missionary Society and Committee on Colored Congregations to meet and converse with Russell. He felt sure that Russell's "modesty, intelligence, and other evidence of worth, will convince us that we should not hesitate to give him an education, and, unless God orders otherwise, let him go to work in Brunswick and Mecklenburg [Counties]." Dashiell's prescient understanding of James Solomon Russell worked itself out in history. It was Dashiell's observations and Pattie Buford's support of the young Russell that give us a sense of Russell's personal character and demeanor. And clearly, Russell was a young man of faith, commitment, high character, preparation and purpose. One can reflect on Russell's long career and then read Dashiell's early description of him as a rising star as an accurate foreshadowing. But what were Russell's religious experiences as a teenager and a young man in Mecklenburg County?

Origin(s) of the Zion Union Apostolic Church

There are at least two stories about the origin of the Zion Union Apostolic Church. At the end of the Civil War, according to the first story, in Lunenburg, Mecklenburg, and Brunswick Counties, colored Methodists were no longer permitted to worship in the white churches. Without a church home and with no desire to affiliate with the colored Methodist denominations, these worshippers were displaced until the arrival of James R. Howell. This story allows that Howell was an African Methodist Episcopal Zion church minister from New York City. Together the displaced colored Methodists and Howell organized the Zion Union Apostolic Church in 1870 in the town of Boydton, with Howell as its first president. Five years later, Howell was elected bishop for life, reflecting a polity change in the Zion Unions from a congregational to an episcopal structure. Personal dissatisfaction arose among some members with Howell's new role, and the Zion Unions drifted and became disorganized until 1882, when it was reformed under John M. Bishop, one of the original founders with Howell. The new church took the name of Reformed Zion Union Apostolic Church (RZUA).[5] This background provides some of the context for Miss Pattie Buford's several ministries during the time of the Zion Unions' period of disarray and the emergence of the young James Solomon Russell. It is not known whether Buford, Dashiell, or the Episcopal Diocese of Virginia were aware of the struggles among the Zion Unions themselves, because in Dashiell's accounts of the evangelization of these 2,000 people, no mention of Zion Union disarray is documented in letters, reports, or other known communications in Episcopal Church publications. The extant documentation in third-party journals is about mission or evangelization, conversion, union, and emerging leadership among both whites and blacks in Southside Virginia and no mention of any internal squabbles.

This version does not record the circumstances and details of Howell's arrival from New York to Southside Virginia. What is recorded, by Miss Pattie Buford, is that Howell was full of hatred for whites, and the combination of his arrival with his racial attitudes and the dismissal of the colored Methodists from Southside churches made easy the formation of the Zion Union Apostolic Church. The ZUAC's discipline and polity were fundamentally Wesleyan. However, the fact that the North had already separated into black and white Methodist church groups prior to the Civil War gives credence to the assumption that there would have been some doctrinal deviations between the ZUAC and mainstream Wesleyanism.

The second story of ZUAC's founding is different. According to research conducted by Professor Estrelda Alexander, the Zion Union Church was a black Holiness denomination and did not have its origin in any schism from a mother church, as so many other black denominations did.[6] Instead of an AME Zion heritage, James R. Howell came from the rival African Methodist Episcopal Church, and he was from Philadelphia, not New York City. Never himself a slave, Howell was an abolitionist, not highly trained theologically, and unable to obtain an AME pastorate in Philadelphia. He was sent as a missionary to Virginia to evangelize the newly freed. Howell moved to the Tidewater area (Norfolk, Portsmouth, Hampton) in 1864 and earned money as a carpenter by day, working as a preacher at nights and on Sundays. He eventually moved to Boydton, Virginia, more than one hundred miles west of Norfolk, to establish his ministry because his evangelistic work was unsuccessful in the Tidewater.

A persuasive speaker with a somewhat charismatic character, he pulled his new denomination together by convincing several displaced congregations who had left the Episcopal, Baptist, and Methodist churches of their former slave masters. In 1869 Howell organized the Zion Union Apostolic Church at first as "Zion Societies." The name "Zion Union" was used because Howell believed that the Bible portrayed Zion as "the dwelling place of God among men." Because Howell was a strong leader and dealt with his membership in a heavy-handed manner, the Zion Union church went into disarray for a period of time, probably due to a change in its polity in 1874. ZUAC switched from a congregational to an episcopal polity, similar to the AME church. Howell was made bishop for life. There were other problems as well. Many members wanted the liturgy to be less emotive and more structured. The church eventually voted to merge with the Episcopal Diocese of Virginia, but that never happened. The ZUAC did eventually reorganize, but under a new leader, in 1881–1882. The new church took the name of the Reformed Zion Union Apostolic Church, a church that today has congregations mostly in Virginia and North Carolina.

Given the two versions of the origin, development, and temporary dissolution of the ZUAC, it is not known, as a matter of record, whether the leadership of the Episcopal Diocese of Virginia knew of all the problems within its proposed ecclesiastical partner. Our purpose here is that we must consider the young Russell, a teenager. In 1870, the year of ZUAC's founding, Russell was thirteen years old and lived within five to ten miles of Boydton, Virginia. We know from his *Autobiography* that he, like other freed African-Americans, thirsted for an education, and that much of his early education

St. Paul's College Military Unit B, 1916 (Russell Memorial Library, Saint Paul's College, Lawrenceville, Virginia).

was within a church. Which church denomination, Russell never said in his writings. Given the evidence cited above, he eventually attached himself to the ZUAC. His description of church and Sunday schools invites interpretation. Russell wrote favorably about those white men who helped him and his family, both when they were in slavery and when free. But the bias or slant in Russell's writing was always toward religion and a great desire to know more. His mother, obviously a religious person, was strong in her opinion that young James should be a preacher some day. White church school superintendents assisted the young Russell, and eventually Russell himself became a church school teacher and superintendent as a teenager. It is quite probable that the adults — both white and black — who surrounded him saw a "rising star" in their midst. Russell identified the Apostles' Creed as the turning point in his young life. The Creed was a clear statement of belief. Later he coupled the Apostles' Creed with the *Book of Common Prayer* (BCP) as being determinative in his decision to join the Episcopal Church. Because of Russell's imprecise dating of some events, it cannot be reckoned exactly when he made his decision. We learn precious little about his childhood church encounters from his *Autobiography*. We know from *The Churchman* article that in 1878, when he was probably nineteen or twenty years old, he was the secretary to the Annual Conference of the Zion Unions. Perhaps Russell was secretary to a faction representing a large remnant of the Zion Unions. We do know that Russell and his uncle Macklin were presented to the representative of the Episcopal Diocese of Virginia as secretary and minister, respectively, of the Zion Union Apostolic Church. We know that Russell and some Zion Union members eventually joined the Episcopal Church. Russell betrays a bias toward the Episcopal Church by citing the Book of Common Prayer. Russell, it appears, had made up his mind about entering the ministry of the Episcopal Church. From this we can assume that Russell was a strong-willed young man at that time. We need to recall several items. Howell was described as a hateful man initially, with a strong, charismatic, and imposing character, who held sway over his people. By the time Howell and Russell met with the Rev. T. Grayson Dashiell, Howell was a changed man. His transformation had been attributed to Miss Pattie Buford, and indeed she may very well have had an effect on Howell's transformation. But Russell, as a ZUAC insider, may have had more influence on Howell's turnaround.

The split in the ZUAC occurred when one faction wanted a more liturgical or structured church order. The mere fact that Howell's office changed from president to bishop suggests, at least at first glance, that he was part of the "formal" church faction. Howell's possible background was as an AME or an AMEZ elder would support the notion of a more formal church structure headed by a bishop. But Dr. Alexander's study identifies Howell's new church in Boydton as a Holiness or Pentecostal church, either one being congregational (and not episcopal) in governance and structure. This latter perspective also makes sense because the holiness/Pentecostal churches in the South were biracial in worship before the Civil War. It was the one place — if only one day a week — where blacks and whites worshipped together and shared the same freedoms. But once the war ended and there was a slow rise of white disenchantment with the conduct of the federal government's political handling of former Confederates, the separation of the races began. Therefore, many colored congregants of the biracial Methodist churches in Mecklenburg County were thrown out and left on their own.

Russell, for his part, writes little about the details of his upbringing. But what we have learned from the consistency of his entire life is that Russell was a man of order and structure. This characteristic led him to appreciate the Apostles' Creed and the Book of Common Prayer because both are structured and represent a fixed order. Russell was also a family man and did everything he could to teach and preach about how a family should live, work and pray. He showed an entrepreneurial spirit and knew that economic stability was a necessary component of a stable family. He knew that the key to success for former slaves was education. We learn from his book that he was an observer of human character. As a boy he could deal with anyone, and his abilities to interact with all people proved to be a lifelong strong suit. So it follows that what Russell saw in the formerly established Anglican Church of Virginia and its structure and belief system was not only a solid faith, but economic and political powers. We can assume that even as a man in his early twenties, Russell was developing his personal life's plan, which required working with all types of people from the weakest to the powerful. James R. Howell and his transformation may have been Russell's earliest effort at preaching the gospel to effect personal transformation — of his bishop, in this case.

Given his high drive for an education and a religious connection, it may be that the young James Solomon Russell discerned problems or contradictions living within not only the new American social arrangement in the South, but in his Zion Union church as well. He may have seen the imperfect, but living, biracial churches in the South disintegrate before his very eyes after 1865. He probably knew about the separate black denominations decades old in the North, and was curious about the rationale for the style of worship and the separation. Most likely the immediate presence of the attitude endemic in the ZUAC struck him as theologically contradictory of how a church should live its life. Russell also had to know, from a practical point of view, that the Episcopal Church had more money than the ZUAC, was more organized (split briefly during the Civil War and reunited afterwards) in its structure, and had a much longer ecclesiastical history, notwithstanding any historical continuity linked by schisms. These factors are probable influences in his decision-making. It is also not impossible to conjecture whether or not Russell, even though a young man in his twenties, had a religiously transformational effect on James R. Howell. An observation made by historians of the ZUAC state that Russell was a young delegate from Penuel Church to the Fifth Annual Meeting of the Zion Union Apostolic Church in August of 1876. That meeting was held in Warren County, North Carolina, at Russell Union Church. Russell offered a resolution to the effect that: "It is the sense of this body that no man ought to attempt to read in public who cannot read correctly, nor must any[one] take text who cannot read, nor shall any attempt to preach more than one hour."[7] Earlier, Russell had been elected recording secretary of the annual conference. Giving fuel to the theory that Russell (in addition to Pattie Buford) had an influence on Howell, the historians of Reformed Zion Union Apostolic Church (RZUA) write, "Russell loved order, such as to be found in the Episcopal Church, and he loved education.... He wanted to see a trained ministry, less emotional worship and more orderly procedures."[8] When observing the work of Miss Pattie Buford in Brunswick County with Howell's churches and her eventual surprise at Howell's "born again" transformation, it is not difficult to conclude that Russell was working in the background to effect the changes.

Personal objections by some ZUAC members to Howell's election as a bishop caused ZUAC to break apart. The disintegration probably did not sit well with Russell—it was disruptive to an orderly church life: a split in the church, whether racially, personally, or politically motivated, was contrary to the teaching of the Gospel and the catholicity of the Body of Christ. The Zion Unions had split over at least two issues: governance—episcopal or congregational; and liturgical—highly emotional or Pentecostal in manner versus the less emotional and restrained, ordered liturgy as found in the Episcopal Church. Russell was engaged in these ZUAC struggles and participated in finding resolutions. Therefore, before Russell, his uncle Macklin, and Bishop Howell even approached the representatives of the Diocese of Virginia of the Episcopal Church in 1878, Russell had lived through and thought through many significant theological, liturgical, organizational, financial, and sociological issues. He was prepared. For Russell to have been secretary to the Zion Union's annual conference suggests that he held a talent for organization and structure. In an organization of more than 2,000 people, that kind of work does not normally come easily.

Racial Identity

Dashiell's use of the term "bright mulatto" is informative, if not potentially misleading. In the beginning chapter of his *Autobiography* Russell writes briefly about his ancestry, saying that his mother's grandmother came to Virginia on a slave ship. One perspective of his ancestry is to assume that Russell's maternal side is of pure African heritage. If Russell's mother was African or black, in order for him to be labeled a mulatto, by some definitions, his father would have been white. No record has been found to date on the race of his father Solomon, or even Russell's mother. Young Russell grew up on a plantation in south Mecklenburg County, Virginia, with his mother. Russell's father, it is reported, worked on a plantation in neighboring Warren County, North Carolina. Since Russell's autobiographical account of his early life is brief and displays no interest in ancestor worship, showing at best an attitude of benign neglect, we are not told much in the way of ancestral facts. But one can assume that if Russell's mother was indeed black his father had to be, at minimum, mulatto. That would make Russell a quadroon, meaning that three of his four grandparents were black and one white. Both parents could have been mulatto; thus Russell would be the same. But why concern ourselves with Russell's racial identity? Perhaps Russell's written attitude toward ancestral heritage indicates, in part, his approach toward racial and social reconciliation of the races in the United States. This is explored in these chapters.

Four times in his *Autobiography* Russell writes about being mistaken for a white man. If he did not really care about his race, why would he cite examples of mistaken identity? In the many pictures of Russell, one can see that the hue of his skin is light, almost white. Russell himself said that he never intended to take advantage of his appearance, but he sometimes did not bother to correct an observer's error if it paved a smooth road for his purposes. As we will learn later, Russell was quite adept at dealing with people, both white and black. In Lawrenceville he writes of little difficulty in purchasing land for his school. Russell always dealt with white men when acquiring land or materials for his college. His deals in Lawrenceville were secured by his signature, no cash. That fact alone indicates a high level of trust in Russell by Lawrenceville's white businessmen. Many of Russell's benefactors, however, were white Northern philanthropists and clergy, and given the North's altruistic and paternalistic attitudes toward the former slaves in the South, interacting with them may not have been as extraordinary an effort as that of dealing with Southern white men who had not yet relinquished or transformed their Confederate inclinations. Still, white men of the South may have been curious and uncertain about Russell's racial identity. White businessmen in Lawrenceville knew that he was building a school for colored children. So why did they deal with him? They may have truly wanted him to succeed or they simply wanted to make a financial transaction for their own personal benefit. But that argument does not hold, at least in the initial analysis, because Russell and his wife signed transactions without offering cash or collateral. The probable reason that Russell was so successful — with all people — was due to his integrity. The signs of Russell's personal integrity were evident in 1878 when the Rev. Mr. Dashiell and others met with him. Russell's descriptions of himself, the reactions of others to his racial identity, and his personal and business dealings with other people, clearly demonstrated that he was not only a faithful Christian leader but a practical utilitarian, a principled man, a man of his word.

In the nineteenth-century United States a person was considered either black, white, or Indian. Some states passed laws designating Negro as a person with at least one-eighth African blood. The cases made or attempted to be made for classifications of races as mulatto, quadroon, or octoroon were social and not legal. Brazil, for example, did not, and does not today, use the North American black-white dichotomy; it embraces a spectrum of color in gradations of skin tone from the darkest Negro to the lightest, white European.

Personal economic gradations also appear to be a factor. The histories of the two nations are similar only insofar as both were active at one time in the slave trade and slavery. And even though the United States officially ended the slave trade and slavery eighty and twenty-five years, respectively, before Brazil did the same, it is Brazil that seems to have incorporated its racially mixed population more successfully. This is not to say that Brazilians do not discriminate; they do. Brazilian discrimination runs along the boundaries of both class and skin color, not just color alone. For example, a wealthy mulatto in Brazil is considered white. The definition of mulatto there is different from that in the United States. The difference lies within each nation's concept of race: in Brazil there are dozens of recognized (but unofficial) skin and class gradations; in the United States there is simply black and white.[9] There are many social, economic, and other historical factors contributing to each of the two nations' development which will not be explored here. As one reads through literature of any period of American history, race is binary. But the American identification of only black and white is not so "black and white," pun not intended. Racial identity in the United States was and is sometimes confusing, and James Solomon Russell, being the practical man that he was, took advantage of that occasional confusion.

From the time of his youth, with the encouragement of his mother, Russell developed his personhood to a strong and mature degree before he stepped foot into Hampton Institute and the Branch Divinity School (later renamed Bishop Payne Divinity School). Once ordained into the ministry he would learn that he had to deal with current-day issues amassed from a history over which he had no control. The post–Civil War years from 1865 through the first third of the twentieth century brought to light many difficulties faced by the freed slaves as they embarked on a totally new life. In one sense, uncertainty was an apt description of the future. In another sense, hope filled the hearts and minds of those who wanted to make sure that their lives would become better, not only economically but socially as well. The Union or federal government put in place programs such as the Freedmen's Bureau to assist primarily African-Americans during the period of Reconstruction. The Bureau's responsibilities included not only economic assistance, as it acted as a mini-government throughout the defeated Confederate states and assumed all executive, legislative and judicial powers for a set period of time. The Episcopal Church, as well as the other denominations, had to deal with the aftermath of the war — not only with results of the war's physical and economic destruction of the South, but with the change in the social status of its African-American communicants. Regardless of any presumed warm, filial affinity between the white slave owner and his black slaves, the new reality was that Emancipation and the end of the war legally ended that relationship. American

Southern culture had endured seemingly unchallenged from seventeenth-century colonial days up to the Civil War of 1861–1865. The style of Southern living was a given fact for all those years. Although the South was stuck within its structure, there were always rebellions or uprisings trying to cause change for what seemed to be just. Church theology taught what was right and just, but the church in the South persisted in all but ignoring the civil and human rights of their enslaved black brothers and sisters.

Plausibility Structure or the Social Realities of Living

Sociologist Peter Berger coined the phrase "plausibility structure." For a society to continue its existence from day to day, year to year, and so on, that society requires a base of its people to live as if their social structure constituted reality.[10] Such a social reality was labeled the "reigning plausibility structure." Everything, or almost everything, makes sense when the people accept their culture as reality. All is well in a society as long as it meets with no serious challenges to its legitimacy. Societies, over time, define their realities. But since all societies are composed of people, people affect society. Conversely, but not in contradiction, the society affects its people. The relationship is one of growth: dialectic between individuals and their greater society constantly is in motion.[11] Change certainly takes place, but change can be so gradual as not to be noticed. Change can be so insignificant that it represents little or no challenge to the structure. Even so, within the larger social structure or culture, the subculture of slavery caused slaves to act out all that social suppression bred. In 1800 a slave by the name of Denmark Vesey won a local Charleston, South Carolina, lottery, he took half of the proceeds to his slave-trading owner, John Vesey, and purchased his freedom. For more than twenty years afterwards, Denmark Vesey worked his own businesses and became a prominent if not wealthy citizen of Charleston. As a freeman, Vesey could walk the streets of Charleston unencumbered and without restriction. Yet Vesey, it is purported, plotted one of the most ambitious insurrections ever in the United States by an African-American. Multilingual and with a personality that befriended anyone, Vesey was able to secretly plot his insurrection using a large number of slaves. If successful, the plot called for the slaves to board ships in Charleston Harbor and set sail for Haiti. Some of Vesey's conspirators were servants of the city's elite political establishment, including the governor and the mayor. Word leaked out about Vesey's plot, and the city fathers set about to stop the planned rebellion. How did this plot lose its secrecy?

Some of the servants of the town's elite got cold feet and the word of the rebellion spread rapidly. The conspiratorial servants, who were both black Africans and mulattoes, caved in. Vesey had at one time held their confidence. What happened? Life was, in a limited sense, good in Charleston. Slaves were given virtual freedom on weekends to shop the markets. Slaves on assignment from their masters could bandy about town to fulfill chores directed by their masters. Life was fairly calm, so it seemed, in Charleston. The few slaves who disobeyed or tried to run away were placed in a workhouse near City Hall. Those slaves would be beaten with straps until their skin peeled. Everyone knew about the beatings.[12] But there were always small rebellions or rumors of rebellion which kept whites on guard at all times. Whites did not want any change to their existing structure, so they put in place mechanisms to thwart insurrections and uprisings. A case could be made that the Charleston slaves, in the end, were co-opted by Charleston's reigning plausibility structure. Slaves knew that their bondage was wrong because most of them went to church every Sunday. The true Christian gospel could not be preached as promoting slavery. The Old Testament story of Moses and the Jews coming out of Egypt was an oft-told message. Vesey, too, was regular in his church attendance and preached occasionally. Not much is documented about the white churches and their reactions to the Vesey plot except that they usually sided with the government. But the slaves knew the consequences of challenging the way of life in that era. They were trapped. Vesey and some of his conspirators eventually went to trial and were hanged in the public square. And life in Charleston went on.

Another rebellion occurred in the Southside of Virginia in the 1830s. Nat Turner's rebellion advanced further than did Vesey's—people were killed during the rebellion.[13] But Turner's challenge made no immediate or significant change to the reigning plausibility structure, except that Virginia imposed stricter controls over blacks, both free and bond. Every rebellion and every challenge, however, had a gnawing effect on society, whether immediately recognizable or not. There is always a reaction. Virginia's experience of Nat Turner's rebellion was more reactionary and led to more bitterness than in the aftermath of the Vesey plot in South Carolina. The reaction of the church to the challenges presented to it by those who were enslaved is one of the issues addressed in this book. Turner was an evangelical preacher and was well-respected because he "stayed within his place" in Virginia society, or so it seemed to white evangelicals. So his rebellion shattered the complacent and settled attitudes of white churchmen to the extent that life in Virginia would never be the same. Vesey's plot could be seen as merely local in its effect. Vesey and some of his conspirators were hanged and his AME ministerial associate Morris Brown, who pastored a large church in Charleston, escaped to the North. In both cases the scandalized white populations reacted swiftly to repress any further uprisings, but Virginia's reaction was stronger. White churchmen in Virginia, previously comfortable in biracial congregations, no longer held high levels of trust in their African co-churchmen. Virginia had been different from most of the other southern states. Its potential for developing racial harmony was sidetracked by its reaction to Nat Turner's rebellion. As we will discover in later chapters, the Episcopal Church in Virginia made advancements in race relations both in antebellum days and the immediate post–Civil War decades. There existed contradictions between social and ecclesiological structures, but evidences of a clear understanding of the concept of human dignity from political and church leaders was a driving force not to be denied.

Sociologically, the dialectical relationship between an individual and the society is "conversational" and fundamental. A slave rebellion is a form of conversation necessitated by the failure of a previous nonviolent conversation. A slave always understood his reality regardless of what the dominant or reigning plausibility structures enforced. Whether the dominant race liked it or not, the suppressed race always conversed with the powers-that-be in order to inch closer to a just order: a new plausibility structure. Those who define the reigning structure would have great difficulty visualizing a reality totally alien to the status quo. The church, such as the Episcopal Church, was itself a society within the greater civil society. In colonial days the Anglican Church was virtually one with the colonial government as the "established" church of the Virginia colony, for example. In that role the church had been viewed as meta-social or meta-civil. But it was not. The government controlled the church, and as such, the Anglican Church was one of the supports for government. One could examine the development and the operation of the church up to the time of the Civil War and quickly come to a conclusion that the church's endorsement of the reigning plausibility structure was hardly challenged and thus remained static in its beliefs. Such a conclusion would be mistaken. In the "biracial" evangelical churches of the South it was the African-American member, unafraid and free to speak up, who provided the language of correction, and challenged the church's norm.

In the years following the Civil War many Southern religious institutions found themselves unable to justify their centuries-long status quo. Berger points out that "the fundamental problem of the religious institutions is how to keep going in a milieu that no longer takes for granted their definitions of reality."[14] The options available to religious institutions (and civil society at large) are accommodation and resistance to the high impact of the milieu. To the Episcopal Church in the Southern states the larger society was the re–United States of America operating under a new set of beliefs and unfolding structures. Slavery was dead. Blacks were free citizens legally. The social status among citizens would have to change and the details of change were to be worked out socially, and in some cases were imposed through more laws. Historically, there are differences between the social orderings of South Carolina and Virginia. Those two colonies and Louisiana experienced not only similar but contrasting methods of class distinction and their churches operated differently from one another. South Carolina and Louisiana had larger populations of mulattoes and free blacks than did Virginia in colonial days and the early days of the Republic. But Virginia, because it was the first English colony and the place of the establishment of the first colonial government — the House of Burgesses — played the leading role in the establishment of the United States of America. It was Virginia that produced Washington, Madison and Jefferson. It was Virginia that first recognized the error of slavery and the recognition of freedom for all people. It was Virginia that first experienced the spiritual confrontation of the Great Awakenings in the South, its aftereffects on slavery, and the eventual emergence of a new republic. And it was Virginia that produced Booker T. Washington, R.R. Moton and James Solomon Russell. Russell's heritage is Virginia's heritage, and his career was affected by those secular and ecclesiastical eras that preceded him.

It should be helpful for twenty-first century-readers to understand the development and continuing undercurrent of racial prejudice in Virginia as it manifested itself in different forms from Reconstruction back to the colonial period. As actors in history, Russell and his peers lived and worked in a social and economic environment historically developed and determined by their predecessors. The Episcopal Church succeeded the Church of England in Virginia and inherited, for good or ill, association with the Church of England, a unit of the hated government of England. It was the Episcopal Church that had to face the surge of emerging republicanism and American individualism, and it was in many ways seen as a loser, or the most negatively affected denomination in the decades following the American Revolution. From antebellum days to the end of the Civil War, many African-Americans fled the Episcopal Church to join the Methodists, Baptists or all-black church denominations. Those former slaves who remained within or even joined the Episcopal Church, along with the church's wealthy, white hierarchy and membership, all had to deal with their new plausibility structure in a church possessing diminishing influence in American life. As a black man, what was Russell's colonial inheritance?

CHAPTER TWO

The Colony and the Commonwealth of Virginia

VIRGINIA OCCUPIES A UNIQUE POSITION in American history, not only as the home of the first English settlement at Jamestown; it also created the first legislative body in the Western Hemisphere, the Virginia House of Burgesses, in 1619. Virginia built a complex, complicated, and successful management of its economic growth over the years since its founding that required many laborers. The fact that indentured servants had to be imported in order for physical work to be accomplished provides a clue about how southern society evolved. The replacement of indentured servitude by slavery was the turning point in the operation of an early management and contract labor relationship of master and slave. This change, occurring somewhere in the middle of the 1600s, was an early and quick transformation. This transformation, embodied in Virginia's free and slave African population and their interactions with English settlers, established the societal presuppositions that continued up to the time of the American Civil War. James Solomon Russell and his peers in the nineteenth and twentieth centuries could not have been unaffected by this history. It is presumed that Russell, consciously or not, embraced not only some Anglo-Saxon attitudes, but American individualism and republicanism as necessary outgrowths of the deep truths embodied in the Christian gospel.

Gentlemen, particularly Virginians in the decades preceding the American Revolution and after slavery became the norm, were not considered gentlemen unless they owned slaves. The gentry in Virginia possessed ecclesiastical power in the form of the vestry in the Anglican Church. How the colonial Anglican clergy were looked upon, how they were managed and manipulated by the (lay) vestry, and the fact that there were no Anglican bishops present on Virginia soil, all combine to form not only this historical character of early Virginia but that of its descendants as well. The Virginia Colony,

Class of 1896. Archdeacon Russell is in the top row, second from right (Russell Memorial Library, Saint Paul's College, Lawrenceville, Virginia).

therefore, is the focal point for understanding how slavery developed in British America.

The Virginia Colony

In 1606 the Virginia Company was organized by a group of English investors in order to develop a colony along the Chesapeake Bay region. Recalling the failure and disappearance of the colony at Roanoke Island (in what is now North Carolina) some ten to fifteen years earlier, the Virginia Company was resolute in developing a plan for a successful settlement in the new world. It was not difficult to recruit settlers to make the grueling voyage across the Atlantic. Most if not all of the adventuresome settlers-to-be, however, were not skilled and not used to a heavy labor requirement for agricultural work. One of the plans of the company was to set up a trading business—a money-making venture trading with indigenous people. What was not part of the company's original plan was the implementation of slavery.

But their avoidance of slavery was not morally based; it was simply a practical matter. They did not need it. For the type of work or businesses that the Virginia Company leadership envisioned, forced labor had no practical appeal. The leaders of the Virginia Company held a grand vision for their colony which was to be based on trade, finding gold or silver, and finding a waterway leading to the Pacific Ocean. There was no plan for sugar plantations because the natural environment of Virginia was inappropriate for such an agricultural enterprise. Over time the settlers and leaders realized that there was neither gold nor silver to be discovered and certainly there was no route to the Pacific through the waters of Chesapeake Bay or the James River, as some had thought. Life was rough, settlers died, new settlers replaced them, and everyone had no choice but to tough it out, for better or for worse. Not until 1619 was there any semblance of a government, when the Virginia House of Burgesses was created. This legislative body turned out to be the very first elected and representative government in British America.[1]

In the years between the settlement of Jamestown in 1607 and the creation of the House of Burgesses in 1619, and due to the failure of realizing the vision of a successful trading business put in place by the original Virginia Company investors and leaders, the company had no choice but to implement a plantation or agricultural model of survival. With sugar cane out of the question, tobacco became the workable, marketable, and successful crop. England developed a long-term, high demand for colonial tobacco which eventually led to production shortages in the colony. It should be noted that many of the settlers came to the Virginia Colony for land. Land was difficult or impossible to possess in England; therefore the new colonies provided opportunities for land settlement. But the Virginia Company, at least initially, was focused on trading and not on agriculture. Circumstances forced the colonists to reconsider their vision and change to a tobacco plantation society. This was another transformation. The English consumption of tobacco created a greater demand in the Virginia colony for land and now for labor.

The English were not the only settlers. Over time Virginia absorbed new settlers from other national and ethnic groups. Although many English customs and practices expressed themselves in the early days of Virginia, a change would take place that would make it appear to be more than or other than purely English.[2] Although English and Negro settlers were the early pioneers, Virginia's population went through much change. There were the Dutch in New York and small colonies of Swedes and Finns in the Delaware River region, all prior to the end of the seventeenth century.[3] But other ethnic groups began to arrive, notably the French Huguenots.

The British ship *Mary Ann* landed at Hampton, Virginia, on July 23, 1700, with more than two hundred French Huguenots. Hampton is located on the point of a peninsula at the mouth of the James River on the Chesapeake Bay, which flows into the Atlantic Ocean. Hampton's location is less than forty miles from the Jamestown settlement. The French Huguenots brought not only men but women and children. The landing in Virginia was of great importance. It was the British monarch William III who asked the Virginia government not only to receive these French Protestants but to give them aid. Royal Governor Nicholson personally welcomed Virginia's new arrivals. The arrangement to get this group to Virginia from France included a circuitous land route from France to Switzerland, into Amsterdam, and then a crossing of the English Channel to England and to Ireland.[4] For this group of new settlers, both the British and the Huguenots were aware of the potential value of resettling in the British colonies, and in Virginia particularly. The Huguenots saw new opportunities not only in religious freedom but in building a new life with plenty of land to acquire. The British saw a dependable workforce and a group of people willing to pioneer the outer boundaries of the colonies: seemingly a profitable venture for both. The British had been receiving the oppressed French Protestants since the revocation of the Edict of Nantes,* but absorbing them into the small area of England and Ireland began to impose difficulties on the British economy and society. So the idea of a resettlement from Britain to the colonies was agreed upon. Individuals like William Byrd I would assist the Huguenots with land settlements in Virginia. He held vast holdings and was interested in assisting in whatever area he could. He was not alone. There were many interested investors in seeing that the Huguenots succeeded. Farm tenancy, plenty of land to develop, and future profits were foreseen. The Huguenots quickly assimilated themselves to Virginia and became productive members of the burgeoning social and economic colony.

The Huguenots pioneered into other areas of the British colonies, especially in South Carolina and eventually Georgia. Though most of the French escaping to America from the oppression by Louis XIV were Protestants, some were Catholic. Many of the bishops of the Roman Catholic Church in early America were French.[5] But the established church in Virginia was the Church of England, sometimes referred to as the Church of Virginia or the Anglican Church, a "Protestant," or more precisely, a non–Roman Catholic Church. Virginia had its own problems dealing with non–Anglicans in its colonial history. Since the Church of Virginia figures significantly in the colony's administration it is discussed at some length. Concerning non–English nationals

---

*Thousands of French Protestants (Huguenots) were slain on St. Bartholomew's Day, August 24, 1572. This was followed by a period of Huguenot wars. On April 13, 1598, the Edict of Nantes was issued, guaranteeing civil liberties and religious toleration. But on October 22, 1685, the Edict was revoked, and because of renewed persecution the Huguenots fled France.

and ethnic groups, so many of them colonized in Virginia that one could argue that the English colony was not very English by shortly after its founding. By the time of the Huguenots' arrival in 1700, slavery in Virginia was an established and taken-for-granted fact. Huguenots either purchased land or were granted headrights. There was no limit to their potential successful future. Another complicated if not confusing factor was the existence of free Negroes living and working in Virginia. As the Huguenots stayed together for their mutual benefit, so did the free blacks.

In their book on Negroes living on the Eastern Shore of colonial Virginia, T.H. Breen and Stephen Innes write that free blacks from the 1620s to the 1680s transacted business with each other not necessarily out of economic necessity but out of a desire to maintain a relationship. The relationships among free blacks formed a network of friends and family—all black. The free blacks were not newly created "English" blacks. Even though they moved about freely and transacted business with whomever they wanted, transactions between blacks was probably motivated by feelings of association and race, not economics. This kind of interaction might have been a natural inclination for one to survive or persevere. Many people, not just Negroes, looked for ways to circumvent laws, standards, customs and other practices that might be perceived as discriminatory.[6] Even though the colonial legal structure recognized free blacks, the normal human tensions between freedom and authority were alive and well. The informal alliance of free blacks meant also that although appearing to be thoroughly "English" in temperament, the Negro would have been acutely aware of his African heritage and would not relinquish it. Evidence, as shown in court records in the Eastern Shore counties of Northampton and Accomac during the seventeenth century, does not support sharp racial categories nor racial animosities. But by many accounts most residents were treated fairly by the law.

Indentured (contracted) servitude was the method of the times for securing labor. Most of the indentured servants were white English men and women, and some children. British subjects jumped at the opportunity to come to the colonies to work for seven years and then receive land, thereby creating an opportunity to build a new life. But over time the occurrence of slavery appeared in legal documents of the colony. Negro landowner Anthony Johnson, who lived on Virginia's Eastern Shore, owned several black slaves, and other free Negroes were known to have white indentured servants. Therefore it must be said that, at least at its beginnings, colonial Virginia was a land open to immigrants but with English control. So when did slavery as it is understood from the twenty-first century perspective become an established, legal fact in colonial times? Assuming that custom precedes law, the gradual development of slavery in Virginia would have been a series of stages in its social development. But as a colony, Virginia was subject to actions by England. On November 16, 1618, a patent was granted to the Earl of Warwick, Sir Robert Rich, to form a company for the purpose of engaging in the African slave trade. Probable reasoning for the English to enter the business was based on other European powers already engaged. The Moors first introduced slavery to Europeans, and it was Portuguese Prince Henry the Navigator who exchanged two Moors for ten black Africans in 1442. His justification for that transaction was that Africans could be converted to Christianity, whereas the Moors (Muslims or Mohammedans) could not. As weak as that justification was, by the sixteenth century other Europeans had entered into the trade. Spain picked up the trafficking in 1517 because Portugal could not satisfy the demand. The Englishman John Hawkins* took it on in 1553 and France in 1624. It was after the French that Holland, Denmark and the English colonies entered the slave trade. As for the Earl of Warwick, his trade was not profitable and he let his charter expire. But a second attempt was made by Charles I in 1631 and a third company chartered in 1633. The Royal English companies were monopolies and enjoyed a profitable advantage. In 1688 the Glorious Revolution brought the monopoly to a close, but not the slave trade. The business of slave trafficking was opened by William and Mary to the entire nation, making it competitive. A complex business arrangement was established among European nations engaging in the slave trade. At its height, just before the American Revolution, there were more than 190 ships employed in the movement of African slaves: British as well as colonial ships were involved. Approximately 47,000 slaves were imported annually into the American colonies.[7]

Later, as a sovereign state, the Commonwealth of Virginia prohibited slave trading by an act of its first Assembly in 1778, thirty years before the British government acted. It was also before the new United States government enacted the same. Historically, Virginia was the first government anywhere in the world to put a legal end to slave trafficking.[8] But as a British colony, Virginia spared no effort in preventing the imposition (and expansion through natural procreation) of slavery within its jurisdiction.[9] It was in 1619 that the first known Negro landed in Virginia. The ship *Treasurer* held a cargo of Negroes and landed a Negro woman at Jamestown, but because the Dutch project was turned away, *Treasurer* sailed for Bermuda with twenty-nine Negroes on board. The cargo of Negroes was the result of the British company's plunder of Spanish commerce in the West Indies. The number of Negroes in Virginia grew slowly, with other ships bringing in few over the

*John Hawkins was an English "privateer" and pirate. He formed a group of wealthy English merchants which invested in the slave trade. Most historians cite Hawkins's action as England's entry into slave trading.

years. By 1625 there were twenty-three Negroes and approximately two thousand five hundred white settlers in Virginia. By 1659 there were 300 Negroes, but not primarily from importation during those thirty-plus years. The rapid expansion of the colony required more labor, prompting the colonial legislature to opt for importation of Negroes. By 1671 there were 6,000 white servants and two thousand slaves. By 1683 the number of servants doubled, the number of slaves grew marginally, and the Royal African Company — under an exclusive charter and owned by the king and the Duke of York — began to import more Negroes into Virginia. The company and the king, seeing the higher profitability of slave labor, stopped the supply line of indentured servants from Britain through a series of legal enactments.[10] Historically, the earliest known legal or statutory recognitions of colonial slavery are found in 1641 in Massachusetts, 1659 in Connecticut, and 1661 in Virginia.[11] (See Appendix A — Colonial Statutory Recognition of Slavery.)

The Church in Colonial Virginia

The Anglican Church was the established church in Virginia. The Quakers and Congregationalists dominated the New England colonies. The history and influence of Anglicanism in the Virginia colony, and later in the Commonwealth of Virginia, provide part of the background for Russell's life and career. Given the knowledge of the rise and decline of the Anglican Church in Virginia, meaning its support structure and its virtual destruction in the decade following the American Revolution, why would any aspiring clergyman — and a former slave at that — want to join the Episcopal Church? The American form of Anglicanism was dominant in the southern colonies, particularly in Virginia. The Church of Virginia, as it was often called, was at one time the strongest church in the British American colonies, and it was no wonder. As the established church of Virginia it received its support from the legislature, the Virginia House of Burgesses. It was a state church, but unlike that of its mother Church of England, its governance or oversight was anything but episcopal. The Bishop of London and not the Archbishop of Canterbury was the designated overseer. But neither Virginia nor the other southern colonial Anglican churches were traditionally administered as part of the Diocese of London, nor by a missionary jurisdiction. Canonically the Church of Virginia, as well as the Anglican Churches in the other colonies, were seemingly a missionary jurisdiction because the Bishop of London held oversight. The fact that the bishops of London displayed little to no interest in governing or disciplining the colonial clergy and churches did not matter. The absence of a bishop in the colonies made it difficult to practice the faith in an orderly, catholic manner. It was particularly difficult for colonial Anglican clergy. Given that the founding of the church in Virginia was sanctioned and supported by the House of Burgesses, a nontraditional system of church governance was developed.

The vestry system was the form of governance for individual Anglican churches or missions. There was no aggregation of churches (or parishes) and missions into anything remotely similar to a diocese, convocation, or synod. Effectively, the Anglican parishes in Virginia would have been viewed as "congregational" in their governance had it not been for the development of the putatively representational vestry system. The governance of the Anglican Church of Virginia was neither episcopal[12] nor congregational. It was something in between. Composed usually of twelve members, the vestry made all of the decisions governing the individual parishes.[13] Clergy were few and far between, and any member of the clergy hired would be given only a one-year contract by the vestry. At the end of that period either there would be a renewal of the contract or the vestry would award a contract to a new pastor (priest). Anglican clergy were dependent on the whim of the vestry. One can readily understand why there were not many clergy. The Virginia Anglican churches also developed an aristocratic-looking leadership as compared with Anglican churches in other southern colonies. In South Carolina, for example, churches elected their twelve vestrymen according to agreed-upon rules: vestry membership was voted on by all church members. South Carolina's system was democratically representational. But when a Virginia vestryman died or resigned his position, it was left to the remaining vestry members to decide his replacement and not the general church membership. This had the effect of keeping control of the church in the hands of an elite cadre of men. The Virginia vestry system was self-perpetuating, composed of "gentlemen." The gentry were one of those retained English social orders evident in colonial Virginia. Those with large estates or those with secular political power, or who came from well-known families, were the only people eligible for vestry leadership. The vestry also had the power to impose taxes for the upkeep of the parish and to maintain a collection for the poor. These, plus other activities of the vestries, gave the appearance of an ecclesiastical aristocracy.[14] Suffrage, it must be noted, during that period of colonial history, was the privilege only of landowners; so the development of the established church and the development of colonial government were coincidental and concomitant. The issue of church and state separation had not yet come into consciousness by the end of the seventeenth century.

During the entire colonial period not one bishop of London ever set foot on British-American soil. Through these actions, or lack thereof, one can understand how lay control of the Anglican churches in America, and especially in Virginia, developed over time. The general public had no need of bishops, either, but that sentiment was mostly benign until the middle of the eighteenth century. Clergy in early colonial Virginia were not necessarily considered reputable citizens. Bishops, had there been any, would have disciplined clergy for their conduct, and would have challenged the authority of the vestry. The Bishop of London, having de jure (though inactive) jurisdiction over the Anglican churches in the colonies, did, however, have a representative or vicar in each colony. That representative, a clergy person, held the position of commissary.

The Colonial Church Commissary System

James Blair was a Scottish clergyman who in 1681 refused to recognize the Catholic James II as head of the Scottish church. Because of his refusal he was forced to leave for London, whereupon he met up with the Bishop of London, Henry Compton. Compton eventually assigned Blair to Henrico County in Virginia, recommending him for the post at Varina Parish. Clergy in colonial Virginia were not held in high regard and ranked low in the social scale, primarily because they were at the mercy of the vestry and they were not properly educated. Blair, unlike his fellow clergy, was successful in his social interactions because he possessed an effective diplomatic manner. Because of his own social capabilities he married, within two years of his arrival, the daughter of one of Surry County's, and Virginia's, strongest men. The marriage certainly placed Blair in the environs of the highly respectable Virginia gentlemen, something unheard of with Anglican clergy. Compton, noticing the skills and effectiveness of Blair's pursuits, designated him as his commissary (1656–1743) in Virginia. As commissary or agent of the Bishop of London to Virginia, Blair was charged with improving the lot of clergy in Virginia. Seeing that the general level of preparedness of the clergy was weak (many were drunkards or misfits), he proposed the development of a college for the purpose of training new clergy. He believed that educating native Virginians whose families' character was known in advance would be the remedy to the situation he encountered. He traveled to England in search of financial support, and when successful he returned to Virginia and founded the College of William and Mary in 1693.[15]

Blair, a man of many abilities and skills, was not shy in promoting whatever cause he deemed worthy.[16] His style was polemic and in the process he developed many political enemies. He was critical of colonial government and was continually working with or meddling in the affairs of state. Not on just one occasion did Blair have disputes with colonial Virginia governors.

But his assignment as commissary was meant to be an effort to improve clergy and to raise the level of clergy respectability in the Virginia colony. Many of the colonial clergy were natives of England, Ireland, Scotland, and Wales, as well as from Germany, France and Spain. Many lacked college training and some read for orders, meaning they trained under other clergy. Even though some of the Anglican clergy were highly trained (at Oxford, Cambridge, etc.) they still were considered second-class.

The commissary usually pastored the largest parish in a colony and took on a variety of duties. Commissaries presided over meetings or conventions, enforced church doctrine, attempted to discipline wayward clergy, and reported to the bishop. The commissary was not a bishop and therefore possessed no traditional ecclesiastical authority. A commissary could not ordain or create new priests or deacons. New priests had to come from the Old World, and even those called to the priesthood while in the colonies had to make the dangerous round-trip ocean voyage to receive Holy Orders from a bishop. Philip Slaughter, long-time historian of the Diocese of Virginia, wrote in 1883 that when the Church of England "sent her daughter to Virginia, she gave her for dowry her Constitution and Canons. But the daughter left her head behind her, her task-master (the British Government) not allowing her to have a Bishop. She lived for nearly two centuries a widow in the wilderness, her head beyond the seas, having good ground for a divorce: an Episcopal church without a Bishop — a contradiction in terms."[17] The vestry did not quibble with this. As long as the vestry was running the show there was no need for new priests or a bishop anyway. Were a bishop to arrive on the scene, the vestry, as well as the general citizenry, might revolt. As the colonists began to think of themselves as Virginians or Americans and not as British, the mere sight of a bishop might generate angst. English bishops were members of the upper class, held seats in the House of Lords, and were viewed by some as tyrants. American colonists were gradually experiencing a freedom never enjoyed in England, and as a result they did not want to return to the British status quo. The Anglican Church, as contrasted with Dissenters (the Baptists, Congregationalists and Presbyterians), was seen by the people as an aristocratic and tyrannical representative of royal government. This perception did not bode well for Anglican churchmen as the American consciousness developed. Many Anglican clergy owned slaves and preached sermons justifying the Crown's institution of slavery in the colonies. This is not to say that other denominational clergy did not own slaves. But the Anglican Church, as the established church, was perceived to be part of the British government in America, and as such had a role to fulfill for the benefit of the Crown as America matured.

When the English government and its merchant class realized what was happening economically in America and other overseas colonies, they foresaw a new empire in the making and wanted to capitalize on this emerging reality. Anglicanism, according to its English leaders, was to monopolize religion in the American colonies, replacing Puritanism and Quakerism in the hope that all would unite faithfully under the Book of Common Prayer. The Society for the Propagation of the Gospel (SPG) was organized and funded in order to achieve this goal — but it failed. Even though the SPG itself was a lay organization, it nonetheless had trouble with the American Anglican churches led by powerful lay persons. The vestries possessed far more power in Virginia and the other colonies than lay persons ever did in England. Even though American Anglicanism was the church most widely spread over the colonies, its membership was disproportionately wealthy. Anglican Church memberships included the poor, persons of moderate means, the illiterate and eventually Negro slaves, but it was a "gentry" church and over time held less and less sway over its membership. The pre–Revolutionary rise of the Great Awakening and republicanism, and the immediate post–Revolution decades of American individualism, would prove difficult for colonial Anglicans and post–Revolution Episcopalians.[18]

Proximity to the Chesapeake Bay meant one would find more Anglican churches than inland. When Cecilius Calvert, a Roman Catholic English subject, received a charter from the English Anglican monarch to create his new colony, Maryland from its very beginning had to "tolerate" the established Anglican Church. "Catholic" Maryland's population was initially a Protestant majority, but in time, religious dissenters, atheists and the irreligious outnumbered both Roman Catholics and Anglicans. In 1649, Calvert, Maryland's proprietor, and his Protestant legislature gave religious toleration to all Trinitarian Christians.[19] "Not until mid-century did an Anglican priest arrive in Maryland. By the 1670s only three Anglican clergy were at work among the more than twenty thousand settlers. When Maryland temporarily became a royal colony in 1691, Governor Francis Nicholson noticeably expanded the number of Anglican churches and clergy. In 1700 fifteen clergy from several parishes came to Annapolis to meet with the first personal representative, or commissary, sent to the colony by the bishop of London."[20]

In 1623 at Jamestown, an African couple named Isabelle and Anthony were baptized into the Anglican Church along with their son William. That was a unique event because Virginia planters in the seventeenth century resisted efforts by Anglican clergy to evangelize their slaves. Their opposition was based on at least a feeling of African-American inferiority, but also on the fear that baptism would lead to manumission. The fear of manumission caused four colonial governments to pass official acts to disclaim baptism.[21] Anglicanism, in colonial America as well as in England, supported the structures of society and taught respect for authority — a critical difference between

Anglicanism and Puritan republicanism. Anglicanism, therefore, supported slavery, as did many ancient systems of religion.[22] "The surge of work with African Americans came after 1800 during what historians have called the Great Second Awakening.... The total number of African American Episcopalians in the antebellum south approximated 35,000. Missionary work was most successful in South Carolina, where an estimated fourteen thousand African Americans were Episcopalians at the time of the Civil War.... Relatively few African Americans became Episcopalians in the nineteenth century. They joined Baptist and Methodist churches in far greater numbers. Despite its head start over other denominations, the Episcopal Church failed to evangelize African Americans for many reasons."[23] How? Why?

The Great Awakenings in Colonial Virginia

Two events, or two movements over the years in the eighteenth century, had devastating effects on the Anglican Church: the first was the Great Awakening and the other was the American Revolution. The growths of these two movements were either parallel or dependent. It can be argued that had it not been for the Great Awakening, the American Revolution might never have come about. The linkages between the two are tight. Furthermore, it can be argued that had there been no vestry system in the colonial Church of England in full control of each church, and had there been no commissary but a bishop instead, the American Revolution might never have taken place. But there were too many variable exigencies to positively conclude what might have happened otherwise. The facts on the ground explain the situation. The colonial Church of England had uneducated and wayward clergy; clergy had no high social status in the church nor the colony; the vestry controlled the clergy; there was no bishop but a resident commissary for each colony; clergy worked on short-term contracts and always asked for more salary at contract renewal; lay people resented the clergy's requests for salary increases; the church was established and attendance was mandatory, and taxation for ecclesiastical support was the order of the day. Bishops, since they were identified as representatives of the English government, were not wanted in the colonies; therefore the colonial Church of England could not operate according to its fundamental order. Not only were there problems in the colonies, there were social and church problems in England as well. The movement in England led by John and Charles Wesley was taking hold. But it was one of their followers who burst onto the scene, first in England and then in the colonies, who would begin to bring about spiritual changes affecting all of the colonies. That spiritual change, it can be argued, led to the eventual political change that lit the fires of the American Revolution.

Methodism and Evangelicalism in Virginia

George Whitefield, a disciple of Methodism within the Church of England, came to the colonies in 1739 and 1740 to conduct a preaching tour. More radical in his beliefs than the Wesleys, Whitefield alienated fellow Anglican clergy by veering astray of traditional Anglican tenets and order. Whitefield preached a personal, spiritual renewal and repentance. He spent little to no time in adhering to the Anglican doctrine of apostolic succession of bishops, which made him popular among non–Anglicans, or dissenters. At first welcomed to preach in Anglican churches in the colonies, he quickly became persona non grata. He was not allowed to preach in Anglican churches from New England to Georgia. The one exception was in Virginia. Blair, the Virginia commissary, allowed Whitefield to preach at Bruton Parish Church in Williamsburg, but queried the Bishop of London about Whitefield's canonical status in the church. In other words, if the Bishop of London were to write that Whitefield was canonically inhibited, then Blair would not allow preaching in the Virginia churches. What was Whitefield's message and why was it so powerful?

Whitefield attacked tradition, particularly where he thought tradition was not spiritually efficacious. In his preaching he was, wittingly or not, allying himself with the deep beliefs of the colonials. He also attacked the vile treatment of slaves. In South Carolina especially, Whitefield chastised slave owners and government for the manner in which they treated fellow human beings; he called them into account, suggesting that final judgment would not be welcomed. The times were changing, and Whitefield was able to pick up on this sentiment; and since his brilliant preaching skill was coupled with emotional evocation, many colonials followed his every word. It was the evangelical and emotional route, and not necessarily the intellectual and logical route, that Whitefield preached. He had the ability to preach to large crowds that their own individual conversion and personal conviction were what was important in life. Baptism and other sacraments played second fiddle in Whitefield's preaching and teaching. His own conversion seems to have been the catalyst sparking his entry into the ministry. He joined the Wesleys at Oxford in their "Holy Club" and thereby began his own learning and understanding of the gospel. In the end it was a personal conviction of the individual to accept Christ and then to change his life — a transformation, a turnaround, repentance. The net ecclesiastical result was that the colonial Anglican Church opposed the preaching of Whitefield; the non–Anglicans were more than accepting. The Anglican Church was on the wrong side of a spiritual movement.

As the "awakening" took life over time, some of the emotionalism evident

Office of the president, early 1900s (Russell Memorial Library, Saint Paul's College, Lawrenceville, Virginia).

in Whitefield's preaching style was beginning to wear off, but the sentiment remained. Revival, personal conviction, and personal transformation were alive and well in the hearts of many colonials because the call for revival in 1739–40 was strong. However, some of Whitefield's followers, especially the Congregationalists and Presbyterians, were split by the events of the Awakening.

The situation evolved into an "either/or" situation — you were for the Awakening movement or you were not. Those not totally on board, although supporters, believed that baptism was indeed a sign of adult awakening, so they broke away from the Congregationalists and Presbyterians and became "Baptists." There existed a Baptist Church — a denomination or sect — before the advent of the Awakening which eventually grew large in numbers afterwards. Other Congregationalists and Presbyterians began to take issue with Whitefield's anti-doctrinal stance because it interfered with or totally ignored traditional theological formularies. These examples were experienced mostly in the New England colonies. The so-called middle colonies saw growth in the Presbyterian Churches especially because of the area's Scotch-Irish presence. Even though Anglican clergy opposed Whitefield's tactics and beliefs, as did many New England non–Anglicans, some Anglican laity left the church. Despite the unusual circumstances brought about in all churches by the Awakening, the Anglican Church grew in the middle colonies.

We pause for a moment to take note of the fact that within this Great Awakening movement, an undercurrent of change taking place may have been missed. Even though each colony supported an established ecclesiastical organization, be it Congregational, Quaker, or Anglican, religious dissenters were everywhere. Whitefield's preaching certainly awakened a spiritual life heretofore repressed, but he engendered not only an emotional release of religious fervor; he also caused many churches to reflect on their traditional creeds and covenants. Those reflections generated anti–Awakening action, certainly unexpected by Whitefield, but perhaps by all. Believing that there were errors in the Awakening's message, Anglicans thought education would correct many if not all of them. This led the way for the seemingly impossible task of creating Anglican colleges in the colonies. So in New York a group of Anglicans developed King's College, today which is Columbia University.

The Virginia colony was initially untouched by the Awakening even though it was the first southern area to experience it. The Church of Virginia's numbers neither improved nor deteriorated during early Awakening of 1739–40. It was not until Whitefield's fifth and sixth trips to the colonies (1754–1755 and 1763–1765) that Anglicans made some changes in their attitude. In Virginia, as well as in all the colonies, a rollover or change of clergy naturally took place. Younger clergy began to accept Whitefield's message. But his message, and certainly his criticism of Anglicanism, had been modified. Instead of being locked out of Anglican churches, Whitefield was invited to preach in the interest of avoiding Anglican disunion. In Virginia one person affected by the Awakening was Deveraux Jarratt (1733–1801). Responding to the message of the Awakening in a Presbyterian church, he subsequently traveled to England to seek ordination. While in England he heard both John Wesley and George Whitefield preach. After returning to Virginia he became rector of a church in Dinwiddie County (in Virginia's Southside) and preached a message of personal conversion. Like Wesley, and unlike Whitefield, Jarratt established small religious societies in and around his church. In addition to clergy, there developed an effective lay leadership in the Anglican Church as a result of the Awakening.

Apostolic succession, the belief and practice that the church's ministry has continued in an unbroken chain through the consecration of bishops since the time of the Apostles, was never abandoned by Anglicans even in the 1760s and 1770s. But the style of preaching changed and the call for personal conversion was stressed. The colonial Church of England was not unaffected by the Awakenings. Some of the changes seemed late but necessary, especially for women and African-Americans. The status of women in the church rose gradually. And even in the early days of the Awakening—1739–40—the Anglican Church extended it ministry to black Americans, slave and free. This was also the period of a great increase in the slave population. But it was later in the 1760s, after the Awakening had its grasp on Anglicanism, that the church may have conducted its most effective work with African-American slaves. Whatever the reasons, the Great Awakening and the Anglican Church's ministry to blacks were concurrent. Other changes, such as a call for bishops in the colonies, were to be acted upon and are discussed in a later chapter. But our focus turns to the evangelization of black Americans.[24]

According to one historian, evangelicalism was a biracial enterprise in colonial America, and by 1792 "all observers knew that to be evangelical meant to share spiritual experiences across racial lines."[25] Again, it was George Whitefield who stirred the emotions of his hearers as well as opposition to his message. After visiting with and preaching to the southern colonies, Whitefield wrote a circular letter to those southern, mainly Anglican, churches. In it he wrote that he was touched by the miserable conditions of their Negroes and that God had a quarrel with the church for their cruelty and abusiveness toward the Negroes.[26] This was a message well-received by non–Anglicans. Indeed, well-known preachers of the Presbyterian and Baptist traditions attracted large numbers of African-American members. Whitefield's message, however, stressed personal conversion and avoided any mention of equating Christian conversion with emancipation, manumission, or civil freedom from bondage. Nonetheless, the evangelical message had its attraction to both dissenting whites and African-Americans.

Dissenting preachers in Virginia could not directly attack the established church for fear of losing their license to preach, but they would take an indirect or circuitous route, criticizing the Anglican Church by implication. Those dissenting preachers who picked up on Whitefield's message were similarly successful in attracting followers, especially blacks. Large numbers of slaves attended evangelical church services. Presbyterian Samuel Davies was successful in the calling together of more than one thousand Negroes in his weekly services in the 1750s in Virginia. The Society for Promoting Religious Knowledge, based in London, supplied Davies with books. Anglicans still could not agree among themselves on the movement. Also in the 1750s two groups of Baptists made headway in Virginia. Those Baptists were divided into two groups called the "Regulars" and the "Separates." They, too, would challenge and criticize the established church. The "Separates" were the more evangelical of the two and even received criticism from the "Regulars." Both were aligned in their beliefs and in their attitudes toward African-Americans. The Baptists, actively seeking black Virginian conversions, were still low in numbers by the 1770s but were more successful than Anglicans. Anglicans did, however, begin to baptize African-American infants, but the only effort by Anglicans with some success came in the educational endeavor of an international Anglican missionary organization. The real missionary effort by Anglicans was made by its "Methodist" sect.

The Methodists preached to black and white alike. They held small meetings, thereby making an open arrangement for slaves to attend. Deveraux Jarratt believed that blacks welcomed the Methodist movement.[27] And he was right. There was in Virginia a social divide among the whites. The gentry were the upper class of Virginia, and the yeomen, many former or descendants of former indentured servants, were the lower. There were political differences between the two, with the gentry holding political power. Though the creation of the House of Burgesses created a representative government, it was still the gentry over time who dominated the political structure of Virginia. There was a natural distaste by yeomen (or farmers) for the gentry. And although Anglican clergy were not gentry, yeoman or the rank-and-file citizens of Virginia held an equal distaste for them also. The established church was viewed as the government, and the Virginia citizenry in the eighteenth century was beginning to experience a sense of individualism and a distinct difference from English society. All of these elements are thrown into the mix of a changing set of attitudes lending itself to a radical readjustment in traditional religious beliefs, slave and free.

Brunswick County and Southside Virginia

Dinwiddie County, Virginia, is one of the Southside counties, along with Mecklenburg, Southampton, and Brunswick. One hundred years or so before the birth of James Solomon Russell (1857) in Mecklenburg, Deveraux Jarratt and his area of evangelical influence enveloped the Southside. The Methodist

Episcopal Church in the new United States declared its independence in Philadelphia in 1784. In May of 1785 it held its first quarterly meeting in Brunswick County, Virginia.[28] During the early 1780s in St. Andrew's Anglican Parish, Lawrenceville, the Rev. Mr. Thomas Lundie was performing such a large number of marriages that there was a waiting list. Concurrently in nearby Bath Parish in Dinwiddie, Jarratt, the Anglican-Methodist, was preaching with fervor about the "Christian experience." Instead of preaching the all-so-common sermon on the moral lessons, he spoke of what was personally required of the believer. He preached not only in church buildings but in open-air meetings attended by large crowds. This Anglican was preaching in a most unusual way for an Anglican at that time, and it was Brunswick County where he first made his preaching journeys. He always received, it is reported, a warm welcome. Jarratt and other Anglican-Methodists began to preach all over the Southside. In 1773 a Methodist pioneer named Robert Williams met with Jarratt in Petersburg, and a new and inspiring relationship developed. Williams was sent to the colony from England by John Wesley. Finding it difficult to preach and to minister in Norfolk, Jarratt encouraged Williams to minister in Brunswick County. In 1774 Williams formed the Brunswick circuit, the first Methodist circuit in colonial America. His work was highly productive and covered a large geographical area. To many, Brunswick County, if not the fount of colonial Methodism, is the cradle of Methodism in the South. Jarratt and other leaders preached that the Methodists came to build up and not to divide the church.[29]

By 1775 the Methodists in the Brunswick circuit claimed 800 members, and they were still within the established church and not a separate denomination at that time. The number had more than doubled the next year. It was larger than any other circuit in any of the other colonies. With a renewal of faith of such magnitude, John Wesley appointed five preachers to the Brunswick Circuit: Roger Glendenning, Robert Lindsay, George Shadford, Edward Dromgoole, and Robert Williams. Shadford was probably the most successful, but he returned to England at the outbreak of the Revolutionary War. All the others, with the exception of Dromgoole, eventually returned to England. Dromgoole, an Irish immigrant in 1770, was a Catholic who converted to the Methodist form of Anglicanism. Dromgoole was also a patriot devoted to the cause of freedom. He preached until the age of eighty-four but discontinued his circuit preaching much earlier, when his son died. What needs to be pointed out is that Methodism had its greatest impact in the short term on Virginia's Southside. And Virginia's Southside had the largest concentration of African-Americans, mostly slaves, who were affected by the Great Awakening and its aftermath. Even though the Revolutionary War affected all of the colonies, the Brunswick Methodist Circuit flourished and the established church — the colonial Church of England or the Church of Virginia — was undiminished in its influence.[30] In a letter to Dromgoole in 1788, Jarratt, who actually left the Methodists and joined the Protestant Episcopal Church when still a dominant Methodist figure in Virginia, wrote that because the Bible made references to slavery and the issue of slavery in the church was becoming so divisive, "white evangelicals should refrain from discussing it within the church."[31] Jarratt had made a turnabout in his ministry: he now objected to criticisms of slave owners, who were prevalent in the Episcopal Church. His prescient letter to Dromgoole outlined the eventual settlements of the slavery issue with Baptists, Methodists, and Presbyterians in Virginia. He now considered the issue of slavery as solely a civil and not an ecclesiastical matter — a consideration adopted by a few Episcopal bishops in the antebellum era. This point of view and its eventual implementation among evangelicals would have its consequences.

In Virginia as elsewhere in the new, post–1776 republic, the ethics of slavery was the major issue. The Methodists were in the forefront of criticism, including Francis Asbury, the founder of American Methodism. Edward Dromgoole bequeathed most of his land in southern Brunswick County to black people. He also attempted to educate African-Americans. The first Methodist meeting in Virginia was hot in debate over the issue. As a result a Mr. Owen of Norfolk freed his slaves and settled them in Brunswick. Many whites left Brunswick feeling perhaps that the county was far ahead of its neighboring counties in this new, liberal thinking. At the time that Methodists were working well with Baptists and Presbyterians developing close friendships and social ties, the Episcopal Church was becoming marginal. In 1790 the Rev. Mr. Lundie, rector of St. Andrew's Church in Lawrenceville, resigned his post and became a (denominational) Methodist. In 1814 at the General Convention of the Episcopal Church, only seven clergy and eighteen laymen from the entire state of Virginia attended. The Episcopal Church's identification with England, the tithes, restrictions and other modes of taxation during colonial times, and its ineffectual clergy, effectively destroyed the Episcopal Church for decades after the Revolution. The Great Awakening had introduced a new way of thinking, not only in Virginia but in the other former colonies. Moral issues such as slavery became more important, and personal conviction in the faith was more important than church doctrine. The Episcopal Church waned and reappeared only in 1827 as a mission.[32]

The Great Revival

There was a period between 1785 and 1792 referred to as the Great Revival. The Baptists, particularly in Virginia, were the leading beneficiaries.

Virginia's white Baptists received the most number of African-American converts. But the whites were divided on slavery and some sought a Biblical justification. With the disestablishment of the Anglican Church in Virginia in 1779, all evangelical churches were engaged in discovering their appropriate role within a republic. Methodists were more orderly than Baptists in their organizational structure and therefore could interact with other churches outside Virginia; Baptists were more independent and congregational. Methodists still held slightly to both Anglicanism's hierarchical model and Wesley's own personal skill at organizational mechanics. All of the churches tried to work their way through the single issue of slavery in their own ways, and struggled to determine each church's polity in that regard. In what should have been a straightforward move toward abolition lingered a longer-term debate which was seemingly never-ending.

Evangelical churches, led by whites, simply could not agree among themselves their polity regarding slavery, so they split into factions and formed new churches, or they refused to deal with the issue. In not dealing with slavery, the general assumption was that since slaves were in bondage, their status, both civil and ecclesiastical, was settled. From that point forward a paternalistic social philosophy prevailed. African-American evangelicals having no choice in the matter, even though some were quite vocal, continued to worship with whites, as the day of worship was in one respect a day of relative freedom. And so it went until 1831 when Nat Turner and some of his followers went on a killing rampage in Southampton County, Virginia. Whites were scandalized. How could a Christian evangelical minister, albeit a slave, lead such an insurrection with the killing of white people? In the aftermath the evangelical churches tightened their reins over what blacks could do within the church. White naiveté or their submission to the centuries-old social plausibility structure blinded them to the reality that slaves really did not want to be held in bondage. The Southampton insurrection was inevitable. Perhaps the surprising thing is that there were not more rebellions and insurrections for all that time since the advent of African bondage. Nonetheless, the rules changed, and fear became the fundamental driver of church and civil polity. White evangelicals as well as the general white southern population developed the theory that God gave to the superior race the responsibility of rearing and teaching the inferior African race. This type of rhetoric was widely used and believed. But after Southampton any level of trust between masters and slaves, whites and blacks, disappeared. Any solution to slavery that could have been settled in the elongated and massive spiritual spread of the Great Awakening was lost. After 1831 there could be no legislative, spiritual or canonical resolution.

Historically there have always been political, social, ideological and religious differences between American colonists in northern or mountainous parts and their fellow southern or eastern citizens. As slavery developed, its strongholds were in the southern portions of the colonies, and eventually, the states. For example, the northern or mountainous parts of Alabama had virtually no say in the politics of the state. The small and almost landless yeomen worked their own fields, few having any slaves at all. So by the time of the advent of the Civil War they had no interest in secession. Likewise, the upstate of South Carolina and the mountainous or western regions of Virginia had similar social structures and sympathies. In Virginia the differences were so wide between west and east that the state of West Virginia separated from Virginia during the Civil War. For those upstate citizens or those on the Border States, seceding from the Union was at the least not a popular item. Evangelicals in Virginia — though Southerners with conflicting beliefs about race and slavery — were never truly Confederates at heart. If anything, they were reluctant secessionists. The contradiction between their justifications of slavery and a sense of mission to "the inferior race" was an ingrained saturation of their lives.[33] It is likely that some white evangelical Confederates viewed the Civil War as a holy war that would eventually justify their social beliefs and social system. African-American evangelicals were not part of the Confederate cause, and therefore may have held a holy-war perspective on a far different basis.

Prior to the Civil War, Brunswick County experienced tensions between the differences of power as exercised by the state government and the federal government. The fundamental issue was the existence of slavery. From that starting point it became, in the eyes of the state, a constitutional issue. So this one county in Virginia was not unlike most counties of the Southern states. After South Carolina seceded in December of 1860, Virginia's citizens actually looked for a way to avoid the developing conflict. Virginia wanted to avoid secession. In April 1861, Virginia had not seceded, and its State Convention or General Assembly voted 88 to 45 to remain in the Union. But after South Carolina's militia fired on Fort Sumter and Abraham Lincoln ordered 75,000 soldiers to put down the rebellion, things changed rapidly. Feeling a strong sister-state kinship, Virginia could not find its way to fight against South Carolina. On April 17, 1861, the Virginia Convention voted to secede by a vote of 88 to 55. The statewide referendum garnered a majority of 128,884 to 32,134 in favor of secession in May. Brunswick, like the entire state of Virginia, was not fully locked into the Confederate cause, but sent men into war. Brunswick County had only 1,288 white men of the age to fight in the war. Slave owners were required to send their able-bodied slaves to Petersburg and the Peninsula (Hampton, Newport News area) to build fortifications and other defense structures for the Confederate troops. Some Brunswick free blacks offered to enlist in the Confederate Army but were denied entry. The 1860 census shows that Brunswick County had 671 free blacks and more than 9,000 slaves. With most of the white men off to war, it was the free blacks and black slaves who operated the plantations.[34]

Geographically Virginia was in the "Upper South." It was closer to the Northern states and therefore had the unfortunate wartime experience of being overrun by both Union and Confederate armies. Most of the plantations, farms, and businesses were ransacked, looted, and pillaged by troops from both sides. Livestock and truck crops were taken or stolen by troops in order to feed themselves. Brunswick County's troops, the Brunswick Guards, the Brunswick Blues, and the Brunswick Greys, all experienced fighting in some of the great Civil War battles. The Blues fought in South Carolina, Georgia and Florida until 1864. They were called back to defend Richmond and Petersburg against General Grant. They were instrumental in holding back the army of Union General Benjamin Butler. The Blues retreated from Petersburg and Richmond on orders from Confederate General Robert E. Lee, and they fought their way westward. Those Blues who remained fought at Appomattox Court House and eventually surrendered with Robert E. Lee on April 9, 1865. The other two Brunswick regiments had similar service in the Confederate effort. There were other units from Brunswick County that fought in the Civil War.[35] This information is presented here in order for the reader to get an understanding of the social, civil, and religious environment in which Virginia and Brunswick County found itself in the immediate decades following the end of the war.

The demographics of the churches in Virginia began to drastically shift during and after the Civil War. The once biracial evangelical churches began to fall apart. The personal but restrained emotion of hatred between black and whites between 1831 and 1861 would manifest itself as quickly as Union troops entered the South and set up physical lines of protection for emancipated slaves. For example, at the beginning of the Civil War, the Virginia Methodist Conference membership contained more than 3,000 African-Americans, but one year after the war only 1,000 remained. Virginia's experience was a microcosm of other churches in the South at that time. More than 80 percent of black Methodists in the entire commonwealth left their former biracial churches. Black evangelicals left to form their own independent churches. The separation was quick and widespread. By 1890 there were living in Virginia more than 635,000 African-Americans, 238,617 of whom were members of black-only churches. Those numbers contrast with up to 70,000 African-Americans who were members of biracial evangelical churches in Virginia just prior to the Civil War. The exodus of African-Americans from white or biracial churches was of large-scale proportions.[36]

According to historian Charles F. Irons, white evangelicals thought the new black churches would enjoy the same "paternal" influence proffered in the past, but they were rebuked. Not yet able to understand rejection, white evangelicals felt hurt, were suspicious, and eventually became angry.[37] At its most superficial level it can be said that at least an attempt had been made by southern, white evangelicals to create biracial churchmanship. The eye-opening initiated by the Great Awakening was at minimum a beginning at trying to correct the social wrongs of their era. But there is another side of the story to be told.

The Methodist movement in colonial and republican America was strong. Its practical and simple methods of spreading the gospel took hold on the hearts and minds of many people. But in the North where there was no legal slavery, black Methodists separated from the church. In 1816 there were African-Americans who hoped for greater freedom and to become more useful in the church. Restrictions on blacks in northern Methodism were widespread enough that a small group of black Methodists called for a separate denomination. A convention was called in Philadelphia and the African Methodist Episcopal Church (AME) was born. Richard Allen, who at one period in his career considered joining the Episcopal Church with Absalom Jones, was elected its first bishop. Allen, already a presbyter or elder or minister for seventeen years in the Methodist Church, was consecrated bishop by five other presbyters. Morris Brown (who was associated with Denmark Vesey in South Carolina) was made bishop in 1828, and their third bishop was consecrated in 1836. Doctrinal differentiation between the AME and Methodist Episcopal churches was hardly distinguishable. What was crystal clear was their separation from one another. The separation was indicative of African-American discrimination of some level among the Methodists.

Earlier, in 1786, some sixty colored members of the First Methodist Episcopal Church in New York City pulled out of their church to form the Negro Methodist Society in America. Their leader was James Varick. This group held their services in the same church building but separate from the whites and at alternating intervals. Eventually they moved to a new edifice. Naming themselves the African Methodist Episcopal Church Zion (AME Zion), they had four preachers initially — Abraham Thompson, June Smoot, Thomas Miller and William Miller. All received their exhorter's licenses from the Methodist Episcopal Church. AME Zion did not incorporate itself until 1801 but wasted no time in establishing itself as an outspoken organization endorsing religious freedom and working to rid the country of any racial prejudice that inhibited or restricted African-Americans' civil liberties. Like the later AME organization, the doctrinal and "methodological" pragmatism of the Methodist Episcopal Church were hardly distinguishable. Perhaps more than the AME, the AME Zion Church was seen as the ultimate racial church in America, promoting the best of Negro hopes and desires. Despite all of the positive motivations in promoting Negro advancement in the creation of these two churches of the North, the simple fact is that they, the African-Americans, called for separation from their white churchmen. The irony is that the evangelical churches of the South called for racial community, albeit not a perfect community. But the separation within Methodism continued through the Civil War period. Other separated churches were the Colored Methodist Episcopal Church; Congregational Methodist (Colored); African Union Methodist Protestant; Union American Methodist Episcopal; and the Colored Contingent of the Methodist Episcopal Church. Other denominations were formed, such as the Colored Baptist; Colored Protestant Episcopal; Colored Presbyterian; and Colored Roman Catholics.[38] (See Appendix B — Colored Churches Membership 1900, and Appendix C — Methodist Churches in the United States as of 1900.)

Of these colored Methodist churches, mostly organized in the North, the AME and AME Zion were the two largest. Smaller colored Methodist churches organized were the Reformed Methodist Union Episcopal Church, with approximately 5,000 members; the Union American Methodist Episcopal Church, boasting 18,500 members; the African Union Methodist Episcopal Church, with about 4,000 members; and the Zion Union Apostolic Church, with approximately 3,000 members. Only the Zion Union was organized in the South and not as a spin-off of a northern church.

It is the Zion Union Apostolic Church (ZUAC) that invites further investigation. From various reports we learn that James Solomon Russell was secretary to this church's annual conference. ZUAC was a "Methodist-like" church, it was all black, and it was separatist, or anti-white, in its origination. The Zion Union Church was more influenced by Russell, as a young man, than the other way around. This future educator and clergyman was formed by his childhood experiences (including some years as a slave), along with the Zion Union connection, his education, and his interactions with persons of leadership.

CHAPTER THREE

Influences

R USSELL'S *AUTOBIOGRAPHY* IS THE LOGICAL STARTING POINT to learn about him, for it is from his descriptions, mostly summary accounts but with selected detail of significant or pivotal events, that the reader gets a sense of his view of the span and meaning of his life. He wrote the book less than a year before his death, having the benefit of reviewing his life through the filters of seventy-six years and a matured, perhaps memorializing perspective. Much of what Russell claims is corroborated in disinterested journals and periodicals and is noted throughout this book.

Russell wasted no time characterizing slavery: "On December 20, 1857, I unceremoniously became one more slave on the plantation of Mr. Hendrick.... This matter of producing slaves was as important as breeding animals."[1] The life of a slave was a structured life, not a good life, but a structured life. A slave-master determined what his chattels would do or not do, how they would live, and when they would procreate. Even though a personal or civil relationship might have developed between a master and his slave, the structure of the Southern social environment did not allow for its public display. But Russell betrays a concern for (if not a personal relationship with) his master and his master's family when he writes, "All through the Civil War, my mother and the other slaves remained on the plantation, but the news of the strife was always around us; three of our master's sons were away with the Confederate forces, *and concern for them also gripped the slaves* [emphasis added]."[2]

Most African-Americans[3] prior to the Civil War and Emancipation lived in highly structured and controlled environments. So when Emancipation finally arrived, it is no wonder that James Solomon Russell would write that they were thrown out to fend for themselves. No longer did he and his mother know where their next meal would come from or where they would shelter themselves. "This poverty stood out all the more because, following the Emancipation, we were left to fight our own battles and to manage our own lives;

Clergy of the Episcopal Diocese of Southern Virginia, circa 1920s. Archdeacon Russell is at front left (see arrow) (Russell Memorial Library, Saint Paul's College, Lawrenceville, Virginia).

we were cast upon the billowy deep to paddle our own canoe, to what destination we scarcely knew. One thing we soon found out; no more could we look to our master for shelter, sustenance, care, and direction; we had gained Freedom and with it the responsibilities—dire responsibilities, at first—of being our own masters."[4] Russell's brief account of his former owner does not read like a harsh description of how he and his family were treated while in bondage. The absence of malice in the printed word by Russell toward his former slave master suggests that Russell nurtured a mindset of forgiveness and a temperament to move forward. After all, his was a transitional generation, and he was a former slave eager to make his own way in truly uncharted waters.

According to some accounts, many former slaves sought no structure at all and became like wild animals. Years after Emancipation the attitude of whites, both Northerners and Southerners, toward the freedmen changed little. For example, at the Pan-Anglican Congress at London in 1908, the Rev. W.A.R. Goodwin, twice rector of Bruton Parish Church in Williamsburg, Virginia, known also as "the Father of [the restored town of] Colonial

Williamsburg," and a future diocesan peer of Russell, said, "The negro sadly needs what the Church has to give — moral education, spiritual enlightenment, ordered worship, and the loving discipline of the order and authority of the Church."[5] It should also be noted that many if not most freedmen did not flee to the North, but stayed fairly close to the homes of their old slavemasters. It was the slaves, after all, who worked the land, cooked the meals, washed the clothes, and tended to the real day-to-day activities of the plantation. Slaves escaped their masters during the Civil War and fled behind Union troops' lines. There they found a temporary means of subsistence. Some fled to the North via the Underground Railroad. Attempts by the federal government to come to the assistance of former slaves were fraught with mistakes, errors and fraud. The Freedmen's Bureau[6] was created specifically to provide aid and governance. The periods of Presidential and Radical (Congressional) Reconstruction were governmental attempts at improving the lot of the newly emancipated. Reconstruction began[7] when Russell was a boy of six and continued through 1877 when Russell was twenty. Russell's early years of freedom were marked by government programs aimed at making major improvements for former slaves.

Araminta Russell

Young James Solomon Russell, like many other freed slaves, sought out an education. It was a common belief that education would solve any present or future problems. Several events and persons had an effect on Russell's development. His drive for structure, education, religion and racial uplift were initially supported by certain influences in his young life. Russell always believed he had a future despite his early experiences as a slave. Although Russell did not spend many pages in his *Autobiography* singling out those who influenced him, evidence exists not only in his book but in his speeches, sermons and annual reports to the church showing that his young-life experiences prepared him for his life's work.

His mother, Araminta, had a plan or at least a vision for her son and she made sure that he understood what she had in mind. His mother's purpose for him might have been the dominant influence — her purpose embodied the concept of structure. For example, his mother named him Solomon not only because it was his father's name, but for King Solomon of the Old Testament. She hoped and prayed that James would be as wise as she heard the "white minister preach and the Negro lay-reader exhort."[8] This also was the first reference in his autobiography to any notion of faith, church or religion — a spiritual influence that began early in his life and played a significant role in his development. It also provides evidence that the Russell family, even as slaves, were a Christian household. For Russell to make an issue of his mother naming him Solomon might betray a trace of self-grandiosity. As we will see, Russell was a purposeful man, and given the times he lived in he had to work diligently against many sorts of man-made or social obstacles; therefore he worked with aplomb and with a certain level of self-promoting hyperbole.

It is risky to make too close a comparison between these two Solomons, but there are some points in common to highlight and some points of departure to cite. First, Russell was reared in a faithful and religious family — this was foundational to his formation. King Solomon, on being faithful to God and keeping Israel faithful to God, would be honored by God and Israel would thus prosper. Secondly, Solomon was a great builder, not only of a new Temple but of alliances of nations. Russell, as we will see, was a developer of groups or networks of supporters, adept at acquiring land and properties for his school; a builder of church congregations; and the founder of an educational institution. St. Paul Normal and Industrial School and Russell are virtually tautological.[9] Russell understood at an early age the potential effectiveness of power, prestige and perseverance.

Russell acknowledged the heavy burden or problems which befell his mother before, during and after the Civil War. Once freed, they were on their own and did not have the protection of their master. He observed her work and dedication toward a family life. During slavery, James's father Solomon did not live with his family on the Hendrick Estate plantation in Mecklenburg County, Virginia, but on the Russell plantation in nearby Warren County, North Carolina. Solomon Russell joined the family after the Civil War ended and together the family worked the land as tenant-farmers and took jobs in order to survive.

Apostles' Creed and the Book of Common Prayer

During his short tenure at Hampton Institute, Russell's home was in Mecklenburg County, Virginia. It was as a child and again in his teen years that he discovered the Book of Common Prayer (BCP) and the Apostles' Creed, and determined that one day he would enter the ministry as a priest in the Episcopal Church. Although Hampton Institute was a secular institution, founder Samuel Chapman Armstrong infused the daily school routine with the practice of religion and regular chapel attendance by all students. Armstrong used the Book of Common Prayer, and the Creed was heard at every service; therefore Russell's calling to become a priest was actually strengthened by his Hampton experience.

Just months before his return to Hampton in the autumn of 1877, Russell's aunt, Jennie Fain, urged him to consider the African Methodist Episcopal Church, and she arranged a meeting with her pastor. But Russell had already made up his mind about the Episcopal Church. Russell writes, "Having no one nearby to guide me toward the priesthood, I called upon Mrs. P.E. Buford of Lawrenceville, who was much concerned about missionary work among the colored people."[10] Russell writes:

> Mrs. Buford became interested and referred my case to the Rt. Rev. F.M. Whittle, then Bishop of the undivided Diocese of Virginia. Bishop Whittle directed the Rev. Robert White, evangelist, to go to Hampton and ascertain what he could concerning my qualifications and character, but when Mr. White reached the Institute I had already left to open my school in North Carolina. Hence, I did not see Mr. White. Bishop Whittle later appointed a commission composed of the Rev. Alexander Weddell and the Rev. T. Grason [sic] Daschiell, who met me at St. Andrew's Church, Lawrenceville, in the summer of 1878 — within a stone's throw from the property now owned by the St. Paul School. This body ultimately agreed to give me my opportunity by starting a branch of the Theological Seminary of Virginia at St. Stephen's Church, Petersburg. This "branch" became the Bishop Payne Divinity School for the training of colored men for the Episcopal priesthood.[11]

Russell makes no mention in his *Autobiography* of his association with the Zion Union Apostolic Church (ZUAC).

After reading through the entire Book of Common Prayer, Russell said that he became a spiritual member of the Episcopal Church. The Book of Common Prayer represented structure to Russell. The prayers were impressive and he said that he made use of them whenever called upon in public.[12] Mostly likely it was the fixed format or structure of the prayer book that provided young Russell with an orderly way to structure his future. To Russell the BCP may have been the rationale or plausibility structure of the Church. It is not known whether Russell was aware of the practices of the Episcopal Church in the American South, or that he was aware that many Episcopalians, including bishops and priests, owned slaves. Recognizing the BCP as the document of church structure, Russell knew how the church was called into being and how it should operate. It was the Methodist Church in the South that practiced a more open attitude toward slaves. Many of those who were Methodists, even during the American Revolution, were opposed to slavery. Many Methodist slave owners who could not free their slaves due to economic reasons freed them in their wills, and Methodists were suspected of harboring fugitive slaves over the years.[13] The practices of the Episcopal Church did not enjoy a similar reputation. The attractions of the Episcopal Church to Russell seems to be its collective high intelligence, wealth and social status. Russell, although influenced by the BCP, the Creed and the Episcopal Church itself, later in life was to be critical of the Episcopal Church's neglect of ex-slaves. Although he understood why many former slaves bolted Anglicanism for other churches — mostly for the African Methodist, Baptist and African Methodist Zion — he called that a mistake.[14] What was it that Russell understood about Anglicanism that made him label the black exodus as a mistake?

In his book *Yet with a Steady Beat*, Harold T. Lewis documents the mass exodus of blacks from the Episcopal Church in the years following Emancipation and the end of the American Civil War. "In the Diocese of South Carolina, where before the war nearly half of the communicants had been black [South Carolina had 3,000 black communicants in 1860 — not even half that number could be found in all the dioceses in the North or South], there were only 395 black members in 1868.... In Alabama ... only two congregations remained after the Civil War.... In Virginia, only 64 black Episcopalians remained; a mere 1 percent of the membership of the diocese. Even the great St. James', Baltimore, having been founded by free blacks, could not boast fifty members in 1867."[15] Why this exodus? Whites blamed blacks for being too emotional in their worship and for their adverse reaction to white instruction. Low morals were a common reason used by whites. Southern whites also blamed Northerners, carpetbaggers and the like. Blacks had another explanation: they wanted to be free of the white man's domination, and the black churches made it possible for black leadership to develop. The gap between white and black Episcopalians was to be found in their respective understandings of "catholicity." Whites believed that God's house had many rooms and some of those rooms were better than others. The rooms differed according to social status. This view of "catholicity" had no absolute, objective standards. Lewis said that this understanding meant that the church's life was to remain stratified, as was society in general. Blacks' beliefs about catholicity were based on the epistles of St. Paul in Romans 12:2,[16] that mankind should not conform to the patterns of the present world (where there are no absolute, objective standards), and Galatians 3:28,[17] that there is neither Greek nor Jew, nor bond nor free, but that all should be one in Christ Jesus.[18]

To the young James Solomon Russell, the Episcopal Church and its BCP must have seemed catholic and true. There were standards, order, and structure. And the worship was less emotional and more restrained than what he experienced in the Zion Union Church. Although not yet intellectually or scholastically aware of the stated theology in the BCP nor aware of the pre- and post–Civil War history of the Episcopal Church, Russell nonetheless sensed an unchanging standard of Christian belief and Christian living that provided him a vision of how his new emancipated life should be worked out with his former owners. To the older, more experienced Russell the *mistake* that the church-exiting former slaves made after the Civil War was a mistake of political naïveté. Bishop Meade said that the African-American slave population in the Episcopal Church was large enough to become a problem. Russell, in his *Autobiography*, wrote:

> Notwithstanding the strong position taken by Bishop Meade, soon after the War colored Churchmen began to mistrust their white brethren who were laboring among them and the list of colored communicants rapidly decreased. This, of course, was a great mistake made by the colored people, and yet the Church should not have held this illiterate and lately enslaved race accountable for its error in this particular. For it was about this time that Northern Churchmen did not have too much confidence in the efforts that were being put forth by the white missionaries of the South laboring among their colored brethren, and that there was severe prejudice from Southern whites against those who undertook the task of educating and uplifting the former slaves. Hence, in these exciting times the Negro found himself between the upper and nether millstones religiously, with the result that he was crushed out of the Church for the time being. On the other hand, he was clay in the hands of designing politicians who used him as a tool often against his best interests, and thereby widened the breach between him and his former owner: yet, in this hour of his weakness the Church withheld her sympathy and support to an alarming degree, although her missionaries had the endorsement and moral support of their Bishops.[19]

Had former slaves remained in the Episcopal Church they would have had at least a larger numerical percentage of communicants than they eventually did, Russell believed. Politically that would have meant that blacks would have had the potential of a large measure of clout within the ranks of the Church. Russell, knowing the spiritual, social and political natures of the church militant so vividly, believed that the freedman would not only uplift himself through the social and economic strength of the Episcopal Church but he would be strong enough to positively influence the church's necessary transformation. The next two chapters chronicle and analyze Russell's beginnings in the Episcopal Church and follow the steady, but slow, inclusion of African-Americans into the Episcopal Diocese of Virginia.

Overseers and Teachers

From time to time the overseer of the Hendrick Estate, Thomas Wade, would take Russell riding on horseback as he went about his work of the farm. Russell, a young slave boy, would bombard Wade with "countless questions," which Wade always attempted to answer. Nothing more is written about Wade, but it is presumed that Russell mentioned this relationship in his *Autobiography* to show not only that he, Russell, was inquisitive in his youth, but that a significant employee of the estate gave him time and support. It is assumed that Wade was a white man (even though many plantation owners appointed black men as supervisors) and that the young colored slave boy was learning how to interact with whites in an effective and productive way. Perhaps young Russell understood that his future life involved interacting with all people: Emancipation did not mean that Southern white people would disappear, and it did not mean that white people were going to easily relinquish whatever remaining control they might have in politics, religion and social order. That interaction with Wade had to be important to Russell or he would not have included the episode in his book.[20] The superintendent of the white Sunday school, John E.P. Wright, was another person encouraging young Russell. Wright decided to help the small "colored" Sunday school program get on its feet in the spring of 1870 when Russell was thirteen years old. We are never told the name of the church of Russell's youth. All that we know from this *Autobiography* is that his church was located in Mecklenburg County, Virginia, near Palmer Springs.

Another white man, "Mack" Dugger, was the superintendent, and Russell and two of his cousins were the first pupils. Another well-wisher, according to Russell, was a man named Mr. Cheeley, a distinguished educator. We are told that Mr. Cheeley tutored the children of the slave-master Hendrick. The only remark Russell attributes to him is that Cheeley often told Russell's mother, "'That boy will someday be a good preacher' and my mother always kept the prophecy with her and worked for its fulfillment."[21] Armistead Miller, an aged white man, owned a private school in Palmer Springs. Since Russell's family moved from place to place looking for work after the Civil War, Russell had to drop out of whatever school he was attending. His schooling was mostly in a Sunday school. When his family returned to Palmer Springs, Russell attended Mr. Miller's school, but the tuition became expensive. Therefore Russell offered to work at the school to cover the cost. This is meaningful because this "work study" concept repeats itself in Russell's future education and life's work. Once free public education became law in Virginia in 1871, Mr. Miller's school closed. Russell attended public school when he could, but much of his time was spent helping his parents as tenant-farmers. Regardless of his situation, Russell makes the point that he was always studying. It was the superintendent of public instruction of Mecklenburg County who suggested to Russell that he consider attending a boarding school in Hampton, Virginia. This happened on a day when the superintendent was visiting Russell's public school in Palmer Springs. Russell was caught by surprise when the superintendent called him aside and told him that he had completed all that he could at the public school and needed to move on. This was a pivotal event in the young Russell's life. Not only had he now decided to attend

Hampton Normal and Agricultural Institute, but for the first time in his life he was to leave home.

Samuel Chapman Armstrong

Hampton Institute represented a portion of the fulfillment of his dreams for a better education. A realist, Russell believed that the widespread reputation of Hampton was out of proportion to its brief existence.[22] But Hampton was one of those early schools after the Civil War that was meant to be a haven of education for former slaves. So he packed up, left home, and made his way via train and boat to the Virginia Peninsula. Surprisingly, Russell writes little about the principal of his first boarding school, Samuel Chapman Armstrong. Russell's educational format for St. Paul's School is similar if not identical to the format, structure, and order that he experienced as a student at Hampton. For many years, St. Paul Normal and Industrial School, along with Hampton, was a leader in the education of former slaves in Virginia. Armstrong, a former Union brevet brigadier general and a Northerner, came to Hampton, Virginia, as an agent of the Freedmen's Bureau. His purpose in the Bureau was to assist emancipated slaves. A child of missionary parents when growing up in Hawaii, Armstrong had a strong religious sense and worked always in an altruistic — some say a paternalistic — manner. As an agent of the Freedmen's Bureau he worked directly under General O.O. Howard. Howard, a white man like Armstrong, founded what is now Howard University in Washington, D.C.—for many years the major African-American college in America. It was Armstrong who founded Hampton Institute after requesting the American Missionary Society to fund a school for ex-slaves in Hampton. Armstrong did not expect to be the school's principal, but after the missionary society's first choice declined the position, it was offered to Armstrong. During the early years after the end of the Civil War the American Missionary Society was, in Armstrong's opinion, the greatest financial power interested in Negro education. Armstrong suggested Hampton as a site for a school not only because there was a 159-acre site available for sale, but because of the concentration of former slaves, known as contraband, that had gathered in the Hampton, Virginia, area.[23] Hampton was also historically rich: Jamestown was not far away, and Yorktown, where General George Washington defeated Cornwallis during the Revolutionary War, was nearby.

An understanding of the use of the term "contraband" is appropriate at this point. One definition of "contraband" is that of a runaway slave during the American Civil War who either escaped to or was brought within Union lines. A Freedmen's Bureau officer told Armstrong that we have "a great lot

St. Paul's Choir, year unknown. Archdeacon Russell is at the left (Russell Memorial Library, Saint Paul's College, Lawrenceville, Virginia).

of contraband down on the Virginia Peninsula and can't manage them; no one has had success in keeping them straight. General [O.O.] Howard [commissioner of the Freedmen's Bureau] thinks you might try it."[24] General Howard himself connected the term "contraband" with "colored" refugees in Washington, D.C., in his dealings with Congress. He said that in Washington "there was a great population of colored refugees—contrabands, as they are called."[25] Union General Benjamin Butler is credited with using the term "contraband of war" as applied to escaped slaves in 1861. This became known as the "Fort Monroe Doctrine." The Union forces controlled the Virginia Peninsula at Fortress Monroe and the Confederate Army and Navy controlled Norfolk, which is south of the Peninsula across the body of water known as Hampton Roads. Three slaves under the control of Confederate Colonel Mallory escaped and crossed over to Hampton, where they were seized by Union troops. Mallory sent an agent to General Butler demanding the return of the three slaves. Butler denied the request, citing that Virginia, as a belligerent to the United States, cannot claim the return of the "contraband" because Virginia was now a foreign nation. Butler declared the escapees as "contraband of war" and retained them for his own services. The irony of the situation is that the North, prior to hostilities, honored a law[26] requiring the return of escapees to the Southern masters.[27] That Armstrong and others continued to use the term after the end of the war most likely was a convenient way to describe former slaves encamped in his area of responsibility, where more than 7,000 former slaves (contrabands) lived without provisions or work.[28]

It was Samuel Chapman Armstrong who created the concept and method of industrial education for former slaves. Though not a new idea, it had been experimented with and failed at other institutions in years past. The notable failures were at Northern schools such as Wellesley College and Oberlin College. These institutions gave up on the experiment because their young women students were not used to manual work in the first place and the work interfered with their studies. Oberlin was a manual-labor school at its beginning but failed in its goals. Armstrong knew public opinion concerning these schools' experimental failures, but he believed that "the Negro, inured to toil, tough in physical fiber, and without the highly developed American nervous system, could undertake a daily routine that would kill a New England girl; he thought, too, that by a certain skillful arrangement of work and study he could avoid the failure of either farm or book work."[29] Armstrong's methods and educational philosophy not only impressed former Hampton Institute student and graduate Booker T. Washington, it also affected other Armstrong students like R.R. Moton[30] and James Solomon Russell.

Historians differ on the soundness of Armstrong's educational methods and some charge him with an attitude of paternalism. According to historian Robert J. Norrell, Armstrong was an unapologetic paternalist. Blacks should look to whites for help. Armstrong meant to teach the former slaves industrial skills in order to secure economic independence. Armstrong had virtually nothing to do with the classical curriculum. The education at Hampton was basically equivalent to a current-day middle school curriculum.[31] The school was highly structured, coupling order and strict discipline in his method of educating his students. Armstrong's paternalism was uncontroversial at this time. Altruistic whites, whether Northerners or Southerners, wanted to do something that was considered good for the former slaves. Slavery ended once and for all by 1865, and not only Southerners (who accepted the new law of the land) but Northerners, too, carried traces of held-over negative racial attitudes. Everyone had to live within new social structures, but breaking away from the old structures was difficult because it required personal transformations. Altruistic whites acted on what they thought they must do at the time. Refinement and clarity of purpose would evolve over time. The reigning plausibility structure of Southern society had suddenly changed legally and would evolve into a new understanding or reality sociologically over time.

Neither Russell, who attended Hampton, nor Booker T. Washington, who graduated, ever expressed any understanding or evaluation of Armstrong as put forward by Norrell. Although Norell's description was perhaps accurate, other attributes of Armstrong were more positive and practical in their immediacy. For example, Washington and Russell modeled their schools after Hampton and were quite successful as school entrepreneurs. Both were not just educators, they were effective community leaders and organizers of white, and African-Americans. Russell and Washington absorbed and believed in Hampton Institute's methods and philosophy of education in the founding and ongoing operations of their own schools. Armstrong's story is worthy of elaboration because he was responsible for developing an educational method that worked in the early years after Emancipation. It is important to pay attention to the positive impact Armstrong made on Russell. One will see in the chapters that follow that Russell's methods in education mirrored those of Armstrong. Russell had already made his two-pronged decision not only to get an education but to enter the Episcopal priesthood. He recounted in his *Autobiography* that when he wrote to Armstrong that he had decided not to return to Hampton in order to attend a new seminary for black Episcopalians, Armstrong responded, "It was savage of the Bishop of Virginia to take you away from Hampton."[32] We know Russell wanted to enter the priesthood, and now we need to know how the pieces fell into place, making it possible.

Booker T. Washington

Russell and Booker T. Washington knew each other later in life. Though Washington was born less than 150 miles from the place of Russell's birth and he was 18 months older, their paths never crossed until after Washington graduated from Hampton in 1875. Both were reared in the care of their mothers on Virginia plantations, and their early upbringings were similar. Though Washington and his family moved to the newly created state of West Virginia after Emancipation, both young men, with similar motivating causes, gravitated toward Hampton Institute for their initial educational training. It was later in their careers that Washington had an influence on Russell. On a train tour of black schools in the South, Washington spent one night in Lawrenceville to observe the daily operation of the St. Paul School. His tour report commended the work not only of the college but of Russell himself.[33] This was also a time when Washington was engaged in a national public debate with W.E.B. Du Bois about the kind of education for former slaves—whether their studies should be liberal arts or industrial arts. Washington received the full force of Du Bois's invective against industrial education. Russell had struggles on the local level similar to those Washington faced at the national level. The problem, nonetheless, was real and challenging. Washington, after graduation, eventually went to Alabama to found Tuskegee Institute, and Russell founded St. Paul Normal and Industrial School. Both schools were similar in direction, curriculum and leadership style. The big difference was that Tuskegee was a secular school and St. Paul was affiliated with the Episcopal Church. Given the daily routines of students in both schools included daily prayers, chapel attendance and the like, few would have discerned any differences in student life, school management, or governance.

Giles Buckner Cooke

Giles Buckner Cooke became the first principal or leader of the new Episcopal seminary for African-American men located at St. Stephen's Episcopal Church in Petersburg, Virginia. A white man and a wartime member of the staff of General Robert E. Lee, Cooke became an Episcopal priest and not only led this church but opened a normal school for ex-slaves on the church's premises. The Committee on the State of the Church report in 1878 cited Cooke for his missionary zeal among African-Americans at his church in Petersburg. Apparently Cooke was tutoring men for the ordained ministry of the Episcopal Church. This method was and still is known as "reading for orders." The Committee stated that it rejoiced in noting "indications of success in his work, and especially the fact that two of this [tutoring] class, drawn from his school, are now candidates for holy orders."[34] These two candidates were, most likely, J.H.M. Pollard and Thomas W. Cain. Russell would attend the school later when it became chartered as the Branch Divinity School of the Virginia Theological Seminary in Alexandria. Pollard, Cain, and Russell would become the first three ministers of the emerging black cadre of Virginia.

Russell and Cooke became close friends quickly and that friendship lasted a lifetime.[35] It turned out Cooke provided Russell with many lessons of life, which in turn provided the structure Russell was always seeking. And there should be no doubt that Russell's early aims were met when Cooke's theological school was opened: Russell wanted to become a priest in the Episcopal Church. There was no time to ponder further this new opportunity: it was a matter of action to Russell and he took it. Whether Cooke and Armstrong were racial paternalists or not probably mattered little to Russell. Russell's desire for order and discipline was found at Hampton; his natural inclination toward friendships was found at St. Stephen's in Cooke. With the short-term but foundational training at Hampton Institute and Cooke's structured education at Branch Seminary, Russell was content to be pursuing his call to the priesthood and to his future.

Peter G. Morgan

The life and work of Russell's father-in-law, Peter G. Morgan, represented a model to emulate if not a direct influence. Peter G. Morgan was an "outstanding figure of Reconstruction"[36] and a delegate to the Virginia State Constitutional Convention. Part of Morgan's responsibility as a delegate was to craft a new post–Civil War Constitution of Virginia that would be the means whereby the former Confederate State of Virginia would be readmitted to the Union. It is important to note that Russell cited the new Virginia Constitution as the longest lasting of the "reconstructed" constitutions before yielding to changes and amendments.[37] Russell understandably held his father-in-law in high regard and points out in his *Autobiography* that Morgan was a member of the African-American elite in Petersburg, Virginia.[38] Morgan fought existing laws, habits and prejudices promoting official references to "black or white."[39] Morgan wanted the new Constitution to lack any reference to race. Russell, in the future, would challenge church canonical law in the same way. In an interesting exchange of correspondence during October 18–23, 1920, between Russell and Monroe N. Work of Tuskegee Institute, Russell provided information that Work requested on Morgan's life. From documents Russell gathered from Morgan's sons he learned that Morgan had been a carpenter by trade but later acquired the skills of a shoemaker, a trade he followed before the Civil War. Morgan was twice sold as a slave, and purchased in installments his freedom for $1,500.00. The final payment was made on the Fourth of July, 1854. In 1858 he purchased his wife and children and thereby, according to Russell's description, became a slave-owner himself. Morgan moved his family to Petersburg, became a self-educated man, and after the Civil War, educated his children and neighbors. Not only did he serve as a delegate to the Virginia Constitutional Convention, he later served two terms as a delegate to the Virginia General Assembly, 1869–1871 and 1871–1872.[40] (See Appendix D — Virginia Legislative Assembly African-American Membership 1872–1892.) Peter G. Morgan, then, was a respected Virginia *gentleman* of the new order.

Russell documents the material wealth of his father-in-law and many other prominent blacks in Petersburg. He provides statistics of land holdings of freed slaves and mentions prominent black families in the Episcopal Church. It is no wonder that Russell considered membership in the Episcopal Church — to be within its socially powerful and economically elevated atmos-

phere — something to aspire to regardless of misguided and unbiblical inter-
pretations from its leadership.[41]

George Freeman Bragg

George Freeman Bragg, Jr., recognized the valuable work of Pattie Buford
in helping former slaves in and around Brunswick County. He ascribed to
her, as a cultivated Southern lady, his most laudatory accolade — an angel of
mercy. Mrs. Buford, Bragg implies, was not only an angel of mercy but was
a powerful person within the Episcopal Diocese of Virginia. It did not hurt
Russell to seek her for assistance in securing him a meeting with the Bishop.[42]
It is important to recognize the connection Russell made with Pattie Buford.
She, like many other Russell connections, served with a group of concerned
local citizens working for the welfare of the freed slaves. Despite obstacles
faced by Russell in his beginnings and his future, it is noteworthy that he
made friends not only with other former slaves and their children but with
whites, all of whom managed to deal with their own sets of economic and
social problems.

Russell lived with the Bragg family in Petersburg for much of his four-
year education at the Branch Divinity School. So Bragg and Russell knew
each other while still in their twenties. Both men would become leaders in
the African-American group of the Episcopal Church. Bragg would eventually
follow Russell into seminary, and like Russell, would be a star pupil. In that
era, Bragg transitioned from the diaconate to a presbyter (priest) in a shorter
period of time than the other African-American clergy candidates, including
Russell. Russell remained a deacon for almost five years. Bragg was a deacon
for less than two. Both men started in the Diocese of Virginia, but by the
time the new Diocese of Southern Virginia was formed, Bragg was gone. For
some years Bragg was rector of Grace Church in Norfolk, but in early 1892
he accepted a call to Baltimore. There he would make his career as rector of
St. James's and publisher of the church periodical *The Advocate*. For the few
years that Russell and Bragg were together in Virginia as clergy, they operated
as a team. Several occasions when the black clergy objected to a resolution
or presented a resolution of their own to Annual Councils, Bragg would be
the person who vocalized the objection or resolution, and Russell made his
signature the first on the document. These items will be elaborated in the
next two chapters.

Even when he was a young teen, Bragg's talent as a writer was obvious.
On more than one occasion he won writing awards in his schools and St.
Stephen's Church. His talent would serve him well as a writer and publisher

in matters religious through his career. He, along with Russell, would become well-known in the Episcopal Church, as evidenced by their nominations for Bishop Suffragan of Arkansas in 1917. The two men split on some important issues affecting African Americans in the Episcopal Church. For example, on the issue of separate colored jurisdictions, Bragg favored them, but Russell did not. Nonetheless, their career-long work within the Episcopal Church cast both men as pioneers in civil rights in secular and church realms.

CHAPTER FOUR

1877–1885 Annual Councils of the Diocese of Virginia

C HAPTERS FOUR AND FIVE provide analyses and commentary of the reports found in the journals of the diocese's Annual Councils. The analysis is selective in terms of observing how the diocese worked with its African-American communicants in general, and how Russell developed himself and his ministries after ordination in particular.

James Solomon Russell began his seminary studies in 1878 at the new Branch Divinity School in Petersburg. He would have a successful academic career, graduate, and receive his diaconal ordination in March of 1882. A son of the Zion Union Apostolic Church in an Episcopal seminary, Russell may not have had much contact with his former church during these years and he may not have been aware of the negotiations between the two churches while he was studying. But one thing is certain: the Episcopal Diocese of Virginia was at that time, and had been previous to the Civil War, a mission-minded, evangelistic church. The evangelical orientation is due primarily to the initiatives of the diocese's second and third bishops, Richard Channing Moore and William Meade. Much of the diocese's activities are chronicled in their journals of Annual Councils. From those documents we learn much of the evangelical movement in general and its association with the Zion Unions.

The gathering of the diocese's Annual Council was usually in the month of May. Delegates to the council were clergy and laity, all male. The issues discussed in each council meeting occurred from the end of the previous council meeting to the current gathering. The journals of the Annual Councils include detailed committee reports; voting on resolutions, constitution and canonical amendments; and addresses by the diocese's bishop. Each bishop's report details his church visitations for the previous twelve months in addition to his address. These journals record not only the details of the diocese's Annual Councils, they paint a landscape in words, sentences, and paragraphs

Archdeacon Russell (second from left) and St. Paul's administrative staff, year unknown. At the front of the picture stands Major Whitehead, dean of men and the military unit (Russell Memorial Library, Saint Paul's College, Lawrenceville, Virginia).

of their minutes detailing the growth and development of the church and its membership through the years.

83rd Annual Council — St. Paul's Church, Lynchburg (May 15–18, 1878)

James Solomon Russell entered the Branch Theological Seminary in Petersburg, Virginia, in October 1878. As he studied for the next three and one-half years, his diocese continued its evangelical or missionary-minded calling. There are no records available to show how much Russell kept up with the workings of his church diocese during his years of study, but we do know that he must have had good interpersonal, organizational, and managerial skills to have been appointed secretary to the Annual Conference of the Zion Unions at an early age. In other words, he was already a leader. Although his attraction to the Episcopal Church came from his understanding of the Apostles' Creed and the Book of Common Prayer, his knowledge of his new church's history would have been scant. His seminary training in church history would cover much territory for him, and matched to his personal skills, he would be a young man ready to engage in church mission upon seminary graduation.

The Episcopal Diocese of Virginia was a highly mission-oriented church, and it had been even before the Civil War. But a look at its organization and its work following the Civil War shows an impressive but not perfect effort in their calling. For example, the Diocesan Missionary Society of Virginia was its strongest and most-funded agency. The diocese was constantly working on ways to plant new churches across its huge geographical area. When the West Virginia Diocese was formed out of Virginia after the Civil War, the Virginia diocese covered the entire state of Virginia, parts of western North Carolina and eastern Kentucky. The leading and oft-repeated names in the Missionary Society from year to year were Bishop Francis M. Whittle, T. Grayson Dashiell (the diocese's council secretary for 29 years), and A.W. Weddell. In addition to the Missionary Society was the Standing Committee on Colored Congregations. Although small in number, there existed several black Episcopal churches soon after the end of the Civil War. The prominent names on this standing committee were Bishop Whittle, Dashiell, and Weddell, as well as the Rev. Pike Powers and the Rev. Thomas Spencer. Spencer would be a professor and head of the Branch Divinity School in Petersburg. Five laymen served on the Standing Committee for Colored Congregations. None of the committee members was an African American.

In 1878 there were two colored men who were candidates for Holy Orders: J.H.M. Pollard, a candidate for deacon's orders; and Thomas W. Cain, a candidate for priest's orders, meaning that Cain was already a deacon. In the journal of the 1878 Annual Council, both men's names were parenthetically tagged by the word "colored." It is noteworthy, however, that once these men were ordained, their names appeared in the clergy list without the tag. The African-American deacons usually served five years before ordination as a priest or presbyter. White deacons were made priests anywhere from six months to one year. F.M. Whittle was a very active and mission-minded bishop and worked diligently to plant black or colored churches throughout his diocese. His annual visitation schedule was mind-boggling. In the 1877-78 season he visited 139 churches from Alexandria to Norfolk to Lexington to Richmond. He ordained 8 deacons and 15 priests. He received six clergy into the diocese and lost 11 by resignation or transfer to other dioceses. In that same year the diocese had thirty-one clergy on the payroll of the Missionary

Society. Clergy supported by the Missionary Society were either church planters or were attempting to rejuvenate churches that had become inactive. Of course, none of these plants or missions was financially self-sustaining. It was the Missionary Society that supported the ministry in the field. The Rev. Robb White, for example, was the missionary to St. Andrew's Church in Lawrenceville, a church that had been inactive for some years. Founded in 1720, its current edifice as of 1878 had been constructed in 1829. One of St. Andrew's notorious rectors was Goronwy Owens of Wales, a poet who was considered one of the finest writers in the Welsh language. But in 1878, Robb White was St. Andrew's rector and soon to be evangelist to the Zion Unions.

Another interesting event took place in 1878. The diocese was divided into geographical convocations, smaller units that were unofficial and voluntarily organized. But the Petersburg Convocation presented a proposal to the Annual Council to form official convocations across the diocese. The purpose was mission driven and not political. It was proposed that such convocational districts would contribute to the rapid growth of the church in each region of the state. The proposal stated that "canonical" convocations would not only have the advantages of the voluntary convocations, but by being attached to and sanctioned by the diocesan council, the work in the field would be rendered more efficient and would become valuable to the work of the Missionary Society. Church missions or church planting would be more formal with a plan and structural control. The convocations would be officially connected to the bishop, and the church at large would have a better appreciation for the official work of the church. Official convocations with geographical boundaries defined by the council would not overlap. A similar structure in the neighboring Diocese of Maryland had been already in place and proved adequate to meet its goals. Of significant spiritual and social significance was that within the boundaries of the Diocese of Virginia the highest concentration of African-Americans lived, worked and sought shelter. The Peninsula of Virginia (Hampton) had a significant number of African-Americans living there. But the Southside of Virginia, an area from Petersburg southward to the North Carolina line, had the most. The Diocese of Virginia, year by year, refined its missionary practices and continued to follow its evangelical calling.

The journal of the 1878 Council stated that the large colored population of the state of Virginia "claims our attention and culture," an interesting mix of words which betrays a class structure still existent in the minds of many. The Committee on the State of the Church reported: "Furnishing as this class does the labor best adapted to our particular wants, and at the same time the least turbulent, most orderly, and on every account most desirable, which capital anywhere controls, it is little to expect, and, to say the very least, impolitic and unchristian to withhold provision for the spiritual as well as temporal necessities." It was Giles B. Cooke, a former Confederate major on Robert E. Lee's staff and rector of St. Stephen's Church in Petersburg, who was cited for his evangelistic enterprise among central Virginia's African-Americans. Cooke was a white priest in a black church. His church was also the original home of the Branch Divinity School. The 1878 Council called for support of Cooke's missionary needs. Cooke was also preparing two African-American men, J.H.M. Pollard and Thomas W. Cain, for holy orders in a process known as "reading for orders" since there was no seminary at the time. The journal recorded that these candidates would create a "ministry of their own race." This was assumed to be their most imperative need. The notion of a missionary enterprise among African-Americans coupled with the idea of a separate ministry for each race, appears to be a subtle and unchallenged assumption at that time.

The church that Russell would be assigned to later in 1882, St. Andrew's–Lawrenceville, reported two adult baptisms, both colored; 9 white infants and 1 colored; 5 white confirmations and 3 colored; and the Sunday school had 5 white teachers with 20 students, and 5 colored teachers with 100 colored students. Robb White was the "missionary" in charge. The diocese reported its active communicants at 12,345; a total of 127 clergy with 15 having no charge. Confirmations, a sign of growth, were recorded at 1,328.[1]

84th Annual Council — St. George's Church, Fredericksburg (May 21–24, 1879)

The Diocesan Missionary Society continued its strong leadership. Pike Powers was replaced by the Rev. F.M. Baker, who acted as secretary. Mr. J.L. Williams was the Society's treasurer in 1878 and 1879. The Standing Committee on Colored Congregations replaced the Rev. William M. Drake with the Rev. C.R. Haines. Bishop Whittle maintained his heavy travel and visitation schedule, visiting 146 churches and missions. He confirmed 1,032 persons — 992 white and 40 colored. Whittle ordained J.H.M. Pollard to the diaconate on June 28, 1878 (after the Annual Council held in May 1878). Thomas W. Cain, a deacon, was still listed as a candidate for priest's orders in the 1879 *Journal*. In his report to the Annual Council, Bishop Whittle made special note of the Rev. Giles B. Cooke's ministry in Petersburg, which was "constantly enlarging...." Whittle also mentioned Mrs. Pattie Buford of Lawrenceville as "a devoted blessed lady" for her work with former slaves and their families in Brunswick County. He also said that in 1878 he appointed the Rev. Mr. Dashiell and the Rev. Mr. Weddell, both members of the Committee on Colored Congregations, as his executive missionaries to the

Zion Unions. These two priests were charged with engaging in conversation with the ministers of the Zion Union organization for the purpose of discerning what the Zion Unions wanted to do with the Diocese of Virginia.

Dashiell and Weddell reported that the Zion Union sought to be "taken into the care of our [Episcopal Diocese of Virginia] church." The Zion Union church members had a conference on April 29, 1879, and voted unanimously to place itself under the care of the diocese. In addition to stating this fact, Dashiell and Weddell remarked, basically, that this organization of colored people, in seeking union with the Episcopal Diocese of Virginia, were not under the same influences as others who would seek union. The Zion Union Apostolic Church was not in a position to argue about the validity of their clerical orders or about the legitimacy of the office of bishop. They had not progressed that far at that time. Instead, they sought union, in Dashiell's and Weddell's judgment, due to "the glory of God and to the credit of our [Episcopal] church." This was an opportunity to minister to the large Zion Union population in the Southside of Virginia, and Dashiell thought that with proper care they could become loyal "children" of the ecclesiastical household. This report established the beginning of work between the Diocese of Virginia and the Zion Union Apostolic Church. No union was made at this time, but work toward a union was now underway. The details of the size and scope of the Zion Unions did not go unnoticed. The Zion Union Apostolic Church had its own bishop, more than twenty ministers, and more than 2,000 communicants spread over mostly Brunswick and Mecklenburg Counties. But there were problems evident between the two churches. The Zion Union, for its part, was a faction or a remnant of a larger church that had its own problems and splintered. Zion Union Bishop James R. Howell led a faction seeking a certain kind of union with the Episcopal Church, perhaps as an attempt to hold his own remnant together.

The leader of the Virginia Episcopal Diocese's special committee on colored work, Dr. J.S. Hanckel, said that there existed something "uncertain" in ZUAC's application for union, a vagueness that was "embarrassing." Hanckel believed that because of the present state of negotiation and development, he and the committee were not certain of what ZUAC wanted and therefore did not know what to provide them. ZUAC Bishop Howell had proposed a relationship similar to Methodism — before it became a denomination — within the Church of England. Hanckel suggested that the diocese take a slow approach and restrict itself to teaching or "disciplining" them, and to aid them by every means possible in a Christian manner. In light of that matter, Bishop Whittle ultimately appointed the Reverends Robb White, R.A. Goodwin, and E.B. Jones as evangelists to the Zion Union Apostolic Church. These appointments constituted the first of eight resolutions enacted.

The second resolution added the name of an attorney, J.R. Jones, Esq. to the group of three evangelists, and the four of them would constitute a special committee to take charge of the entire Zion Union work. Another resolution authorized this committee to employ as many Zion Union ministers as catechists, under their direction, as they deemed expedient. Both the executive committee of the Diocesan Missionary Society and the Committee on Colored Congregations were charged with supplying books needed for Sunday and/or day schools. A portion of the sixth resolution would create some difficult decisions in the future. Looking ahead, the resolution recommended that since the colored ministers would be ordained into the Episcopal Church, they would be received with seats and all privileges of members of the Council. Any Zion Union congregation would be received in the status of any existing colored Episcopal congregations and to lay representation in the Councils. The seventh resolution asked that Bishop Whittle and a special committee of two address a cordial letter of welcome and Christian sympathy to the colored preachers and people of the Zion Union. This letter would be read directly to the Zion Union people by the evangelist in charge in Brunswick County, the Rev. Robb White.

Finally, this seventh resolution contained words of hope and promise as well as an assumed status quo of colored churches. The diocese directed their deputies to the next General Convention to bring this matter of the Zion Unions to the House of Deputies as a question of expediency of giving to the colored people of Virginia and the other Southern states a full and complete organization of their own race, within the constitution and canons of the Episcopal Church. This should have been a priority of the General Convention. Given all that the Diocese of Virginia had done up to this point in history, it had demonstrated its faithful consideration of ministering to all African-Americans within its canonical jurisdiction. Its commitment to evangelism clearly evident, the Zion Union interaction appeared to be the perfect model in which to move forward, not only in Virginia but in the entire Southern church.

In the meantime, James Solomon Russell was in Petersburg undergoing his seminary studies. The Rev. Thomas Spencer, a professor and leader of the Branch Divinity School, reported the details of the past academic year. His student roster included three Episcopalians: Thomas W. Cain, James S. Russell, and George [Freeman] Bragg, Jr.; also included were two Methodists and one Baptist. Spencer worked with Cain and Russell on "Evidences of Christianity" three times a week. Cain and Russell practiced homiletics [preaching] every Friday, and Russell studied "Townsend's Elements of Theology" three times a week. Russell, Cain, and Bragg took Greek grammar lessons daily, but only Russell studied Hebrew twice a week for four months, though in the current academic year he sat for Hebrew lessons daily. Russell and Bragg took "Mental Philosophy" three times a week. This report cited Russell's first year of studies. One can readily see the expanse of his training as well as understand the rigor of such a pace of study. Russell's development was on its way.

Although the Diocese of Virginia maintained records of its Annual Councils in a journal, it had no organized way to further chronicle the history of the diocese. In 1878 the Council moved to have a committee study a proposed position of historiographer. In 1879 the committee presented its report and moved that the Rev. Philip Slaughter be appointed historiographer of the diocese. Slaughter was appointed "with authority to proceed to collect the material for said history..." [vestries of parishes, vestry books, and other materials] history. Subsequent to this appointment Slaughter introduced annual historiographer reports with interesting facts from the colonial church up to his own time. Slaughter also wrote a history of the diocese and many other books about the church and about Virginia. In 1855 he published *The Virginian History of African Colonization*. Slaughter was also a delegate to the two triennial councils of the Protestant Episcopal Church of the Confederate States of America in 1862 and 1865.

It is interesting to compare the 1878 and 1879 statistics of St. Andrew's–Lawrenceville. It is important to keep in mind that Lawrenceville is the geographical center of Virginia's black belt. Brunswick County's ratio of blacks to whites in 1879 was 3 to one. In neighboring Mecklenburg County to the west, a significant African-American population resided. Russell's hometown of Palmer Springs was only a few miles from Boydton, where the Zion Union Apostolic Church was formed in 1869. But St. Andrew's proximity as the center point posted an impressive increase in its school: there still remained 5 white teachers and 20 students; there was only one colored teacher (compared to 5 in 1878) but 150 students, up from 105 in 1878. These numbers do not include what Miss Pattie Buford was doing in her school at the Chapel of the Good Shepherd. The diocese itself reported active communicants of 12,616 and 127 clergy. There were 1,032 confirmations. Impressive was the number of Sunday school students at 13,702.[2]

85th Annual Council— St. Paul's Church, Petersburg (May 19–22, 1880)

From May 1879 to April 1880, Bishop Whittle's work pace did not diminish. He continued his episcopal duties by visiting 140 churches and missions, confirming 881 people (50 of whom were African-American), ordaining 7 people to the diaconate and eight deacons to the priesthood. The diocese enjoyed a net increase of three clergy. On November 23, 1879, he visited St. Andrew's Church in Lawrenceville. In the morning he preached to the white congregants and confirmed four people. In the afternoon he preached, in the same church building, to the black congregants and confirmed nine. The next day he visited, with the Rev. Messrs. Robb White, R.A. Goodwin and E.B. White, the Colored Mission of the Good Shepherd to the Zion Union churches, about three miles from Lawrenceville. Whittle reported that he, White, and Zion Union bishop Howell gave addresses to the people. On December 21, 1879, Bishop Whittle ordained Thomas W. Cain to the diaconate in St. Paul's Church in Petersburg. Cain was the second African-American to be ordained in the Episcopal Diocese of Virginia. It should be noted that a candidate for priest's orders at that time, J. Green Shackelford, would eventually receive diaconal orders and make his first assignment at St. Andrew's Church a year before Russell's arrival.

At the Annual Council of 1880, Thomas Spencer made his yearly report on the Branch Divinity School and the progress of its students. Although he had been hopeful of reporting on Zion Union students, none were sent that year. The Diocesan Missionary Society reported thirty-two clergy missionaries on its payroll and mentioned that Robb White severed his connection with the Society, probably due to the fact that his salary from St. Andrew's Church and support from the special committee on Zion Union evangelism were sufficient for his maintenance. Thomas W. Cain was added to the list as the missionary deacon to St. Philip's Church in Richmond, a charge he would keep for several years. The missionary work with the Zion Union organization was taking on increasing importance to the diocese. The Zion Union leadership, it appeared, could not be precise enough in describing the closeness of a union between the two churches. When they were asked "How close do you wish the union?" the reply was always "As close as we can get." This imprecision in purpose by the Zion Union was puzzling if not disturbing to the special committee overseeing the project. However, both groups continued to forge ahead in mission and ministry. But given the lack of a clear commitment to a union, the diocesan special committee recommended, and Zion Union Bishop Howell agreed, that Howell's ministers should not be confirmed at that time. When Bishop Whittle visited the Chapel of the Good Shepherd, many Zion Union members were presented for confirmation, some of them ministers. By receiving the laying on of hands in confirmation, those Zion Union clergy would become lay persons in the Episcopal Church. Although desirous of ordination in the Episcopal Church, the ministers were found not ready, and if they became Episcopalian laymen they could no longer serve as ministers in their former churches. The result of such a move might cause the Zion Unions to scatter even further and the Episcopal Diocese of Virginia might lose any influence it had earned to date. The committee noted that the ministers were godly and earnest men, some of whom may have been ready for deacon's orders. In the end, however, with the nature of a possible union of the two churches still unspecified, the mission of mutual cooperation, education, and ministry continued. The committee recommended that the diocese establish a school of "higher grade" in the center of the Zion Union geography.

Robb White wrote a letter to Bishop Whittle on April 30, 1880, less than a month before the Annual Council meeting. In that letter he summarized the Zion Union activity in Brunswick County since July 1879. He first mentioned that the letter of welcome that was addressed to the Zion Union churches had made a profound impression on them, according to White. Considering the potential closeness between the two churches, the Zion Unions held a conference (not the annual conferences that they hold in August of each year) on March 10, 1880, at Bethel Union in Brunswick County. The special committee of the Episcopal diocese was invited to join them at the conference in order to confer in a full and free discussion about their relationship. When all was said and done, the Conference documented five resolutions that were passed. They resolved to hold "firmly to our church organization as now constituted" with no present desire to make a change. Expressing their gratitude to the Episcopal Church and especially to Mrs. Buford for her faithful Christian teaching, they expressed their desire to continue working together bound by common principles. Their third resolution commended the use of the Book of Common Prayer of the Protestant Episcopal Church in the Zion Union churches as the ministers found it practicable. In the fourth resolution they again thanked Mrs. Buford for her untiring work. Finally, the Conference requested of the Diocese of Virginia that the Rev. Robb White continue as missionary to the churches of their communion. The Zion Union clergy who signed the document were its chairman George Taylor, Charles Brown, Albert Brown, Samuel Barner, George Williams, Oscar Jones, and William E. Howell. The lay signatories were J.J. Graves and William Burnett. Robb closed his letter to Bishop Whittle with his suggestion that, despite the differences between the two churches, he believed "this to be a great work."

White's direct charge at St. Andrew's Church reported a good year. The Sunday school had five white teachers and 27 students. There were three colored Sunday school teachers with 36 students. The parochial school had two teachers and 138 students. Though not recorded, it is presumed that most of the students were African-American. White also reported that the home of the rector, the rectory, had been paid for and that the deed was recorded. Robb, unknowingly, was preparing St. Andrew's Church for the arrival of

James Solomon Russell in 1882.The Diocese of Virginia as a whole continued its missionary calling around the state. Thirty-one candidates for ordination provide a sign of diocesan support for evangelization and expansion. The active communicants reported were 12,884 with a Sunday School enrollment of 12,089 students/scholars. There were 130 clergy, ten without a charge. Revenue for the diocese was recorded at $193,024, a number that would grow substantially in the years ahead.[3]

86th Annual Council — Epiphany Church, Danville (May 18–21, 1881)

In May of 1881 the chairman of the Committee on Contingent Fund notified the delegates to the Annual Council that it believed it needed to transfer the responsibility of funding evangelists to another diocesan committee or agency. Although the committee believed that their evangelists were efficiently conducting their ministries, the contingency fund was not chartered for evangelical purposes. The committee suggested that funding of evangelism come from voluntary contributions from the people and parishes. In fact, the report on the contingent fund was a detailed reordering of how assessments were calculated from the parishes for the entire diocese. Other programs were also scheduled to be reordered. Seemingly a blow at first to the diocese's remarkable evangelism efforts, the resolution was laid over for consideration by the next Annual Council in 1882.

Once again Virginia's Bishop Whittle maintained a heavy visitation schedule. He visited 130 missions and parishes, down by 10 from the previous year. He confirmed 837 persons, 30 being African-American. There were now 254 churches and missions in the diocese. The bishop did admit that his work had become tiring. He told the Annual Council, "In the past year sickness and affliction in my family, the unusual severity of the winter, and attendance at the General Convention during nearly the whole month of October, have not allowed me to accomplish as much work as I proposed, though I have done more than usual...." Between June 25 and September 12, 1880, he was prevented from his episcopal duties due to the circumstances mentioned above. One of the appointments made by Whittle was the Rev. A.W. Weddell to fill the vacancy created by the Rev. R.A. Goodwin to the Committee on the Zion Union Work. The bishop also mentioned that Robb White had been equally dividing his time between his duties as rector of St. Andrew's Church in the town of Lawrenceville and the Zion Union work in Brunswick and Mecklenburg Counties. The previous council suggested that White work one hundred percent of his time with the Zion Union. But after consulting Zion

Union Bishop Howell, they agreed that White could continue his present arrangement.

The Episcopal Church in Virginia knew its mission and acted on it. The State of the Church report noted, "No subject can engage our attention more earnestly than 'the mission of the church.' The Church of God is a missionary church.... And unless the church goes out in obedience to our Lord's commands, it is dead, and we do not see what claims it has to call itself the Church of Christ." The committee explicitly pointed to its colored membership and claimed that African-Americans were much more wards of the church in a blessed sense than they ever could be claimed as wards of the nation. Recognition was made of the fact that there were more colored Sunday schools in existence than in any previous year and that the Zion Union work was not without good fruit. But the committee also warned against boasting of any documented successes. It was proposed that the executive committee of the Diocesan Missionary Society of Virginia appoint three subcommittees, one of which would be known as the Committee on Work Among Colored People.

Those responsible for the Zion Union work reported at this Council "no material change in the attitude of the Zion Union organization and membership." There was no change in the care that the diocese provided. Work with the Zion Unions had been continuous over the year and uninterrupted, but they still held firmly to their organization. It was believed that any attempt to graft their ministry or members into the Episcopal Church at that time would prove fatal to the overall work. In other words, the progress must continue to be slow, but steady. In their latest Annual Conference the Zion Unions resolved to hold on to their existing organizational structure; to continue to work with the Episcopal Church; and to continue to use the Book of Common Prayer. But the diocesan committee on Zion Union work reported the resignation of the Rev. Robb White as evangelist, with great regret.

Of significance was the committee's recommendation that the office of evangelist be discontinued. The committee believed it was time that the church recognize that the colored people within bounds of a parish were integral to the missionary work of a local parish. The work with colored people was not to be ignored but integrated into the normal working of the church. This move made sense with the Zion Union church membership because they fell within the parish boundaries of Brunswick and Mecklenburg Counties. It was then proposed to the Annual Council that there be created assistant ordained ministers (deacons or priests/presbyters) for parishes of Mecklenburg and Brunswick Counties appointed for special work among the colored people. It was further proposed that the salaries of these assistant ministers be paid by the Diocesan Missionary Society. This action paved the ground for

Russell's appointment, after his diaconal ordination in March of 1882, to St. Andrew's Church in Lawrenceville.

In the meantime Robb White's final parish report for St. Andrew's showed an average Sunday school attendance of 16 white students and three teachers; and 40 African-American students with four teachers. The parochial school had 149 students and two paid teachers. White also remarked that the colored communicants had purchased land in Lawrenceville in the hope of building a church during the year following. "The lot is paid for and deed made, and the subscription has commenced." The diocese's annual contributions grew to $212,099 with a communicant total of 12,778. There were 145 clergy, nine without charge. The Sunday School enrollment consisted of 10,226 scholars with 1,475 teachers. Clearly the Diocese of Virginia was faithful to its evangelical calling.[4]

87th Annual Council — Christ Church, Norfolk (May 17–20, 1882)

On March 9, 1882, at St. Stephen's Church in Petersburg, Virginia, James Solomon Russell was ordained a deacon by Francis M. Whittle, the Bishop of the Episcopal Diocese of Virginia. Candidate Russell was presented for ordination by the Rev. Giles Buckner Cooke, rector of St. Stephen's Church. Over the ensuing years the two men would become close, personal friends. The Rev. Professor Thomas Spencer delivered the sermon at Russell's ordination. Bishop Whittle then assigned Deacon Russell to an assistant position at St. Andrew's Church in Lawrenceville. The deacon-in-charge, J. Green Shackleford, asked the bishop for an assistant to help with the church's colored congregation. Shackleford had little to no experience as rector of a church since his own ordination had preceded Russell's only by months. Shackleford probably did not know how to deal with his colored congregants either. One can only speculate about Shackleford's motivation. Nonetheless, this assignment placed Russell in the middle of the developing, and possibly dying, Zion Union relationship. But after his assignment, Russell wasted no time in reporting to his new ministry.

On April 25 the bishop made an official visitation to the colored congregation at St. Andrew's Church and Deacon Russell presented eighteen people in his charge for confirmation. The next day, at the same church, Whittle confirmed five more persons and administered communion. Some of the confirmands were Zion Union people who had come from some distance to attend the service. The Rev. E.B. Jones had been ministering to the Zion Union people and was relieved by Deacon Russell in March. Jones was the last of the original three diocesan evangelists to minister to the Zion Union organization. Russell's arrival marked the end of the planned discontinuation of special evangelists. From this point forward the ministry of any parish in the diocese was to minister to the colored people of its area as it would all members of the congregation. The unique opportunity facing Russell and the entire diocese was that there were more than 700,000 African-Americans living in Virginia and their great majority lived in the Southside — meaning Brunswick, Mecklenburg and a few other surrounding counties. There was a vast field of people to whom he could minister. By this time Russell would have been fully knowledgeable of the evangelical aggressiveness of his diocese. He had work to do.

As usual Bishop Whittle kept up his pace, visiting 142 parishes and missions. In the months between June 1881 and April 1882 he confirmed 1,033 persons, 82 of them African-Americans. He ordained 24 clergy: eleven priests and 13 deacons. The total number of clergy in the diocese numbered 140 and contributions were slightly up over the previous year. Given its long-term commitment to evangelization of its jurisdiction, the diocese was well-prepared and well-gifted in continuing its gospel-spreading work. In January 1882, the Zion Union church sent five of its ministers to the Branch Divinity School in Petersburg. Professor Thomas Spencer reported that their instruction had been of an elementary character since "the minds of the students permitted no other." Although deportment and religious character of all five were most exemplary, the progress of the five Zion Union students was slow and discouraging, according to Spencer. But as the Council of 1882 discussed their evangelical enterprises, they seriously took note of the huge responsibility of ministry to the 700,000 colored people "which a mysterious Providence" had planted within its borders. Although they considered the work slow but growing, they were more encouraged by the stirring words of their three new colored ordinands who were not only Virginia-trained colored clergy, but Virginia-born. Virginia pride was not confined to secular sentiment; it seeped into the spiritual life of Virginia's churches. Before the close of the first day of the 1882 Annual Council the Rev. Messrs. Pollard, Cain, and Russell addressed the gathering about their work among the colored people. They were well received by all delegates.

One week prior to the Annual Council, May 10, Russell wrote a letter to Bishop Whittle. Russell reported that when he first arrived at St. Andrew's less than two months earlier, he was given charge of its colored congregation. But at the time of his writing he had the care of three congregations: Mercy Seat, a Zion Union congregation thirteen miles from Lawrenceville; the Chapel of the Good Shepherd (Mrs. Pattie Buford's mission chapel) nearby; and St. Andrew's colored congregation. He preached twice a month at each station and he enrolled a membership of thirty-one at Mercy Seat, which had a large Sunday school enrollment. Much encouraged at his work of less than sixty days, Russell had to write to his bishop. This update was part of Russell's operating character. Russell was a self-promoter and this skill was valuable as he planted many churches and as he entered the field of education for former slaves and their families. The annual parochial report for St. Andrew's Church shows for the first time two clergy names: the Rev. Green Shackelford, rector, and James S. Russell, assistant. It must be noted that Shackelford was listed on the record as rector, but he was a deacon. At best a deacon would be a vicar, not a rector. The reports of the annual council, however, reported many deacons as rectors of their churches, particularly among the developing African-American missions in Brunswick and Mecklenburg Counties. The record for St. Andrew's showed nine baptisms of which 2 were African-American; thirty-two confirmations, 18 colored; 14 white persons were added to the membership rolls, 18 African-Americans. There were 6 white teachers and 28 students; 8 black teachers with seventy students. It was noted that contributions were small. This listing actually reported for two churches: St. Andrew's and Trinity, both within St. Andrew's Parish. The diocese itself continued to make progress with contributions reaching $215,337. The Sunday schools reported 10,603 scholars with 1,484 teachers. There were 1,033 confirmations and 1,623 baptisms— 302 were adults.[5]

88th Annual Council— St. James' Church, Richmond (May 16–19, 1883)

The Rev. Mr. Shackelford's tenure at St. Andrew's was not long. By the time of the Eighty-eighth Annual Council of the Diocese of Virginia, Shackelford was in charge of two churches in and around Ashland, Virginia. Bishop Whittle ordained him to the priesthood on June 23, 1882, at the seminary chapel in Alexandria. Thomas W. Cain was ordained into the priesthood in Richmond on April 29, 1882, and became rector of St. Philip's–Richmond, a church he was serving as a deacon. Russell married Virginia Michigan Morgan in December of 1882 and the two of them embarked on their long career in Lawrenceville. The mission-oriented expression of the Episcopal Diocese of Virginia not only continued but took on a great expansion.

Since 1878 Bishop Francis M. Whittle had had the Rev. George W. Peterkin assist him in the opening divine services of the Annual Councils of Virginia. In the 1879 record of the Annual Council, Peterkin continued to assist Whittle in the opening services, but then as the bishop of the newly formed Episcopal Diocese of West Virginia. This relationship between Whittle

St. Paul's College trade class of 1917. Archdeacon Russell is seated at the left, his son Alvin standing directly behind (Russell Memorial Library, Saint Paul's College, Lawrenceville, Virginia).

and Peterkin continued for several years. At the 1883 Council, Whittle explicitly noted: "Having been unwell all the winter, and seeing no prospect of improvement during the spring, I accepted the kind offer of assistance from Bishop Peterkin, of West Virginia, who filled in for me...." In April, one month before the 1883 Council, Bishop Peterkin confirmed 106 persons at twenty-one different churches.

Bishop Whittle reported that the diocese still struggled with how best to work among the colored people. This assertion by Whittle might have been startling to some, given that the diocese had always worked steadily and earnestly with the African-American population. On the other hand, Whittle might have been referring to the organization difficulties with the Zion Unions. Another factor might have been the post–Reconstruction secular temper rising within the general society. So, with that introduction, Whittle expressed joy in receiving a circular letter from the bishop of Mississippi, W.M. Green, asking his fellow Southern bishops to meet in Sewanee, Tennessee, at the University of the South in July 1883 to discuss and then to resolve "the relations of our Church to the late slave population of our States, and the best means that can be adopted for their religious benefit." Whittle knew that he would be physically unable to attend the Sewanee Conference, so he directed the executive committee of the Diocesan Missionary Society to make a recommendation. The Society passed a resolution which requested Bishop Whittle to appoint two presbyters and two alternates to attend. The only other discussion or report about the subject matter explicit in the Sewanee matter was that of the Committee on Diocesan Colored Work. The committee reported that it believed the Diocese of Virginia was as "fully alive" as any in the nation to the great duty God had placed upon the church in this nation.

The committee had in earlier years concluded and stated, that the only solution to the relation between the church and colored people was to give colored people the right to a separate organization. What that meant was anything but clear. A separate organization could mean something similar to what Zion Union Bishop James R. Howell requested of the Diocese — an organization similar to the Methodists under the Church of England. Or it could be a separate ecclesiastical jurisdiction — a racial diocese. But none of that was suggested at that time. What was clear was the Committee's statement of its reasons for a "separate" organization. First, it stated that no white congregation had any intention of calling a black man as their rector. It believed this was a natural response and not a notion of resentment. The committee's assessment here is brutally honest, but it is an assumption that would not hold up over time as more African-American clergy would be ordained and more colored missions were formed. Perhaps the committee was simply rehearsing the sign or temperament of the times. Though brotherly friendliness was genuine and unfeigned among the few colored and many white clergy in the councils of the church, the Committee believed that the lack of significant lay representation at that time was not as it ought to be in a Christian environment. They asserted that colored members of the church "have every right upon this floor with the rest of us, [and] do not feel that they have the same measure of influence which we all would desire for them." Over time this sentiment would not hold among white delegates.

Though a separate organization seemed to be the solution in the grand scheme of things, the Committee was quick to assert that such an organization was not one in which the large "body of our population feel that they are merely patronized." It appears from what was written by the Committee on Diocesan Colored Work that its membership struggled with their internal deliberations to produce an honest assessment of current obstacles to any solution. The diocese would struggle with this issue for the next several years. T. Grayson Dashiell, white, experienced many years of working with colored people in the diocese, especially the Zion Union Apostolic Church leaders and membership, was responsible for seeing that James Solomon Russell was educated in the new seminary. But the membership of the diocesan Committee on Colored Work included four other white men as well as three colored members: Thomas W. Cain, J.H.M. Pollard, and James Solomon Russell. The high personal stature of each of the members provided a finely deliberated suggestion for a solution. The decision to endorse a separate organization for colored communicants turned out to be prescient. Since there were perplexing problems connected with their work with the colored people, the Committee on the State of the Church looked forward to the "happiest results" from the [Sewanee] conference of the bishops of the Southern dioceses. Given all of the positive work developed over the years by the Episcopal Diocese of Virginia toward the colored population, why suddenly did it defer to an ad hoc gathering of southern bishops to find a solution to "the problem?"

Another development during 1883 was the election of the Rev. A.M. Randolph as assistant bishop of the Diocese of Virginia. For several years previous, the diocese had engaged in discussion of having an assistant bishop. The diocese was growing at a rapid rate and was simply geographically large. In the parochial reports, St. Andrew's Church and Trinity Church in St. Andrew's Parish showed a rector vacancy. Mr. Shackelford had already left for Ashland to minister to two other parishes. What was new in St. Andrew's Parish was the report for "St. Paul's Church and the School House." It did not take a long time for James Solomon Russell to plant his first church and new school. The St. Paul Sunday school reported 8 colored teachers and 120 scholars or students. The parochial school started with one teacher and 54 students, all colored. In his report Russell remarked, "Large classes awaiting confirmation at both of the above named churches." The diocese reported having now 151 clergy on the rolls with 14,153 active communicants. The Sunday schools remained large with 11,211 scholars and 1,521 teachers. Contributions reached $222,731.[6]

89th Annual Council — Christ Church, Winchester (May 21–24, 1884)

In his address and report to the Eighty-ninth Council of the Episcopal Diocese of Virginia, Bishop Whittle expressed his appreciation to the people of his diocese for their kindness toward him over the past sixteen years. He made note of the fact that he could not continue the heavy schedule of visitations and other episcopal duties as he had in the past. The assistance of Bishop Peterkin of West Virginia, and the election of the Rev. A.M. Randolph as Virginia's assistant bishop in October 1883, helped Whittle. Out of the country for five months to recruit his health, the bishop said that he could easily fall into ill health if he did not reduce his schedule. In the meantime the growth of the diocese continued. Four new church edifices were consecrated, seventy-six visitations were made, and four hundred nine persons were confirmed. Persons receiving the laying on of hands in confirmation from a bishop usually were above the age of eight and had received instruction through a catechism class or some other instructional opportunity approved by the bishop and the diocese.

Bishop Randolph was not present at the May 1884 Annual Council, so the secretary was directed to publish Randolph's report in the *Journal*. A serious illness of one of Randolph's sons prevented his attending. The assistant bishop's report contained some interesting elements. In December 1883 he visited a "colored mission" in Gordonsville but did not record the number of confirmations. In February 1884 he visited the Normal School in Hampton; it must be assumed that Randolph is referencing Hampton Institute. In March he visited St. Stephen's Church in Petersburg, the large colored church led by its white rector, Giles B. Cooke. Randolph commended the work at St. Stephen's and other colored missions. He said he was impressed with the "prudence, the Christian fidelity and enthusiasm with which these missions are conducted." Seemingly a more reflective and didactic person than Bishop Whittle, Randolph recognized that the Episcopal Church was working more, proportionally, with former slaves than the other Protestant denominations, but cautioned that the "negro [sic] and oriental races" for centuries were without the benefit of the moral and spiritual direction of Christianity. As such, he concluded the concerns about organization and relationships of the colored missions to the governance of the church "can afford to wait." In his first report, Randolph, the future bishop-ordinary of the to-be spun-off Diocese of Southern Virginia, presented his fundamental position on race, either deliberately or unconsciously, for all to read.

Since this Council of 1884 was the first since the gathering of Southern bishops at Sewanee, it resolved: "That a committee of five clergymen and three laymen be appointed to take into consideration and report to the next Council what action, if any, should be taken by this Diocese looking to a separate organization for our colored brethren." Clergy appointed to this committee were E.W. Hubbard, J.S. Hanckel, Kinloch Nelson, Pike Powers, and J.B. Newton. Lay persons appointed were John Allen, Edmund Pendleton, and Joseph Wilmer. In his parochial report, James Solomon Russell reported that St. Paul's Church had one adult and 45 infant baptisms; the Sunday school had nine teachers and 210 student scholars. In his attached remarks Russell said there were large congregations at St. Tammany in Mecklenburg County, and in Sturgeonville in Brunswick. He expected large numbers of

people to be confirmed at the next visitation by a bishop. The diocese itself
reported active communicants at 13,640 with 153 clergy. Financial contributions grew to $241,184. The Sunday school programs reported 10,694 student
scholars with 1,449 teachers. The diocese had been steadily growing.[7]

90th Annual Council— St. Paul's Church, Richmond (May 20–23, 1885)

The action taken by the Committee on the Separate Organization of the
Colored People at the 1885 Council was to ask that the committee be continued. In other words, they wanted more time, or they were buying more time,
to feel out what was happening politically in the secular world. The contin-
uation of the committee's work was an inevitable outcome regardless of the
reasons. Considering the good work of the Diocese of Virginia over the years
with its colored congregations, the Council delegates as well as the committee
members may have experienced a level of ambivalence toward making any
decision. After all, it was the Bishop of Mississippi who called for the Sewanee
meeting of Southern bishops to deal with the perceived problem with colored
members. The Diocese of Virginia at that time was proceeding in a positive
manner with its membership. Had Bishop Whittle not responded to Bishop
Green's characterization of a perceived Negro problem, their futures might
have been different and the call for separate colored organizations might not
have occurred. But a delay was asked for and a delay was given to the committee. As time moved on, the makeup and character of the diocese and its
committees naturally changed. Two of the three lay persons on the Committee
on the Separate Organization of the Colored People were replaced by three
new members, and one clergyman was added. The committee now had six
clergymen and five laymen.

By the time of the convening of this Ninetieth Annual Council of the
Episcopal Diocese of Virginia in May 1885, an assistant bishop, A.M. Randolph, had been on board for two Councils. Since the founding of the diocese
after the Revolutionary War in 1785 was one hundred years earlier, the 1885
council was its centennial. The first convention of 1786 was not followed by
conventions for several years, hence, the ninetieth annual council. The membership of the Executive Committee of the Diocesan Missionary Society of
Virginia was much the same as it had been for many preceding years, the
notable members being the Rev. Messrs. T. Grayson Dashiell and Pike Powers.
Seven African-American postulants for holy orders were studying at the seminary in Petersburg. There would have been eight, but one had died during
the school term. The opening of the ninety-first council led off with morning

prayer, followed by an ordination liturgy priesting four deacons. This was also the first council since 1878 without the guest presence of Bishop George Peterkin of West Virginia. Another interesting event at this council was the resignation of the Rev. Philip Slaughter, the historiographer of the Diocese of Virginia. He would become widely known as a historiographer of the church and author of many books. The credentials committee listed the clergy entitled to seats in the council; among them were the three ordained African-American deacons Thomas W. Cain, J.H.M. Pollard, and James Solomon Russell.

As usual, Bishop Whittle presented his stewardship efforts by reporting of his visitations, this time from June 1884 to April 1885. Shortly after the previous year's council, Bishop Whittle had visited on May 31 the Mercy Seat Church, a large congregation of colored people in Brunswick County. He confirmed twenty-five people and celebrated holy communion. The Mercy Seat Church was a congregation of Zion Union members. Whittle made note of the fact that this church plant was one of two by James S. Russell in Brunswick and one in Mecklenburg Counties. He commended Russell's work to the council and suggested that they consider contributing to this "good and deserving" ministry because they were building a church edifice that required more funding.

The next morning Whittle went to a combined service with members of Trinity and St. Andrew's churches, at the latter's location. There he confirmed two. He mentioned that those two churches had been without a rector for a long time. In the afternoon, while still in Lawrenceville, Whittle went to the St. Paul colored church and confirmed twenty-nine persons. In the morning of the next day he visited the parish school that Russell and his wife, Virginia, had started some three years earlier. Whittle said the school was a "neat and comfortable frame church with a good congregation, a commodious and suitably arranged school building, with two teachers and between fifty and a hundred pupils, and a large lot of ground on which he proposed to build a rectory as soon as kind friends will give him the money." On September 14, 1884, Bishop Whittle visited St. Mark's in Mecklenburg County, about thirty miles from Lawrenceville, where Russell lived. Whittle confirmed seventy-four persons and celebrated communion. The large congregation was developed by Russell from the Zion Union connection. The physical location of St. Mark's location was close to Russell's home town of Palmer Springs, and near Boydton where the Zion Union Apostolic Church was founded in 1869. It would be an understatement to say that Russell was well-connected in Mecklenburg County.

As Bishop Whittle traveled throughout his diocese in 1884–5 he confirmed many African-Americans in "white" churches as well as in colored churches in formation. The number of colored confirmations rose to 216. He was careful to cite where progress was made in the colored churches. For example, he confirmed forty persons on March 22, 1885, at St. Stephen's Church in Petersburg (rectored by a white man, Giles B. Cooke), seventeen at St. Paul's Chapel in Berkley (Norfolk), where the Rev. J.H.M. Pollard was in charge, and thirteen at Trinity Chapel in Lunenburg County, where services were held monthly by the Rev. Thomas W. Cain. The bishop told the council that even though Mr. Pollard was working under "very unfavorable circumstances" his work was encouraging, and suggested that he receive help because he "must have a church building and the means to pay at least for two teachers to make his missions a success." Of the seven African-American postulants listed in the journal, one was William E. Howell. He and George E. Howell may have been relatives of Zion Union Bishop James R. Howell. By 1882 the Zion Union church was a different organization. Most of its various factions reunited as the Reformed Zion Union Apostolic Church (RZUA).

Bishop Whittle's address and report declared that the seminary in Petersburg, by this time known as the Bishop Payne Divinity School, had been incorporated by the legislature of the State of Virginia. The school's legal name became the Bishop Payne Divinity and Industrial School in Virginia, and its purpose was defined as a school for "educating colored persons for the ministry of the Protestant Episcopal Church, or for any secular business." Whittle also said, based on his "daily observation and experience," that the question of Negroes in the church was going to be a difficult and serious matter. Perhaps he meant that "daily observation and experience" was telling him what was happening in the secular world — the emerging Jim Crow realities. Certainly there were political changes taking place in Virginia and in the rest of the South during this decade, now that the failed Radical Reconstruction project had faded away. At this point, certainty as to what Whittle meant was not defined with any level of precision. What was also unclear was his suggestion that his Virginia diocese adopt a plan similar to "other churches around us." He may have meant neighboring Episcopal dioceses or Methodist and Baptist church reorganizations. He stated explicitly, however, that he personally believed that a large majority of both white and black clergy and laity would unite in the idea of a separate black organization. What kind of organization, what kind of structure, Whittle did not say. But he did recommend that "we agitate the question until the General Convention [of the national church] can be induced to take it up and adopt the necessary legislation." The opportunity for the Diocese of Virginia to lead on the issue of racial inclusion was given away twice; once by responding to the Sewanee Conference, and then by deferring any responsibility for a decision to the national church's General Convention. The Sewanee Conference of Bishops suggested to the General Convention in 1883 separate "convocations" of black churches within the dioceses. But the General Convention failed to pass such legislation in the House of Deputies. Only the House of Bishops agreed. Therefore, the Sewanee suggestion failed legislatively.

Assistant Bishop A.M. Randolph filed his report to Council as was canonically required for Bishop Whittle. Randolph told the diocese that on those Sundays when he had no visitation appointments he preached in several churches in the City of Richmond. His visitation report for this period had two occurrences where he confirmed colored persons: the first occasion was at the Chapel at Virginia Seminary in Alexandria on June 26, 1884, with four confirmations; and the second was at the Colored Chapel in Norfolk, where he confirmed seven persons. A sign of the continued growth of the diocese is revealed in his consecration of five new church buildings. Bishop Whittle consecrated one new church during the same time period. Randolph took advantage of this growth by talking and writing about the five he consecrated. St. Paul's Church in Hamilton was located in Loudoun County; Bethel Chapel in Fauquier County; Christ Church in Lancaster County; Immanuel Church in King and Queen County; and St. Luke's Church in Jerusalem, Southampton County. Randolph placed more emphasis on religious education in the diocese, particularly with Sunday school programs. To him Sunday school "is perhaps the important agency" of the diocese. He pointed out that the growth of church missions has "its germ in the Mission Sunday School." But he also made a criticism of the church.

Randolph charged that Episcopalians, and possibly some Presbyterians, had traditions which believed and acted upon the principle that churches grow and have influence in their communities through regular worship, by devout Christian conduct, by teaching their children the catechism and the Bible in the home, and then trusting in these "quiet methods" to influence others. Episcopalians were afraid, he said, of going too far evangelically, as the Methodists had done and continued to do. Methodist prayer meetings and revivals were simply too much for Episcopalians. Randolph believed that Methodists had actually helped Episcopalians go after the lost sheep and "not to stand on our dignity, and wait for them to come to us." He also pleaded for sympathy from the laity for the church's clergy. Laity, he said, must understand the rigors of the work of a parish pastor, and grasp that he is also a man with a family to rear, just like everyone else. Clergy must be provided the necessities of life for themselves and for their families. This was a broad appeal for church people to wake up, to actively engage in evangelism and to support their clergy. These references by Randolph probably indicated a substandard level of clergy compensation that needed correction, in addition to a need for the laity to come to terms with their responsibilities. In many ways, the diocese had tremendous growth over the years after the lull in the years immediately following the Revolutionary War. No doubt Randolph remembered that the former Anglican Church in Virginia, and now the Episcopal Diocese of Virginia, almost collapsed. Most of the non–Anglican churches in the years after the Revolution wanted the former "state church" to disappear. Considering that popular mindset of the day, it's a wonder the Episcopal Church survived, even in Virginia.

The Diocese of Virginia was geographically large. Ten years after the end of the Civil War, the Diocese of West Virginia was formed out of it, and from 1879 to 1884 the diocese discussed the possibility of another division. Bishop Whittle, from 1876 to 1883, was without an assistant bishop. All visitations were made by the one bishop. Prior to Whittle, there were bishops-ordinary and bishops-assistant. Whittle was an assistant bishop to Bishop John Johns; Johns was assistant to Bishop William Meade. After the West Virginia diocese was formed, its bishop, George Peterkin, assisted Whittle when requested to do so. In the 1885 Annual Council the committee on the Division of the Diocese, after stating the history of bishops and their work in the diocese, actually declined to recommend a division of the diocese. Even though they recognized the need to split, and knew that both a new and the remaining dioceses would be financially stable, the committee decided to play a passive role. That passive role consisted of waiting for a regional "movement" to take place among those who would want a division. In other words, they decided to look for a ground-up movement. The committee charged with examining another division of the diocese closed its report by saying that they "are not prepared to submit any practical solution for adoption by the Council at this time."

Thomas Spencer, the head of the Bishop Payne Divinity School in Petersburg, reported that there had been seventeen students under his tutelage. There were fifteen regular students; one Methodist who was permitted to attend classes; and another student who was placed on probation. Another student, Fountain Barner, died of consumption at his home in April 1885. In another report to the Council, the Diocesan Missionary Society reported that over the past year they had forty-five missionaries on their payroll and that for the coming year the number of missionaries supported by the Society would be reduced to thirty-six. James Solomon Russell was on both lists. Their stipends ranged from $100 to $300 per year. At a later time in its history, it would be determined that the clergy salaries were far below that of out-of-state dioceses. Bishop Randolph's remarks about clergy support certainly lent themselves to such a possibility in 1885. This would be an ongoing challenge to the Diocese in its future evangelization efforts. Bishop Randolph's observation about the Episcopal Church's "quiet methods" may have been a contributing factor to their "merger" talks with the Zion Union Apostolic Church.

When the diocese's Committee on the State of the Church offered its report, the emphasis on evangelism continued. After another committee had earlier cited the ills that befell the church after the Revolutionary War, the State of the Church committee referenced the revival of the diocese at the election of Virginia's second bishop, Richard Channing Moore, who served from 1814 to 1841. Virginia's first bishop was James Madison, a cousin of the United States president of the same name. In light of Moore's (evangelical) revival, the committee urged the importance in 1885 of family worship for fear that "the fire has gone out on many family altars." It also cited Bishop Whittle, in his address, who spoke of the importance of the work among colored people. There were 233 confirmations of colored people during this period. Even though the church was growing, and the active membership of the diocese was stated at 15,323, there was always a concern of the diocese's membership and special committees that it was not doing enough.

James Solomon Russell, still a deacon, was doing his work. His Mecklenburg County charge, St. Mark's Church, grew. In his parochial report, Russell remarked that this congregation came out of the Zion Union denomination in August 1882. He had held regular monthly services since then, and his assistants had helped give St. Mark's two services per month. His "assistants" were white clergy. In Brunswick County, Russell reported for both St. Paul's Church and St. James's Church. St. Paul's built a schoolhouse, a building whose major funding came from an Episcopal priest from Philadelphia, the Rev. Dr. James Saul. The building was named the Saul School Building. Dr. Saul came from a wealthy Pennsylvania family. The St. James Church had a new building and all that remained to be done was "plastering and painting." Russell said that the neighbors of St. James, black and white, "rendered valuable assistance in the way of furnishing their teams to haul the lumber...." Confirmations for the three churches over that period of time were seventy-five, sixty-one, and twenty-five, respectively. Diocese-wide confirmations were 1,523; Sunday school student scholars numbered 11,716 with 1,760 teachers; and contributions were $241,609.[8]

Missed Opportunity or Not

Notwithstanding the position taken by the Diocese of Virginia regarding the Zion Unions, one might ask whether its decision to evangelize the Zion Union as a group rather than at the local church/parish level was effective. There was indecision on the part of the leadership of the Zion Union Apostolic

Church on how far they wanted to associate or align themselves with the Episcopal Church. The four-year working relationship between 1878 and 1882 had its productive moments. Indeed, some rare admissions occurred during that period of ministry. The prominent example was the Rev. Robb White apologizing for the wrongs committed against blacks by the Episcopal Church during colonial and antebellum days. And there may have been a deeper reluctance on the part of the Diocese of Virginia to pursue a merger based on the social status of the members of the Zion Unions. Pattie Buford's analysis of the constituencies of the two churches is revealing and might have accurately described the attitude of the Episcopal Church.

In one of her letters, Buford described the position of her plantation-owning father and other men in antebellum Brunswick County, Virginia. "These gentlemen lived luxuriously in their elegant homes," she wrote. Because their house servants took care of them, likewise, the plantation owners trained and took care of their Negro house servants. They cared little for the servants who worked in the fields. Buford distinguished between house servants and "plantation negroes [sic]." At the conclusion of the Civil War, house servants had relatively little problem in securing employment in the cities, towns and villages. Plantation workers were looked down upon by house servants. Even though Miss Pattie drew a distinction, she readily admitted loving her "black mammy" for taking care of her in her motherless childhood. She also characterized house servants as those who would attend churches such as those led by the Rev. Dr. Alexander Crummell in Washington, D.C. Crummell's church membership, according to Buford's point of view, consisted of free blacks, artisans, and former slaves who were house servants. Crummell, at that time near the end of his career, was rector of St. Luke's Episcopal Church in Washington, D.C. He served many years as a missionary in West Africa. Never a slave, Crummell was a grandson of an African tribal king. He was also the first black graduate of Cambridge University. His congregation was upscale. Buford, however, ministered to those blacks who were scorned and looked down upon, those who were the membership of the Zion Union Apostolic Church. She said, "My Zion Unions are composed entirely of this class," plantation Negroes and not house servants.[9]

James Solomon Russell worked with former Zion Union congregations in Mecklenburg and Brunswick Counties, forming new Episcopal churches. One could make the case that Russell himself was of the class of servants and not of the plantation. His mother and grandmother, as slaves, worked in their master's big house. That fact alone would place them in Pattie Buford's category of the privileged slave — one who would attend Dr. Crummell's church. Russell had a light complexion, which might have provided him advantages over darker-skinned slaves. But, as we know, at a young age he held a major position within the ZUAC's Annual Conference. He knew how to deal with people regardless of their skin color. He learned at a young age, probably out of necessity, how to effectively deal with anybody. As a young deacon in the Episcopal Church, he was forced to play the cards dealt him. By the time of his ordination the diocese had decided not to deal with the Zion Unions as a group, but as individuals at the local church level.

Perhaps the local church approach was the best approach, as compared to group annexation. Given the evangelical work conducted within the Diocese of Virginia from Revolutionary to Civil War times, it is difficult to accept a notion of rejection of a "class" of people. Virginia, however, was indeed a class-centric society, but family-oriented, and not unaffected by the explosions of evangelical fervor of the First and Second Great Awakenings. The record of the diocese was relatively good. But there was a revealing statistic that should have been given a second thought by the diocese before making their Zion Union decision. By 1882 the Diocese of Virginia had a membership of 13,951 persons. The diocese, however, was interacting with a faction of the Zion Unions, a faction with 2,000 members. This faction appears to be the only one with any cohesion or structure. There were other former Zion Union members, but they had not settled themselves organizationally. Had an arrangement been worked out between the Episcopal Diocese of Virginia and the remnant or factional Zion Unions as Howell had originally proposed, it is possible that the Diocese of Virginia could have increased its African-American population by 2,000, which would have had a broader footprint or base in the evangelization of other African-Americans. How aware the Diocese of Virginia leadership was of the Zion Union's internal struggles is not clearly known. As mentioned earlier, the Zion Union Church restructured itself as the Reformed Zion Union Apostolic Church (RZUA), but the record is not clear under whose leadership. According to a page on the website of RZUA, the church's Discipline Committee issued a statement in 1882 that reads in part, "In 1881 our Ex Bishop [Howell] went to work to call together the *true* [emphasis added] Zion Union Members. In 1882 they met in compliance with his call. On the eighth day of July and at this meeting each and all agreed to forgive one another and live and die as true sons of Zion." They agreed to meet twenty days later to arrange the affairs of their "fractured" union, neglected for the past three or more years. When doing so, Howell was excused from his duties because the membership thought it best for him not to travel. The Rev. J.M. Bishop, one of the original founders, was elected to a four-year term as president.[10] Both Howell and Bishop, along with three other men, signed the statement.

The status of the Negro in the Episcopal Church in Virginia, as well as nationally, was still uncertain or ill-defined. Perhaps the Episcopal leadership held on to elitist ideologies or they were delaying, certainly in the case of the Zion Unions, any ecclesiastical mergers based on political changes taking place around them. As a result of the Sewanee Conference in 1883 an opposing organization was constructed to challenge the Southern bishops at the General Convention in October of 1883. Even though the Southern bishops' proposal ended in defeat, the status of black Episcopalians remained uncertain. Six years later, at the General Convention of 1889 held in New York City, that same opposition group, named a Conference of Colored Clergy and Other Workers of the Church among Colored People, offered a Memorial and asked, among other questions, "What is the position of colored men in the Church?... We ask the General Convention of the Church to give an emphatic and unequivocal answer to this our interest and almost despairing inquiry."[11] Did the Diocese of Virginia, in dealing with the Zion Unions, miss an opportunity to settle the perceived "Negro problem" for the entire Episcopal Church? Regardless of the diocese's decisions, James Solomon Russell, as an ordained Episcopal minister, evangelized African-Americans in Southside Virginia and later in the newly formed Diocese of Southern Virginia — an area bordered by the James River to the north, extending south to North Carolina, and eastward to Virginia's eastern shore and the Tidewater. In the years between 1886 and 1892 (the year of the creation of the Southern Virginia diocese), Russell and his seminary classmates exercised their expanding ministries with great energy and zeal.

CHAPTER FIVE

1886–1892 Annual Councils of the Diocese of Virginia

THESE WERE THE FINAL YEARS of ministerial service in the Diocese of Virginia for James Solomon Russell and most of his African-American clergy colleagues; these would be the end of Alfred M. Randolph's years as the diocese's assistant bishop. Randolph would become the bishop ordinary of the newly formed Episcopal Diocese of Southern Virginia, which would hold its Primary Council in November 1892. The Councils of Virginia between 1885 and 1892 would engage in serious discussion and maneuvers, mapping out the new diocese and restructuring the original and soon to be smaller Diocese of Virginia. History and emotions interacted in Council sessions, but everyone knew that the venerable Church of Virginia had to break apart for the good of spreading the Gospel.

91st Annual Council — Christ Church, Charlottesville (May 19–22, 1886)

From the time of his ordination in March 1882 to the 1886 Annual Council, James Solomon Russell all but dominated the evangelization of the Southside of Virginia. In 1882 he ministered to four churches or missions in Brunswick County: St. Andrew's, where he ministered to the white congregation as an assistant; St. Andrew's colored congregation; Mercy Seat; and the Chapel of the Good Shepherd, the latter being Mrs. Pattie Buford's chapel. By 1883 he added the St. Paul's Church and School House, and by 1884 he ministered to three congregations: St. Paul's in Lawrenceville and a Sturgeonville congregation (both in Brunswick County); and to a Mecklenburg County congregation in the town of St. Tammany. The diocese designated Russell as missionary in Mecklenburg and Brunswick Counties for 1884–5

St. Paul's Choir, year unknown. Archdeacon Russell is at left, Alvin Russell at right (Russell Memorial Library, Saint Paul's College, Lawrenceville, Virginia).

where he ministered to St. Paul's in Lawrenceville, St. James's in Warfield, and St. Mark's Church in Mecklenburg. By the 1886 Annual Council he ministered to these latter three churches but help had been on the way.

On December 11, 1885, four colored men were ordained to the diaconate at St. Stephen's Church in Petersburg: William E. Howell; D.W. Taylor; John T. Harrison; and Joseph W. Carroll. The number of colored clergy was growing and a significant number of colored congregations had been formed. Russell and a white priest, E.B. Jones (who was also a medical doctor), were ministering to the colored churches in formation in the Southside. These newly ordained clergy would already have charges awaiting them. Also in this same period, the Rev. Green Shackelford, the rector who had requested a colored assistant in Lawrenceville to help him, and the Rev. Giles B. Cooke, Russell's mentor who became a close friend, both left the diocese for the Diocese of Maryland. Thomas Spencer, the head and instructor at the Bishop Payne

Divinity School, resigned his position. A priest from Philadelphia, James Saul, provided a gift of $5,000 to the diocese for constructing buildings for colored schools in the diocese. Assistant Bishop A.M. Randolph reported confirming large numbers of colored people in Mecklenburg and Brunswick Counties between June 1885 and April 1886. Things were happening and things were changing within the Episcopal Diocese of Virginia. There was now a small cadre of black clergy forming in the diocese and it would appear that the steady work of the church with colored people continued unabatedly. But the dark specter of separation never disappeared entirely.

At the 1886 Annual Council there would be reporting and discussions of a separate organization for colored people; an observation about colored people by Assistant Bishop Randolph in his annual address; a report from a Committee on Colored Work; and a legislative maneuver to implement a church law known as "Canon XIII of Colored Missions." Prefacing his message about colored people, Bishop Randolph reported visiting the past year the church and parish school in Petersburg; the Bishop Payne Divinity School; a school and chapel in Gordonsville; a mission station in Nottoway County; a school and chapel in Lunenburg County; St. James's in what is now Warfield, Virginia; St. Paul's in Lawrenceville; St. Mark's in Mecklenburg; St. Philip's in Richmond; Hope Chapel in Manchester; and Holy Innocents Chapel in Norfolk. The geographical breadth indicated by the locale of these church missions provided a glimpse of large areas of Virginia ripe for evangelization. Most of these congregations were located in the Southside counties. Randolph also wanted it to be understood that he was attentive to and knowledgeable of the ministerial opportunities and responsibilities that faced the diocese. Randolph then stated his understanding of the obligations and responsibilities of the white race to the colored race.

Using words previously spoken and published, Randolph suggested, "A doubt exists in the minds of many of our people as to the adaptability of our Church to the religious education of this [colored] race." That doubt was theoretical, according to Randolph. If the gospel and Christian education were presented and executed correctly, with any race, any such doubt anyone may have would vanish. Christian study and Christian living regenerates, and the regenerated person thus would become one of high moral character. Here Randolph attached Christianity, or religion, to the moral life. Later he asserted that those in the "lower stages of civilization" tend toward divorce of religion from morality. The "lower stages" includes the Negro. But he went on to say that such a tendency also exists in the white race except that long years of Christian teaching, discipline, Christian law, the churches, and the Bible had modified and controlled those tendencies. The "lower stage" person, such as the Negro, inherited his tendencies from generations of paganism from the dawn of history. But Randolph was trying to suggest that any person of any race can be transformed by the gospel. Had he been a politician, Randolph said that he would advocate Christian education for the colored people as the strongest ground for the stability of political institutions; as an economist he would advocate evangelizing the race for material prosperity, not only to help themselves but to help the national economy; and had he been an industrialist he would have advocated Christian education for the Negro to elevate all levels of life. These, however, were only incidentals because these were not and are not the motives of the church. Instead of evaluating missionary efforts in terms of material progress, it is better that the church understands that "these [colored] people have souls to be saved." Randolph believed that God had placed colored people into the care of white people by removing them from heathen Africa to Christian America. He was not alone in this sentiment. His description of the situation of the day, though well-intentioned, was nonetheless an oblique justification of the superiority of the white race to oversee the improvement of the black race. At the same time, Randolph warned the church against bringing in new converts simply for the sake of growth. Any unprepared person presented for confirmation was an unacceptable method of preaching the gospel. "We should watch against an ambition for numbers to be presented at the visitation of a Bishop; we should pray against the temptation ... we should pray just as fervently to be saved from the temptation to indifference and neglect of personal effort and solicitude for the individual souls committed to our charge." Randolph was acknowledging not only that the church had a huge responsibility in evangelizing the very large black population, but that proper preparation was needed for all new church members. Greater numbers simply for the sake of numbers would not be appropriate and would not expand the gospel message effectively.

At this same Annual Council a proposed "Canon XIII of Colored Mission Churches" was placed before the delegates. The committee overseeing the development of the canon presented six sections as summarized here: (1) the colored people of Virginia would constitute a missionary jurisdiction within the diocese; (2) congregations formed exclusively of colored people would be canonically lawful within the legal limits of any existing parish and subject to the same conditions as any other mission church; (3) multiple colored congregations, missions, or churches may associate in the form of a convocation; if there are several convocations of colored congregations, they may form a General Convocation with 2 clerical and 2 lay deputies from each of the local convocations; (4) the General Convocation may elect four clerical deputies to represent the entire colored missionary jurisdiction at Annual Council, but only to vote on matters affecting the colored jurisdiction; (5) Colored congregations would not be liable for contingent expenses of the

Diocese; they may hold property of their own, but cannot come into possession of white congregation property except by legal transfer; and (6) as a temporary measure the bishop may appoint an archdeacon who must be a presbyter (priest, not a deacon) and either white or colored. There could be more than one archdeacon depending on circumstances.

The Committee (of 6 members) on Colored Work was split on the Canon XIII proposal. The majority reported that the proposed canon was "inexpedient" at this time and resolved that the bishop instead appoint an evangelist for the colored people of the diocese. One of the three members taking the majority position was Thomas W. Cain, the rector of St. Philip's–Richmond. Two other members recommended the canon as proposed, the minority position. Apparently W.H. Taylor, the sixth member, abstained; though citing approval of the underlying principle of the canon, he thought that a change in the diocese's constitution was necessary. The justification for Canon XIII is illuminating in the sense that it communicates to later generations the thinking prevalent regarding racial issues twenty years following the end of the Civil War.

The Rev. Dr. J.S. Hanckel, rector of Christ Church–Charlottesville and one of the examining chaplains of the diocese, chaired the Committee on Separate Organization for Colored Brethren. He presented the committee's report to the delegates of the Council. It was this committee that wrote and proposed Canon XIII citing, in part, social and ecclesiastical precedents. Race affinity was mentioned as the strongest evidence for separation. The committee concluded, from history, that the colored people themselves withdrew from the white churches to which they once belonged, not only in antebellum days but in the years immediately following the end of the Civil War. The committee suggested that it was the colored race, therefore, that shut out the white race and not the other way around. The report identified Northern as well as Southern denominations as having experienced an exodus of their colored membership, mostly Baptists and Methodists. On this item the committee reckoned that one cannot disregard the teaching of history and of Providence. Since separation had already occurred, to expend an effort to stay as one integrated church would "fight against God," notwithstanding the principle that all races should worship together the common God of all. Integration was "impractical."

Secondly, citing that colored people of the South usually had colored preachers as well as white in the past, the report concluded they would prefer to have their own pastors in the future. Accepting separation as a foregone conclusion, the committee asserted that all it could do was to educate colored clergy for work with colored congregations, but it needed to look for steps to take in order to maintain ecclesiastical union between the races in the same

church (diocese). It cited the extreme importance of maintaining a close affiliation for the welfare of both races. This may have been an allusion to the
failed union between the all–African-American Zion Union Apostolic Church
and the Episcopal Diocese of Virginia four years earlier.

The third point that the committee considered was structure. What
should the relationship between the two sets of racial congregations look like?
Comparing and contrasting the legislative enactments of the United States
federal government and the General Convention of the Episcopal Church,
the committee suggested that, like federal territories created by the U.S. Government, the Episcopal Church had formed missionary jurisdictions with
certain rights. Some secular territories overlapped wholly constituted states
with physical boundaries, and some church missionary jurisdictions overlapped fixed boundary dioceses. And as far as voting was concerned in the
General Convention, the missionary jurisdiction's elected delegates held seats
but had no voting rights. The committee suggested creating a colored missionary jurisdiction within the boundaries of the Episcopal Diocese of Virginia. With these precedents the committee proposed Canon XIII. Thomas
W. Cain, a colored member of the committee, voted with the majority. Without knowing more about Cain's ecclesiology and social views, it is impossible
to determine his motivation in voting for the canon. On the other hand, it is
presumptuous to assert that Cain should have voted otherwise. Twenty-first
century presentism on 19th century issues is a dangerous field to mine.

Once the canon was placed before the Council, amendments and voting
took place. The first three sections of Canon XIII passed and the fourth section
was amended by one word. Section four was eventually struck out, and section
five amended twice. The final vote approved of Canon XIII as amended with
the clergy voting 68 to 18 for the canon, and the laity 72 to 6. Both houses
had more than a two-thirds majority in favor, the requirement for passage.
What took place then was a legislative procedure that lawfully separated col-
ored-populated church congregations from fellow white churches while maintaining that the diocese was unified through structure. The committee used
its understanding of historical fact to promote the acceptance of the canon
and the overwhelming votes of both houses confirmed the committee's
assumptions. As mentioned earlier, the reader should keep in mind that in
the American South during the 1880s and 1890s, the phenomenon of Jim
Crowism was in its ascendency, and the churches of the South were not unaffected. In 1893 the United States Supreme Court would confirm the Southern
practice of "separate but equal" in the *Plessy v. Ferguson* decision.

The Canon XIII episode would not end at this point. Clearly it was fallout
from, or an extension of, the framework forwarded at Southern bishops' conference at Sewanee in 1883. It would have its social and psychological impact

of the creation of black bishops and national black jurisdictions in the 1900s. But this whole issue would have an impact on James Solomon Russell in the not-too-distant future from Canon XIII's enactment. Russell would have to deal with it, as would his brother black clergy. How it was handled, how it was dealt with, met with controversy. Irrespective of the future, Russell and his fellow Southside clergy brothers moved forward in the evangelization of the Southside. Beside J.H.M. Pollard and Thomas W. Cain, four new deacons joined the ranks of the diocese's clergy. Joseph W. Carroll was assigned as a missionary in Mecklenburg County in the town of St. Tammany; William E. Howell ministered to a congregation in the town of Fraternity in Mecklenburg; John T. Harrison was assigned to Brunswick County in the town of Totaro; and D.W. Taylor became an assistant minister at St. Stephen's Church in Petersburg. Pollard was already serving a mission in Norfolk, and Cain was rector at St. Philip's Church in Richmond — a black church organized in 1861. Cain would remain there in service until 1887. His tenure ran for seven years before he transferred to Galveston, Texas. He died in the Great Flood of 1900, the storm surge of a massive hurricane.

Russell continued his ministries at St. Paul's, St. James's, and St. Mark's. Concurrently he was establishing the St. Paul's school. His Sunday School at St. Paul's reported 135 students and 5 teachers in 1886; St. James's Sunday school enrollment was 40 with 4 teachers; and the St. Mark's–Mecklenburg Sunday school boasted 80 students and 5 teachers. St. Mark's had the largest number of communicants of the three charges at 103. Russell eventually passed on St. Mark's to Joseph W. Carroll. The Diocese of Virginia now counted 13,456 active communicants, 376 of which were colored; contributions rose to $202,808; and Sunday schools reported 12,795 teachers and students, of whom 1,572 students and 213 teachers were colored.[1]

92nd Annual Council — St. Paul's Church, Alexandria (May 18–23, 1887)

The expected work of the church continued as evangelization expanded throughout the diocese and pastoral care of the faithful was administered by the bishops and clergy. In October 1886, the General Convention of the national church took place, and upon his return Bishop Whittle for two weeks visited the colored churches and missions in Mecklenburg and Brunswick Counties. Both E.B. Jones and James Solomon Russell accompanied the bishop on these visitations. Whittle could not help but notice the large attendance of these colored congregations and their interest to church life. He confirmed 129 African-American communicants, forty-nine of whom were members of

St. Paul's in Lawrenceville. Russell prepared all of these confirmation candidates. Earlier, on June 28, 1886, one month following the 1886 Annual Council, Whittle had ordained three new colored deacons: William P. Burke, Walter L. Burwill, and George E. Howell. Later, on December 14, 1886, Whittle ordained J.H.M. Pollard to the priesthood in St. Paul's Church–Norfolk. Pollard was made a deacon in 1878, having served eight and one-half years before being priested. At his ordination the Rev. Arthur Selden Lloyd preached the sermon, and the Rev. Beverly Dandridge Tucker, rector of St. Paul's, presented his assistant minister Pollard for ordination. Both Lloyd and Tucker would become bishops in the dioceses of Virginia and Southern Virginia, respectively, and Pollard would soon transfer to the Diocese of South Carolina. Another important ordination took place five days later at St. Stephen's Church in Petersburg. George Freeman Bragg, Jr., would be ordained a deacon. Bragg was perhaps the one colored deacon who was elevated to the priesthood in less than two years, a rarity at the time. Bragg, an irascible person at times, was a bright student at the Bishop Payne Divinity School. He edited a newsletter for Bishop Randolph and prior to seminary won several writing awards. Russell, while at seminary, lived with the Bragg family. Bragg would become rector of churches in Norfolk, Portsmouth, and Baltimore. He wrote and edited an African-American church newspaper, authored a book about the African-American presence in the Episcopal Church. Bragg, Cain, Pollard, and Russell can be viewed as the core, certainly the initial, leaders of the African-American clergy in Virginia. Clearly, Bragg and Russell would become national leaders in the church. On February 9, 1887, Russell would be admitted to priest's orders and would continue to plant churches and expand his parish school into a normal and industrial school.

During the sessions of the Annual Council of 1887, the Rev. E.W. Hubard offered a resolution that many would consider a sign of the times. Hubard, rector of churches in Bedford, Russell, and Hanover Counties, proposed that a committee study the feasibility of colored clergy as members of Annual Council. Hubard cited the precedent of an all-white church since its formation in 1785. He said that the Episcopal Diocese of Virginia was constituted and administered upon the basis of a white membership, a white constituency, and a white convention or council, and that no legislation had allowed for colored ministers to sit in council. He considered it a concern of the day that a change in church membership in the diocesan council would be in accord with the diocese's constitution as originally adopted. Whether Hubard was in favor or not in favor of admitting African-Americans is unclear. It was clear that he was asking for legal examination of the constitution. The resolution was tabled.

In his address, Bishop Whittle reported to the 1887 Annual Council that he had consecrated the new edifice of Grace Memorial Church in Lexington on May 30, 1886. Lexington is the home of Virginia Military Institute as well as Washington and Lee College. Originally Washington College, its name was changed to honor General Robert E. Lee, who served as its president in the years following the end of the Civil War. Whittle remarked that the new building was erected after prayerful and faithful efforts of its former rector W.N. Pendleton "for the praise of Almighty God and in memory of the character and services of the great General Robert E. Lee." He reported not only the ordination of three new colored deacons, and the presbyteral ordinations of Pollard and Russell; he announced that two more colored men had been accepted as candidates for deacon's order: Beverly M. Jefferson and M.F. Nelson. Year by year, the number of colored men entering the ministry of the church continued to grow. Despite any Confederate sentiments felt or expressed, the church in Virginia tried to live up to its understanding of the call of the gospel. Without naming them, three friends of the Negroes enabled the trustees of the Bishop Payne Divinity School in Petersburg to purchase land and to construct new buildings. The amount donated was listed at $9,000.00.

One of the items presented to council was for the restoration of the office of perpetual deacon. The Rev. H.M. Jackson, rector of Grace Church–Richmond at the time, cited the practiced disuse of the historical office of the deacon and thus proposed the restoration of that office to the polity of the church. A perpetual deacon would be identified by a congregation and presented for ordination by the bishop. A perpetual, or permanent, deacon stays in deacon's orders throughout his ministry. The office never is a transition to the priesthood. The colored deacons ordained were never "perpetual" deacons and the plans called for eventual ordination to the priesthood. Many colored deacons remained in that office for years. Joseph W. Carroll was ordained deacon in 1886 and was ordained a priest in 1914 by Bishop Randolph in the Diocese of Southern Virginia. Russell spent almost five years as deacon. This proposal at the 1887 Council was referred to the Committee on the State of the Church.

By 1887 there were established ministries to African-Americans in the Diocese of Virginia, especially in the Southside. Russell ministered at St. Paul's–Lawrenceville, St. James's in Warfield, and Grace Church. John T. Harrison was listed as rector of St. Thomas's Church in Totaro. These were in Brunswick County. In Mecklenburg County, William E. Howell ministered at Peyton Chapel Church and St. Mary's Church in Fraternity. Joseph W. Carroll ministered at St. Mark's and St. Paul's Chapel near the town of St. Tammany (now Bracey, Virginia). Russell was listed as rector of Ascension Church in Mecklenburg, and a man named Solomon Russell was listed as the church's treasurer with a post office address in Palmer Springs. It is doubtful that this man was James's father. The Diocese of Virginia continued to grow and reported rising attendance. Revenue or contributions throughout the diocese rose to $232,099, and 15,892 communicants were recorded. There were two active bishops (Whittle and Randolph), 152 clergy, and 36 licensed lay readers. Confirmations rose to 1,496, and Sunday schools had 13,622 students and 1,710 teachers. Seven new church edifices were consecrated by the bishops in this period from June 1886 to May 1887.[2]

93rd Annual Council — Trinity Church, Staunton (May 16–19, 1888)

On June 9, 1887, one month after the gathering of 1887 Annual Council, three more colored men were ordained to the diaconate: M.F. Nelson; Lafayette Winfield; and Beverly M. Jefferson. Despite the addition of three new African-American ministers, Assistant Bishop A.M. Randolph, in his annual address of 1888, was critical of the diocese's progress in the care of its African-American communicants. His critique focused on the actions and non-actions of the diocese from 1866 to 1886 in attending to the work to be done. He began by citing Bishop John Johns's 1866 appointment of a Standing Committee on Colored Congregations. The committee met annually, but with no action until in 1869, when St. Stephen's Church in Petersburg applied for full membership as an independent church within the diocese. But the bishop called for a "special" committee to consider the colored church's application. At first the committee resolved that the church be "admitted into union" with the diocese, but changed those words to "be taken into the care of this Council," and then stated that St. Stephen's care should be "entrusted" to the Standing Committee on Colored Congregations. St. Philip's Church–Richmond was under no such arrangement. Randolph complained of the little action for this period by asserting that Council legislative action "slumbered" from 1866 to 1883. In 1883, of course, the Sewanee Conference of Southern Bishops dealt with the "problem" of Negro communicants, and the Diocese of Virginia deferred its own decision-making on the matter except for the appointment by Bishop Whittle of yet another committee. Randolph was careful to note that this special committee membership had three colored ministers as well as white. James Solomon Russell, Thomas W. Cain, and J.H.M. Pollard joined in the unanimous vote that suggested creating a separate organization for colored churches. Based on the reality of the times, this appeared to be acceptable to whites and blacks. At the 1884 Council, Randolph noted, another committee was appointed to organize a plan for a separate colored organization. The result of that action was Canon XIII. Randolph's objection to the eventually amended canon was that it was ambiguous, legislatively weak, and had no teeth to effect anything of action. After identifying flaws in Canon XIII, ruminating on the fact that "separate organization" had never been defined, Randolph also expressed his feeling that "a large class of minds [in this diocese] are prone to relegate decisions to the future, with a vague hope that time will bring changes that are needed." With all of this, Bishop Randolph urged the Council of 1888 to take some step toward a definite working plan of organization for the colored churches so that constitutional and canon law changes could be effected by the 1889 Council.

Since Bishop Whittle was absent from the Council due to illness, Assistant Bishop Randolph, following his address, appointed a committee to follow up on the portion of his address about separate colored congregations. Seven clergy and 3 laymen were appointed. Among the clergy appointments were colored ministers George E. Howell, George Freeman Bragg, Jr., and James Solomon Russell. Wasting no time, the report from the Committee on Colored Congregations took on Article II of the Constitution of the Episcopal Diocese of Virginia. The Rev. Dr. Hanckel presented the majority report, which, after making word changes in Section 1, created a new Section 3. In that section it resolved that the colored missionary jurisdiction (whatever it is and whatever it is called) shall provide "four clerical delegates" to then Annual Councils as constituted under the existing Canon XIII. An exception was allowed for colored clergy "now connected with the Diocese," who shall retain their right to a seat and a vote in the Council. No provision was made for participation by colored laity. The minority report, presented by Bragg, objected. In diplomatically parsed language the minority report read: "While we appreciate the earnest desire of the majority of this committee to honestly settle this question in such a manner as they think will best promote the work among our people, yet we are conscientiously unable to concur with them in their recommendation." Bragg, Howell, and Russell signed the minority report. Clearly, under the terms of the majority report, the colored clergy could not entertain the thought of a separate organization or jurisdiction with such limited legislative participation. This point in history may have been the first sign that colored congregations in the Diocese of Virginia did not ever want to have for themselves a separate identity.

Although efforts were made to postpone to the next year's Annual Council the vote on the changes to Article II of the constitution, a resolution was offered by the Rev. Dr. Jackson to defer the Negro question to the General Convention and to confer with the other Southern dioceses to "secure united action." The offering was tabled and another was presented by Walter Taylor, a layman. It, too, was tabled. The Council then proceeded to vote on the Report of the Committee on Colored Congregations, the majority opinion.

It passed 63 to 17 with clergy, and 56 to 11 with the laity. What was stunning, upon examination, was the number of white clergy who voted in favor of the report and resolution, considering their aid and support of colored congregations since the Civil War, and some before. For example: T. Grayson Dashiell, the secretary to the Annual Councils for almost 30 years and the person most responsible for securing Russell's seminary education; Green Shackelford, the rector of St. Andrew's who asked for Russell to come to Lawrenceville after his seminary training; Thomas Spencer, professor and one-time headmaster of the colored seminary in Petersburg; Pike Powers, who had worked on committees for colored congregations for years; and Beverly D. Tucker, a priest who would be elected bishop coadjutor of the Diocese of Southern Virginia years later due to an endorsement speech by Russell. But there were also white clergy who voted against the report, notably D. Francis Sprigg, rector of Moore Memorial Church in Richmond and an early supporter of the Bishop Payne Divinity School for colored men in Petersburg.

After discussing other matters of the church, both at the diocesan and General Convention levels, Bishop Randolph announced that he would not

Archdeacon Russell is at bottom row left, with the faculty (Russell Memorial Library, Saint Paul's College, Lawrenceville, Virginia).

attend the 1886 Lambeth Conference in London. Randolph said that he and other bishops received letters of cordial invitation from the Archbishop of Canterbury to attend the conference in the summer. "I saw no intelligent reasons for the Conference, and thought that I saw some reasons against it, at least so far as concerned the Episcopal body in America," Randolph explained. Therefore Randolph did not accept the invitation nor did he attend the Conference.

Despite the legislative arguments over colored congregations, the Diocese of Virginia continued to grow and prosper. Its contributions in 1888 were at $229,953, with 15,443 active communicants (804 colored). Sunday schools enjoyed an attendance of 13,640 regular students, of whom 1,980 were colored. There were 1,219 confirmations—1,082 white, 132 colored, and 5 Indian. The diocese reports attendance in its parochial schools of 36 teachers and 1,424 student/scholars. Russell was listed in the parochial reports as rector of four missions: Grace Church, St. James's, and St. Paul's, all in Brunswick County, and Ascension Church in Mecklenburg. His largest church was St. Paul's with 99 active communicants. Edwin H. Green (white) was now rector at St. Andrew's–Lawrenceville; William E. Howell ministered at Peyton Chapel and St. Mary's Church in Mecklenburg; and Joseph W. Carroll ministered at St. Mark's Church in the town of St. Tammany in Mecklenburg.[3]

94th Annual Council— St. Paul's Church, Lynchburg (May 15–17, 1889)

The Annual Council of 1889 would experience more amendments to Article II of the constitution and Canon XIII, both affecting colored congregations and colored clergy. One month following the conclusion of the 1888 Council, Assistant Bishop A.M. Randolph ordained two deacons at St. Stephen's Church in Petersburg: Benjamin Franklin Lewis and Basil Benjamin Tyler. Another deacon ordained earlier, M.F. Nelson, died at the age of 26. He was in charge of St. Philip's Church in Richmond. George Freeman Bragg, Jr., was ordained to the priesthood on December 19, 1988, at St. Luke's Church in Norfolk. Earlier on August 19, 1888, Grace Church in Norfolk was organized. Bragg would eventually become rector of the historic church but later removed to Baltimore. Randolph, never at a loss for words and one who never delivered a short annual address to a Council assembly, attempted to explain to the delegates of the 1889 Council the high calling of people in the participation of the governance of the church. In an effort to explain potential Negro participation in legislative affairs of the church, Randolph asserted that participation was not a question of race but a question of capacity of character, of faculty, of ability. The system of government that the church maintained, according to Randolph, was based upon the assumption of the "possession of certain elements of moral character, of knowledge, of personal self-control, and dignity, which, in some degree, belong to the white race in all communities." These voters were heirs of the ages of civilization. But the Negro, though genial, kind, and eloquent in speech, might not be capable of adjudicating situations in which he was unaccustomed, according to Randolph. So he rhetorically asked what "seems to be the line of our [white people's] duty to these brethren of another race?" The duties enumerated were teaching, training, guiding, helping and lifting them. Besides being patient with them, "we must pray for these children of our Father whom He has given to us to train." Throughout the post–Civil War days many, not just Randolph, understood their duties as the superior and civilized race to care for and train the newly freed. As seen above, when St. Stephen's Church applied for admission to the diocese as a full and independent member, the church, instead of admitting them, decided to take them under their care — to legislate for them, in other words. As is evident, the white members of the church always struggled in their Christian understanding of their relationship with their colored brethren, not seeing them as equals but seeing them as childlike and needing assistance. These examples support a paternalistic sentiment, even though in many documents the church stated that it never intended to act paternalistically. It had to be an unfolding and evolving process for the church to recognize their real duties.

The continuing changes to Article II and Canon XIII took center stage. Proposed amendments to Section 3 of Article II included scrapping four clerical delegates in favor of two clerical and two lay delegates. Those delegates would have the privilege of voice and vote and the right to vote only on matters affecting the colored convocation of churches. They would not have the right to vote on other matters. Colored delegates were severely restricted in how they cast votes. Another amendment allowed colored clergy connected with the diocese prior to May 1, 1889, to retain their full voting rights, unlike the voting rights of colored convocation clerical delegates. But the May 1 "grandfather date" was soon changed to May 17, 1889. The vote was taken, and the amendments to Article II passed 67 to 23 in the clerical ranks and 73 to 6 in the lay voting. Nine black and 14 white clergymen voted against the amendments. All of the eligible African-American clergy voted "no."

Prior to the voting the colored clergy protested. The protest was presented to Council delegates by George Freeman Bragg, Jr. The signatures of all black clergy covered the protest document, led by James Solomon Russell. The protest stated, in part, that the colored congregations strongly disapproved of the amendments to the constitution of the diocese. Each of these congregations and their convocation had duly considered and discussed this issue of a separate organization but did not favor these constitutional amendments. The protest closed by affirming their belief that "the adoption of the aforementioned amendment will put an end to the growth of the work of the Church among our people." Beside those of Russell and Bragg were the signatures of John T. Harrison, Lafayette Winfield, D.W. Taylor, B.F. Lewis, William P. Burke, George E. Howell, and William E. Howell. White clergy voting in favor of the amendments included T. Grayson Dashiell and Pike Powers, but this time it also included Robb White, the first evangelist to the Zion Union Apostolic Church communities. Arthur Selden Lloyd voted in opposition of the amendment. Lloyd would later become a bishop of the Diocese of Virginia and continued to be a close friend of James Solomon Russell.

Although the African-American communities within the boundaries of the Diocese of Virginia were being evangelized, the attitudes of the church leadership still held on to patriarchal and paternal sympathies. It was difficult for them to make some changes, but changes were gradually evolving. It was equally if not more difficult for black clergy and congregations to acquiesce to the legislative maneuvers of the diocese's Annual Councils. Russell, who would be presented with even tougher, but not unrelated, situations in the future, was a man of order. He understood how assemblies worked, as evidenced by his participation in the Zion Union Church before the age of twenty. He knew that it took people time to adjust to changing situations. But the work of spreading the gospel throughout the Southside continued. Russell's St. Paul charge in Lawrenceville lost membership through transfers and deaths. In 1888 he reported 99 active communicants, 90 in 1889. His parochial school reported 102 students and 2 teachers (Russell and his wife Virginia). The school that he and Virginia started in 1882 as a parochial school was poised to become a normal school. The diocese's contributions passed a quarter of a million dollars; $254,443 in contributions was reported at the 1889 Annual Council along with 17,283 communicants. There were 1,033 infant baptisms, 393 adults. A throng of 14,457 students and 1,991 teachers posted evidence of the still strong Sunday school program across the diocese. With two bishops, 148 clergy and 31 lay readers were recorded.[4]

95th Annual Council — St. George's Church, Fredericksburg (May 21–24, 1890)

By the time of the convening of the Annual Council of 1890 missionary efforts among colored people were in full swing, particularly in the Southside of Virginia. James Solomon Russell rectored three churches—Grace, St. James's, and St. Paul's—with a total number of communicants at 179; 109 were at his original St. Paul's. John T. Harrison at St. Thomas's Church in Totaro had 39 faithful; D.W. Taylor's work at Blandford Mission near Petersburg consisted of 26 communicants; Lafayette Winfield ministered at Trinity Church in Dinwiddie County with 36 communicants; Benjamin Franklin Lewis rectored Ascension Church in Mecklenburg, which had 17 communicants; B.B. Tyler assisted at the white St. John's Church in Hampton and ministered to the colored members; and Joseph W. Carroll led a congregation of 170 at St. Mark's Church in the town of St. Tammany, by far the single largest congregation in the Southside. Churches outside the Southside were St. Philip's in Richmond and a colored congregation at St. Luke's in Norfolk. The diocese continued to advance its missionary calling to the African-American communities. Bishop Whittle ordained Thomas W. Vaughan and Joseph F. Mitchell to the diaconate in June of 1889, and on February 13, 1890, he ordained Deacon William P. Burke to the priesthood. The Rev. Robb White, the first evangelist (a white man) to the large Zion Union community in Brunswick County, transferred out of the diocese to take a charge in the Diocese of Georgia. The Rev. Dr. E.B. Jones (white) continued as the evangelist to the colored congregations as well as rector of Sapony Church and Good Shepherd Church in Bath Parish, and St. John's Church in Cumberland Parish. These churches had colored members, but Jones, as the diocese's designated evangelist, operated, more or less, as an archdeacon. Canon XIII, though passed in previous years and amended again in 1890, had not been effectively in practice at this point. Soon changes would take place among the many colored missions, but in a newly formed diocese.

In his address to the 1890 Annual Council, Bishop Whittle recommended that a committee be appointed to consider dividing the diocese into two or three dioceses. The work of the diocese had been increasing steadily due to population increase; old cities were becoming larger and newer cities and towns were being created. Future councils of the diocese would provide the mechanism for the division of the diocese, or not. In the meantime the bishop continued to report his annual visits and other significant events during the year from the end of the 1889 Council to the present council. He visited and confirmed many African-Americans, not only in the Southside churches but in other geographical regions of the diocese. In his observation and reporting on work among the colored people, Whittle enumerated that the diocese had at that time five postulants for holy orders, one candidate for holy orders, and thirteen active ministers (priests and deacons). He categorized colored congregations as eighteen churches or missions, six preaching stations (congregations not fully organized), three church rectories (homes for the pastors), and 26 parish schools with 1,067 scholars. In all there were 27 Sunday schools with 2,169 scholars, about 1,200 communicants. He confirmed approximately 1,200 over the year.

Bishop Francis McNeese Whittle also suggested that legislation was needed for the "benefit and protection of this [colored] people and their interests," citing that this particular council would take up such proposed legislation, and that though Canon XIII was adopted some years earlier, the council should take the "time and trouble to improve the canon law." In other words, Canon XIII had not been practical because it was virtually non-executable. Whittle backed up his suggestion by recognizing that legislatively (or canonically) every colored priest or deacon labored in his work at the sufferance of another minister (meaning a white minister) in his parish who could put a stop to the work. But the moral obligation of the church was not to cast off "our colored brethren," but to find ways to strengthen the ties that bind. Whittle asserted that the diocese's colored members "ought to have some voice in the legislation which affects them, and some means by which the influence of their laity may be felt among them."

Assistant Bishop A.M. Randolph in his address reported that the question of the church's relation to the work with colored people taken up at General Convention was the duty of the individual diocese. Again, even after the Diocese of Virginia sought definition from the General Convention, it was rejected and returned to the diocese. Apparently hoping for assistance from the General Convention (GC) and not getting it, Randolph diplomatically ridiculed that decision. He cited conditions imposed by GC for its cooperation in "carrying the Gospel of Christ to an ignorant and half-civilized people...." Randolph, realizing that the work must be done within the diocese, said, "We will try to do it under the conviction that God has given it to us to do. We will give, as we may, the labor and the sacrifice for its accomplishment. Our friends throughout the country must trust us as brethren, and help and pray for us in our efforts to educate and to Christianize the negro [*sic*] race, and may God bless us and them in the discharge of our great responsibility." When referring to the Negro race, most of Randolph's addresses at Annual Councils betrayed his attitude and sentiments toward colored people. He projected a notion of the superiority of the white race while pronouncing any other race as uncivilized and ignorant. Yet Bishop Randolph persevered with his work with the colored people in his charge and would eventually have to make critical decisions on race relations in his diocese.

Canon XIII is a document that presents the mindset of race relations within the Diocese of Virginia at that time. Its sections spell out how the church's thinking developed in the late nineteenth century South. It is Canon XIII that James Solomon Russell would have to live with for the remainder of his ministry: a canon that he would have to deal with one way or another on many occasions. It would affect his future. Russell was also the only African-American appointed to the committee that submitted what would become the canon's final version of actual implementation.[5]

96th Annual Council — Grace Church, Petersburg (May 20–23, 1891)

At the Council of 1891 only two significant issues were discussed: the organizational meeting of the new Colored Convocation in Petersburg at St. Stephen's Church; and the potential division of the diocese into two or more. Not much content was printed about the colored convocation except for the fact that one unnamed clergyman was not there due to illness. Bishop Whittle attended at least one day of the convocation's organizational meeting on December 30, 1890, and Assistant Bishop Randolph gave the sermon in the middle of a day-long liturgy of morning prayers, the administration of the Lord's Supper, and a closing evening prayer. During evening prayer a sermon was preached by one of the convocation's members — the journal does not identify that person. Bishop Whittle also made an address. There were two sessions of the convocation when officers were elected and delegates to the diocese's Annual Council were also elected. Rules were developed for the convocation, which was now to meet every year.

Much of the discussion of the 1891 Annual Council centered instead on what the possible new geographical boundaries of the new dioceses should be. No less than one alternative was suggested. What is of interest today is that the council's original line drawing placed, more or less, the Diocese of Virginia within what eventually turned out to be the Diocese of Southern Virginia. Again, Assistant Bishop Randolph was without brevity in his address to the council. Much of his address was about the division of the diocese and a consideration of the psychology and sociology of its rearrangement. But before delving into this understanding of division, Randolph did make note of two meetings that he participated in with the Commission on Colored People of the national church. Its first meeting was in June 1890 and the second on January 7–8, 1891, both in Washington, D.C. Randolph produced no content of these meetings, but the fact of his participation provides evidence of his ongoing effort to understand what his Christian calling had to be in regard to colored people in the church. He also visited Brunswick County in March 1891 and made a special note of the work he saw with the colored children under the care of James Solomon Russell: "I can recommend this work without reserve to the confidence and the generous help of our people."

Randolph read through his personal, multi-point reasonability test for dividing the diocese. He first declared that a bishop is "married" to a diocese. Non-episcopal clergy and the laity are under no such bond. In this point Randolph suggests that as the people of the diocese change over the years, except for retirement or death, the bishop remains and ministers to his people within his jurisdiction. But the question of dividing a diocese entailed an element of finality. In the future new diocese, some may want to return to the original. Even though that can be accomplished, it can be done only with great difficulty. He also provided the example of the Diocese of Easton created out of the larger Diocese of Maryland. The high-church party in the church, according to Randolph, favors smaller dioceses. He then remarked that many believe that smaller dioceses work better and are more efficient than larger ones. But he stated that facts on the ground proved just the opposite. Large dioceses, he said, possess more resources and can serve communities better than smaller ones. Prosperity was another element in his calculation. Stating that a proposed Los Angeles diocese out of the large Diocese of California was proposed due to the prosperity of the era and area, he warned that material well-being can be fleeting. By the time the proposal reached the General Convention, prosperity had diminished and sufficient operating funds were unavailable to begin a new diocese.

Bishop Randolph recognized that the Methodists and Presbyterians had increased rather than reduced their boundaries. Considering the material prosperity all around them, Randolph believed that "combination, not disintegration, [and] association, not isolation, constitute the law and principle of growth." The Diocese of Virginia had experienced great growth in the twenty-five years following the end of the Civil War. It was doing well. He turned then to the capacity of the bishop to adhere to his responsibilities of office. Using the Diocese of Maryland as an example, Randolph said that the one bishop there was able to conduct his official acts in a diocese with more churches than in Virginia. Randolph, it seemed, was building a case for a diocese to have only one bishop. The existence of an assistant bishop, according to Randolph, was an anomaly in the history of the Christian Church. An assistant bishop operates within a contradiction of constitutional and canonical laws. Constitutionally, a bishop is conferred with all the rights, responsibilities, and discipline of the episcopal office; but canon law removes the very responsibilities conferred constitutionally. In other words, a diocese should have only one bishop. This logic leads to the identity and inseparability of a bishop and his diocese. But in the practical world some issues need to be considered and laws thus modified.

Bishops get sick or become unable to perform conditions of office. Bishop Whittle, for example, had been absent from Annual Councils on

several occasions due to illness. Even Assistant Bishop Randolph was unable
to attend on one occasion due to a traveling accident. The end result of Randolph's monologue on the division of the diocese was to promote the division,
not to keep one large diocese. A division of the diocese would create two
equally sized and growing dioceses. Randolph, after citing the heavy workload
on the bishop, called on the diocese to "relieve your Bishop" from half of the
burdens of administration. Randolph's view is captured in his belief that the
whole state of Virginia would no longer be served by one (canonical and ordinary) bishop, but by two bishops. At this point in the history of the Episcopal
Church, only an "assistant" episcopal office was in place in addition to the
"ordinary." The episcopal offices of suffragan and coadjutor would emerge
later from national church legislative General Conventions. One should keep
in mind that both Randolph and Russell were members of the original Committee of the Division of the Diocese.

The parochial reporting at the 1891 Annual Council demonstrated the
continued growth and prosperity not only of the diocese in general, but of
the colored congregations. James Solomon Russell still had charge of three
churches in Brunswick County: St. Paul's, St. James's, and Grace. These three
churches had a combined communicant membership of 196. Their Sunday
school enrollment exceeded 360 students, and the St. Paul parochial school
had an enrollment of 92 students. Joseph W. Carroll pastored two congregations: St. Paul's and St. Mary's in Mecklenburg County. St. Mary's had a
membership of 183, still the largest single congregation, with 134 Sunday
school students, and a parochial school of 90 students. George Freeman Bragg,
Jr., was the rector of Grace Church–Norfolk with a communicant count of
100. Grace Church also had an enrollment of 82 in its Sunday school and 50
in the parochial school. Nine other African American clergymen pastored
one congregation each. The diocese reported annual contributions of
$309,368.00. According to the report those contributions exceed the previous
year by $31,734.00. Total diocese-wide active communicants totaled 18,697,
of whom 1,289 were African-American and 45 Indian. Sunday schools across
the diocese had a total enrollment of 15,450. A total of 156 clergy served the
diocese.[6]

97th Annual Council — Epiphany Church, Danville (May 18–21, 1892)

The Ninety-Seventh Annual Council of the Protestant Episcopal Church
in Virginia, held at Epiphany Church in Danville, Virginia, was a significant
assembly. The work of this assembly began on May 18, 1892, and ended on

May 21, 1892. This was the last time that the Diocese of Virginia could be called "undivided." It was at this Council that the all male delegates, clergy and laity, voted to divide into two equal dioceses. After five attempts at modifying the original proposal, and a total change in the membership of the Committee on the Division of the Diocese, a compromise was reached. The proposed new diocese would eventually be named the Episcopal Diocese of Southern Virginia with a boundary that was basically south of Richmond and included the Eastern Shore, the Peninsula and the Tidewater, and counties south of the James River and extending westward along the Virginia–North Carolina border. The original Diocese of Virginia would retain its name, and the episcopal residence would remain in Richmond. Significant to the new diocese was placement of the Bishop Payne Divinity School in Petersburg within its jurisdiction. The population divisions were notable. In the restructured Diocese of Virginia the white population was 365,701 and African-Americans numbered 241,617. The population in the new Southern Virginia diocese was 648,979 white and 399,250 colored. The new southern diocese would have 130 white congregations and 18 colored. There would be only three African-American congregations remaining in the Virginia diocese.

Soon after the Report of the Committee on the State of the Church was read and the report itself and its resolutions were unanimously adopted, the Rev. Dr. T. Grayson Dashiell, longtime secretary of the Annual Councils, read a telegram from A.A. Watson, the Bishop of East Carolina. The brief message read, "The Diocese of East Carolina sends love with greeting to the twin Dioceses of Virginia." It was, indeed, a momentous and historic occasion. The old, venerable Church of Virginia, the undivided Diocese of Virginia, was breaking up. The emotion of the council delegates was overwhelming for some. O.S. Barten, chairman of the Committee of the State of the Church, read into the record his and the committee's sentiments by saying, "We are meeting this year under peculiar circumstances, and that the Ninety-Seventh Annual Council of the Protestant Episcopal Church in the Diocese of Virginia must be ever memoriable [*sic*] in the history of the Diocese. It may be the last time that we meet as one body. Another year may find us two bands, but always one in heart and Christian affection." And in the evangelical spirit that always was nurtured in the old Virginia diocese, Barten went on to say they were "living in sober, solemn times ... [but] God has supplied to us ... an instrumentality good and perfect ... the Gospel of Jesus Christ." Near the end of his report Barten said that the Church of Virginia "is safe, is prosperous, is divinely blessed, [and] continues true to her high vantage ground." The mere act of legislating a division, though necessary due to the diocese's incredible growth, was nevertheless a painful undertaking.

Among issues and items that occurred during the past year that might been obscured by the process of dividing the diocese was that the Colored Convocation that organized itself in December 1890 did not convene in 1891 as required. Bishop Whittle was ill and not able to convene an official convocation. That meant that by the end of 1892 there would be a new southern diocese and the responsibility would fall to its new bishop to convene what would become by far the larger number of colored congregations of the two dioceses. The nucleus, the centrality, and the highest concentration of African-Americans among the two dioceses (as well as in the entire South) would reside within the boundaries of the jurisdiction of the Protestant Episcopal Church in the Diocese of Southern Virginia. If there were ever an opportunity to envision an evangelical opportunity for a new ecclesiastical entity, it could clearly be seen in the creation of this new diocese. Southern Virginia would begin its ministries with fifty-five white and 10 African-American clergy, and one bishop. (See Appendix L — Statistics of the Two Episcopal Dioceses in Virginia 1892.) Though the entity was new, its people were not. Trained evangelists, black and white, knowledgeable and experienced in church planting, social integration, and church administration, would now become the driving force in the Episcopal Church's major leadership in ministry to African-Americans. Bishop A.M. Randolph would accept the episcopal seat of the new diocese, and James Solomon Russell would emerge as the natural leader of racial reconciliation within the church.[7]

Later in 1892 the Episcopal Diocese of Southern Virginia held its Primary Council at St. Paul's Church in Lynchburg, Virginia, on November 23 and 24. Colored clergy entitled to voting privileges according to a grandfathering clause were William P. Burke, Lafayette Winfield, and James Solomon Russell. Another, Joseph Fenner Mitchell, was elected by the Colored Convocation as a voting delegate along with laymen H.E. Barnett and Landon Jessup. The Colored Convocation never exercised its canonical charge in the old Diocese of Virginia. This was its first use and test.[8]

CHAPTER SIX

The Trials and
Joys of Black
Entrepreneurial Education

NINETY PERCENT OF AFRICAN-AMERICAN ADULTS in the South in 1860 were
illiterate. This was one of many reasons why former slaves had an
"unquenchable thirst for education."[1] Acquiring an education was central to
the meaning of freedom. Some slaves learned to read and write clandestinely,
and those who could not read and write held those literate blacks in high
esteem. Former slaves were in the forefront, if not the actual leaders, in the
movement for universal, state-supported education after the end of the Civil
War. Most of the Confederate States had made education of the slaves illegal
and the powers of the day, predominantly the planters, made sure that the
status quo was untouched. White political opponents of the powerful planter
elites—yeomen farmers, laborers, and some industrialists—did not offer any
opposition. Planters could continue their social and economic way of life by
maintaining themselves as the ruling class while ignoring the educational and
economic needs of their own economic engine: slavery.[2]

Many of the early postbellum black educators became literate while still
slaves, and that experience motivated their entrepreneurial educational adventures as freedmen. Though the vast majority of slaves never learned to read
and write under the system of social slavery, some did learn either on their
own or by finding themselves in a favored situation. Some who became literate
in the antebellum South were P.B.S. Pinchback of Louisiana, who became a
United States senator, and William Sanders Scarborough, who became an
educator and a Greek classics scholar.[3] Former slaves wasted no time in setting
up education societies and raising money for the purchase of land, buildings,
and teachers. By 1870 blacks had spent more than one million dollars on education in the Deep South.[4] There is no doubt that James Solomon Russell, as

Faculty and staff of St. Paul's College, year unknown. Archdeacon Russell is at the top right (Russell Memorial Library, Saint Paul's College, Lawrenceville, Virginia).

a young slave boy, learned not only how to read and write, but how to interact successfully with other human beings. He, too, had that unquenchable thirst for an education, and not just for reading and writing. He simply wanted to learn as much as he could so that he could help others and move forward. Russell's calling to education and to Christian ministry would serve him and his organizations well over the years. Public education came to Brunswick County in 1871, but it was not an equitable system and not all people accepted it, black or white.

Russell Makes His Way

As a newly ordained deacon in March of 1882, Russell traveled to his first (and more-or-less final) assignment in Lawrenceville, Virginia. The only Episcopal church in town was St. Andrew's, a white congregation with a number of African-American congregants. Although Bishop Whittle considered assigning Russell to churches in his native Mecklenburg County, it was the rector of St. Andrew's who asked and convinced Bishop F.M. Whittle to assign

Russell to St. Andrew's because of the black parishioners there. Lawrenceville was and still is today the seat of Brunswick County, and at the time of Russell's relocation to the county was home to more than 12,000 African-Americans.[5] This large African-American population eventually turned out to be a blessing for Russell's ministry.

Russell, in May, attended his first diocesan council meeting in Norfolk as a voting member. At this Council of the Diocese of Virginia,[6] Russell was given an opportunity to speak, and without hesitation he took advantage of it. By this time in Russell's adventure, the entire lay and clergy membership of the Council should have heard of him. After all, he was a rising star, and the diocese made sure that he acquired an excellent theological education. Not unaware of his potential standing among the council, Russell asked for assistance in starting a new mission and made a plea for a horse. One of the lay[7] members of the council offered a resolution that Council provide Russell with a horse, bridle and saddle, and another asked for subscriptions to support this new deacon's planned church. By the close of Council, Russell had enough funds for a horse and accessories, and an additional three hundred dollars to start his new church plant.[8] In that same year Russell organized the St. Paul Benevolent Society of St. Stephen's Church, Petersburg. At its first meeting, in Lawrenceville, twenty-two people attended and "endorsed a program of mutual helpfulness."[9]

A room in the new chapel was used as the classroom. After a few years, more space was required, and Russell built a 3-room structure with a gift from the Rev. James Saul[10] of Philadelphia. Once the Saul Building was constructed, the expansion of Russell's educational program took off. In 1888 the transformation of the parish school into a "normal"[11] school moved forward, and Russell began acquiring land from several local Lawrenceville landowners. The school had fewer than a dozen boarding students by the time of the start of the normal school in September 1888. It was 1893 when St. Paul Normal and Industrial School was incorporated in the Commonwealth of Virginia. The first meeting of St. Paul Board of Trustees was held in Richmond at the Episcopal residence of Bishop Whittle.[12] No time was wasted in contracting for the construction of other buildings, and financial contributions arrived from people who had heard about the new school but who had never visited it: contributions from Minnesota, Massachusetts and Pennsylvania, just to cite a few. Though criticized for going on a "land-buying" spree, Russell continued to make land deals between 1890 and 1899.[13] By 1899 Russell had acquired 1,600 acres on "The Hill" by signing notes with no collateral — only his word and signature — and by receiving loans from out-of-town people (mostly from the North) whom he had met previously. Enrollments grew steadily at St. Paul School. The school was modeled after Hampton Institute.

One of the disciplinary practices put in place was a military corps format for male students. And for all students alternative methods of tuition payment were made available. For example, very few students could afford to pay tuition for the full term, so Russell implemented a work-study program which made education possible for many former slaves and their children. This, too, was similar to the Hampton Institute model.

Churches in the Virginia diocese provided parochial education for both blacks and whites after the war. In 1871 public (meaning free) education began in Brunswick County, Virginia. There was not much excitement at first about public education, evidenced not only by vocal opposition but by statistics showing that the average daily school attendance was 32 percent and 23 percent for white and black children, respectively. By the early 20th century, when Russell's school was about twelve years in operation, the sentiment for public education had changed dramatically. Public grade schools had become well established, but high school education was considered a luxury. For black students wanting to continue their education through high school, their families had to either pay tuition or the students worked their way through institutions such as St. Paul Normal and Industrial School. This alternative gave black students an advantage which was virtually unique in the state.[14]

Russell's community orientation and his desire to provide training beyond just the classroom drove him to develop extension programs. Farmers' conferences began at St. Paul School in 1902 at a time when "Brunswick County was the least prosperous and the most backward of Virginia counties."[15] Russell claimed, "The Conference enjoys the distinction of being the first organized effort on a countywide basis among Negroes of the State to carry out a definite plan of constructive racial uplift."[16] That the St. Paul Farmers' Conference was the first of its kind can easily be challenged, since schools such as Tuskegee Institute in Alabama and Hampton Institute in Virginia had similar programs in place. Hampton's conferences were started by white school administrators, and perhaps that is the distinction that Russell subtly made in his comment. An article in *The Southern Workman* reported that the series of conferences "established by the Negro schools" have been one of the most effective means of helping "Negroes of the South" improve their condition.[17] In an address at Western Theological Seminary, Robert Strange, the bishop of East Carolina, cited the fact that he attended a farmers' conference at St. Paul School in 1906 and was "much impressed and greatly encouraged for the true progress of the negro." He made that observation as one of two special ways in which he saw the church influencing the "negro race." His address, though high in praise of work done by "negro" schools and conferences, conveyed a not-uncommon attitude of superiority of the Anglo-Saxon race.[18]

According to Russell, the purposes of the conferences were "to encourage our people to buy land, build better homes, churches, and schools; to promote better race relations; to make useful and intelligent members of society; and to publish statistics of Negro progress" in a nonpolitical and nonsectarian program of mutual assistance.[19] Russell would promote not only the school but its farmers' conferences in speeches, sermons, diocesan reports and written articles over the entire life of his ministry. Many of his speeches were laden with statistics. In short, Russell produced an impressive record. At his farmers' conference in 1908 Russell provided hard data supporting progress made in Brunswick County for "Negroes" for the two preceding years. He stated that blacks owned 49,171 acres of land, an increase of 5,962 acres; assessed land value was $332,000; personal property valued at $119,000; and $15,000 in cash was on deposit in the banks of Lawrenceville. Houses were better, crop yield was larger and black families were determined to educate their children.[20] In 1906 it was reported that St. Paul's School paid taxes on real property assessed at a value of $250,000; that Negroes owned from 100 to 500 acres of land, and one in particular owned 1,000 acres; and all had been bought and paid for since the end of the Civil War. Also reported was that the Negroes in Virginia owned or operated 25,000 farms, and started banks and other financial institutions.[21] Most of Russell's speeches and addresses were like this—his speeches were not unlike a political candidate's stump speech. Using St. Paul School as his platform, Russell not only traveled around the country promoting his farmer's conference and the progress made in his Southside Virginia region, he came into contact with influential and wealthy people. This was helpful to his fundraising efforts. The curse of fundraising is that it never ends. Like Booker T. Washington at Tuskegee Institute, Russell traveled heavily to promote St. Paul School simply to keep it operating. This virtual nonstop effort extracts over time a heavy personal toll, usually in the form of ill health. In an article in *The Southern Missioner* it was reported that Russell was "Exhausted and in ill health" and went away for a brief rest.[22] In his *Autobiography* Russell described an incident in 1898 when he was on a fundraising trip in New York City. It was his first outing in behalf of the school after the 1897 typhoid outbreak. On his way from his hotel in Newark to St. Bartholomew's Church in New York City he became ill, weak from exertion. Though late for his scheduled fundraising address, he made his presentation to the women of the St. Augustine's League and received financial gifts toward his St. Paul Memorial Chapel.[23]

Russell's school was a parochial school attached to his church. When it was incorporated, the board of trustees included the bishop of the Diocese of Virginia, making it, at least on first blush, a school owned by the diocese. But such was not the case for Episcopal schools for African-American children.

Just as the federal government created the Freedmen's Bureau to assist in the transition from slavery to freedom, the Episcopal Church, the national body and not the diocese, created the Freedman's Commission.[24] The commission's name was confusing, so the church changed the name to the Colored Commission. The purpose of the church agency was to financially support education in church-affiliated schools for freed slaves and their children in the South.[25]

Financial support for St. Paul School therefore came from the Freedman's Commission and its successor agencies, but the funding was never sufficient and fundraising became a time-consuming enterprise. Russell was not the sort of person to give up — he was a resourceful leader. In order to implement all of the educational programs that he thought were needed for his region of the nation, Russell required significant funding. Between the end of the Civil War and 1902, there was no major organized effort outside the state and federal governments for providing funding of any magnitude. Although Russell gave us little information about the Rev. James Saul and his funding of the construction of the school's first building, he did mention other small donors who had heard about the school. The school needed funds not only for building construction but for operating expenses which tuition payments hardly covered. Russell knew what he had to do, and in his *Autobiography* he wrote: "I have addressed the General Convention and church organizations of all kinds, traveled in many states, and written thousands of letters, all in the effort to secure the wherewithal to build and maintain the Institution. It has been my good fortune to attend eleven General Conventions of the Church—from 1898–1928—and on all these occasions, special mass meetings[26] have been held in the interest of the colored schools."[27]

He tells of speaking at the special mass meeting at the General Convention of 1901 in San Francisco, which yielded him an invitation the next month to speak at the Women's Auxiliary of the Diocese of Pennsylvania in Philadelphia. In 1907 the General Convention was in Richmond, Virginia, a city less than 90 miles north of Lawrenceville. At that convention, he was successful in attracting almost 100 delegates to visit the St. Paul campus. What was Russell's message to them? His typical fundraising speech was like the one given before the special mass meeting at the 1913 General Convention in New York City. Russell was given an additional ten minutes (fifteen in total) to complete his presentation, and those additional minutes were given at the request of the delegates. In that speech Russell said that in Southern Virginia "we have 34 [African-American] churches and 2,000 communicants,[28] and a prosperous, growing work. The standard of morality has been wonderfully raised, and the jails, once full of prisoners, are now empty. St. Paul's School is the largest Church institution in this country; it has 3,500 graduates, and the official recognition of the State of Virginia. It touches the life of every family in Brunswick County and has solved the race problem there, as black and white live on the most cordial terms."[29] Some elements of his speeches may seem out of place, especially the phrase about morality and empty jails. From before the Civil War up until the time of this speech, the principal concern of white leaders, both secular and religious, was the morality of African Americans. But Russell, knowing his audiences, was acutely aware of such thinking and therefore he wanted to assure them that all was well at St. Paul's and in Lawrenceville. This may have been one of Russell's sure-fire phrases that brought in the money, which is important, given that Russell ran up fairly large debts for St. Paul.

Harold T. Lewis's examination of school funding by the church's agencies is insightful. Simply put, the church's missionary work in Japan, China, the Philippines and Alaska were monumental success stories compared with its shameful support of the African-American. According to Lewis, there were multiple factions with conflicting goals within the Episcopal Church's school funding agencies. These conflicts inhibited or curtailed the success of these agencies. Therefore, the church thought it better to dissolve them in 1904. The church needed to re-think its strategies in support of African-Americans in the Episcopal Church. At the same time that the Episcopal Church struggled with the infighting of its educational funding agencies, many prominent and wealthy Episcopalians contributed large sums of money directly to nonchurch schools like Hampton and Tuskegee.[30] Certainly it had to be an embarrassment to the church that its own people contributed significantly to secular schools yet ignored its own. Though the Episcopal Church dissolved its fundraising efforts in 1904, it is important to understand what happened when a new movement emerged in 1902 that set the standard for funding Southern black schools, and how the Episcopal Church reacted to it later in 1906.

The Politics of Financial Black Education

Professors Eric Anderson of Pacific Union College and Alfred A. Moss, Jr., of the University of Maryland studied Northern philanthropy to Southern black schools which had been funding, since the end of the Civil War, Protestant religious societies seeking to elevate the freedmen. Money was always available even after the end of Reconstruction and reached new highs in the early 20th century. The dominant denominations receiving these funds were the Methodist, Presbyterian, Congregational and Baptist churches. These churches were headquartered in the North and were collecting and spending money for black education in the South. By 1906 their expenditures on black education was four times greater than in 1876.[31] The Episcopal Church's record in Southern black education during this same time period was worse. In 1902 a major shift occurred in the funding structure of Southern black education: the Rockefeller Foundation created the General Education Board (GEB). It is necessary to point out the effect of the GEB on the Episcopal Church and the Church's eventual reaction to this new type of funding. There was an intellectual and secular philosophy undergirding it, and was monopoly-like in structure.

In 1901 a movement led by a group of reform-minded men in the North began to address the problems of Southern black education. That movement was known both as the Southern Education Board (SEB) and more famously as the Ogden Movement.[32] There were other funds that existed prior to the creation of the GEB. By 1902 the members of the boards of most of these Northern and common-purposed philanthropies were the same people. In other words, there were "interlocking boards," and a virtual monopoly of school funding came into play. The interlocking boards controlled how funding would be distributed based on their own view of black education. No member of any board was African-American and little input was sought from African-American educators. Token gestures were made to blacks such as Booker T. Washington. The boards never invited him to their meetings held outside the South, but they provided him stipends for speech-making in their behalf.[33] What provoked the ire of Episcopal Church leaders about the GEB and other boards was the fact that the primary contributors to those funds were wealthy Episcopalians.[34] This embarrassment led to the formation in 1906 of the American Church Institute for Negroes (ACIN). The brainchild of New York Bishop David Hummell Greer and with the support of layman and financier George Foster Peabody, the ACIN was born on the assumption that millions of "Episcopal" dollars could be diverted from the GEB and other agencies to the new church-affiliated ACIN. Since the predecessor church agencies to the ACIN were fundamentally failures, Greer, after observing the practices of the GEB, envisioned the ACIN.[35] The first important task at hand was to select the agency's executive director, the person who would run its day-to-day operation.

Samuel H. Bishop, an Episcopal priest, a University of Vermont and Union Theological Seminary graduate, at age 43 became the first director of ACIN. Bishop was highly educated and conducted postgraduate work at Columbia University, Oxford University, and the University of Berlin. He devoted much of his time as a student, and later in life, to the study of philanthropy within modern charities in the South.[36] George Foster Peabody was the one person instrumental in getting Bishop this assignment. Bishop immediately went to work and began making contacts in the black community.[37]

St. Paul's College Choir, year unknown. Archdeacon Russell is standing at the right (Russell Memorial Library, Saint Paul's College, Lawrenceville, Virginia).

Soon after his appointment, Bishop visited the Episcopal Church schools for blacks in the South. The report produced by Bishop of his multi-campus visits, according to Anderson and Moss, was, not surprisingly, in accord with the educational views of Bishop Greer and George Foster Peabody. Three of the schools visited were selected as the first institutions to be affiliated with ACIN: St. Augustine's[38] in Raleigh, North Carolina; Bishop Payne Divinity School in Petersburg, Virginia; and St. Paul Normal and Industrial Institute in Lawrenceville, Virginia.[39] Schools that were not selected by the ACIN began harboring ill feelings toward the new church funding agency. Theodore Bratton, the bishop of Mississippi, expressed the hope of many Southern white Episcopalians that the ACIN would come to the aid of the other schools by creating at least one industrial high school in each of the Southern dioceses. Even though ACIN affiliated with a few more schools,[40] the scale of ACIN's expansion never measured up to Bratton's assumptions. With the original three schools now selected, Samuel Bishop began his work.

St. Augustine's was financially healthier than the two other affiliated schools because it had no debt at the time Bishop conducted his audit. But

St. Paul's School, according to Bishop's visits and surveys, had many unpaid debts, needed a larger revenue stream in order to carry on the industrial education program, and required major sums for a building program and the purchase of equipment for shop classes. Bishop also did not approve of the procedure in place for contracting with teachers. The principal of the school, James Solomon Russell, made rehiring decisions for teachers only at the beginning of a school term. Although the Lawrenceville school could have been overlooked and a similar school selected, by 1906 the St. Paul School was the leader in industrial education of all the schools belonging to or affiliated with the Episcopal Church. St. Paul's was located in Virginia's "black belt," where the highest concentration of African-Americans lived. James Solomon Russell was also very well known by this time not only in the Church but around the country. He began his fundraising campaigns from the time of the school's founding and never stopped. ACIN's initial three-school initiative dealt with three schools with three distinctively different curricula and operational characteristics. ACIN, in other words, picked the cream of the crop for varying purposes. In the case of St. Paul, Russell clearly was widely known as an effective educational entrepreneur and leader. Russell could not be ignored. But Samuel Bishop had other problems to face in the meantime.

As chief fundraiser for the ACIN, Bishop was unable to build a sizeable endowment and became increasingly frustrated not only in his inability to secure ongoing funds in large amounts from wealthy Episcopalians, but in the apparent inaction of ACIN's board to use their influence for the same purpose. The lack of significant funding also meant that the Institute might not be able to pay Bishop's salary. At his wit's end, he wrote his board, "If I stay, the Board has got to 'brace up' and help me get money." Bishop's leverage was a job offer from his alma mater in Vermont.[41] That dilemma and the job offer occurred in 1908, hardly two years into his work. Eventually Bishop Greer found funds for Mr. Bishop's salary, but Greer and the other board members continued to keep their involvement in fundraising a low priority. The ACIN in many ways was no more successful than its predecessor agencies. Bishop did not think he was hired to be a fundraiser but to be an innovative educator. Bishop, though well-connected within the Church, was not one of the wealthy elite as were Bishop Greer and George Foster Peabody. Bishop thought Greer and Peabody should be the fundraisers. Greer and Peabody assumed Bishop should. These misunderstandings or assumptions worked against Bishop's efforts to move the organization forward. In a word, Bishop was frustrated. He needed some successes because success was not coming through ACIN's Board.

In 1893, after the Diocese of Southern Virginia was formed out of the "undivided" Diocese of Virginia, Bishop A.M. Randolph appointed James

Solomon Russell to the post of Archdeacon for Colored Work. Two things here are important: first, Russell's parochial school, although within the physical jurisdiction of his bishop and diocese, was subordinate to the Colored Commission. As the principal of St. Paul's, Russell received his salary from the commission, not from the diocese. Secondly, Russell could not become archdeacon without receiving approval from the Colored Commission, or so he assumed. Bishop Randolph asked Russell to accept the archidiaconal appointment and work out the details with the commission later. Russell preferred to work things out in advance. An agreement was then reached and Russell became archdeacon while remaining principal of St. Paul School.[42] With these two situations in place, in 1893 seeds were sown, prefiguring potential problems revolving around authority and jurisdiction over the school. As Russell tells his story, he, the school's board of trustees, and his local bishop, and not the Colored Commission, were in charge of running the St. Paul School. A failure, the Colored Commission dissolved in 1904. The ACIN was organized in 1906 with new insights, new plans, and a management oriented to progressivism.

Frustrated by ACIN's inability to raise funds from Episcopalians, Samuel Bishop, in 1910, attempted to solicit funds directly from the GEB. But GEB policy provided for distribution of funds to individual schools and not to religious denominations. Therefore Bishop declared that ACIN would pledge itself to the secular, progressive education agenda adhered to by GEB. Although Bishop never mentioned the progressive education ideology of GEB it was a well-known fact that the sponsors of all of the board members of the "interlocking" philanthropic agencies were "progressives" and intended to impart that agenda when funding schools.

ACIN had no African-American members on its board. By 1912 a black priest was appointed field agent. In 1911 Bishop convinced ACIN's board to create an advisory council for the purpose of including not black but white Southerners—mostly Southern bishops—in the decision-making process. The second purpose was for mediation of potential difficulties between ACIN board members (all Northerners) and officials of the Southern leaders in the Episcopal Church.[43] Bishop had to make some changes because Southern Episcopal leaders did not like the ACIN interfering in its Southern schools while having no Southerners on the ACIN board. Bishop did not like the fact that St. Paul's board was dominated by local whites from Brunswick County who approved Russell's style of management. Bishop, like many Northerners such as those in the GEB, did not believe Southerners (white or black) were qualified for the tasks at hand. This attitude held by Bishop was one among several factors contributing to the conflict between him and Russell. It is informative to review some actions of the GEB.

In a private conference in 1915 on Negro education held in the New York City offices of the Rockefeller Foundation (GEB), Abraham Flexner described his idea of a modern school, a vision of progressive education. This was one of the few conferences attended by black educators like John Hope of Atlanta University, W.T.B. Williams of the Slater Fund, and R.R. Moton, the successor to Booker T. Washington at Tuskegee Institute. Flexner, the assistant secretary to the GEB, stated that the GEB was not interested in almsgiving but in framing and developing a long-headed policy which would take years to implement. Though the GEB was interested in Negro education, it actually contributed little funding to black schools from 1902 to 1914. Many friends of black education thought the GEB indifferent to blacks. Significantly, however, the GEB made its funding decisions based on controlling the black population, especially within the African-American leadership group.[44] In other words, Northern white philanthropists wanted to control how Negro education progressed.

Samuel Bishop was a white Northerner, an idealist, a progressive educator, and a bureaucratic executive. James Solomon Russell was an African-American Southerner, a pragmatic, Protestant evangelical, and an educational entrepreneur. Russell would have welcomed a church-related and clear-thinking fundraising arm to assist him in keeping St. Paul afloat. But the independent-minded and self-assured Russell looked upon ACIN in general as a weak and meddling agency. He probably dealt with Bishop suspiciously and with contempt. Russell knew people. He could size them up quickly, and was able to sense the motivations from which they acted. This trait may also explain why Russell was successful at independently raising funds from Northerners and making land deals with Southerners. But in a way, both men, Bishop and Russell, had finally met their match.

Knowing how Russell ran St. Paul's and frustrated with Russell's opposition, Bishop increasingly became hostile to Russell and began a series of attacks on Russell personally, rather than employing a diplomatic correction. Bishop alleged that the school was making profits on contract work (done by students who were laborers) for local businesses and farmers.[45] Profits were large enough that the board of trustees of St. Paul's paid taxes on those earnings. Bishop and the ACIN charged Russell with exploiting his students to the discredit of industrial education. Bishop accused Russell of improper if not illegal financial gain. Between 1908 and 1910 Bishop more and more publicly criticized Russell as an administrator. Bishop Tucker, on hearing these charges by Bishop, actually asked the school's major contributors to withhold contributions until changes were made. The enmity between ACIN's executive director and Russell escalated into a battle for control of St. Paul's School.[46]

As a diversionary tactic, Bishop offered Russell and his son a vacation trip to London. Though skeptical, Russell accepted the offer. There is no speculation about why Samuel H. Bishop offered James Solomon Russell and his son an all-expenses-paid vacation to London in 1911. Russell's smart and strong opposition must not have been anticipated by Bishop, at least not at first. Bishop may have had his way with school principals at St. Augustine's and Bishop Payne, but Russell was another matter. Bishop was an ideologue and not a school operator. He was a declared progressive,[47] uncompromising on educational issues that he believed in, and knowing better than anyone else (he thought) how charitable institutions ought to be run. Bishop also believed — as the Northern philanthropists believed — that he knew best how to educate the freedmen of the South. Bishop needed a quick victory of some magnitude in order to deflect potential criticism of his own inability to raise significant endowments for the ACIN; to investigate and to oversee the operations of the ACIN's school; and to change the attitudes of ACIN's passive board. He needed to get control of St. Paul's School. His solution was to send Russell on a vacation to Europe and get him out of the country. Moreover, Russell was more than an obstacle to Bishop's authority over an ACIN-affiliated school; Russell's continuing presence at St. Paul's stymied Bishop from not only subduing Russell and his school, but implementing his progressive approach to black education in the South.

Russell, sometime after returning from his 1911 "vacation," had no choice but to commence a counterattack on Bishop. Russell persuaded the Board of Trustees of St. Paul's School to issue a memorial[48] stating that Mr. Bishop "attempted to render the government of the principal and the board unnecessary." That memorial was sent to the ACIN trustees and Bishop Arthur Selden Lloyd, a former bishop coadjutor of the Diocese of Virginia and chairman of the Episcopal Church's national Board of Missions.[49] Bishop Tucker and Bishop Greer had conversations leading up to the consideration of Mr. Bishop's dismissal and a reduction in the scope and purpose of the ACIN. Like Russell, Bishop was not to be intimidated, and a compromise solution had to come into play. Bishop had both the St. Paul's School and Archdeacon Russell audited by the Phelps-Stokes Fund[50] educational foundation. The audit seemed damaging to Russell, making the longed-for victory for Bishop appear close at hand. The audit criticized Russell's business arrangements between the school and town and county governments where St. Paul's School was paying taxes of $1,000 per year. The report recommended appointment of a white man as treasurer of the school; appointment of an assistant principal for educational administration reporting directly to the school's trustees and not to the principal; implementation of a revised bookkeeping system; and elimination of contract work involving the alleged exploitation of the school's students.[51] What happened to Russell as a result of this audit?

History records James Solomon Russell as an exemplary leader not only in the church but within the field of education. The settlement between ACIN and the school was that Russell would be principal in name only, an honor in a sense, because even then St. Paul's School and James Solomon Russell were recognized as one. Who was the winner? What good did the ACIN bring to St. Paul's School? Anderson and Moss wrote, "In 1912–1913, as Bishop was challenging what he perceived as the backward, inefficient, and corrupt elements in James Solomon Russell's administration, the school received $18,173 from the [Episcopal Church's] Board of Missions, while the ACIN contributed only $5,011."[52] ACIN officers and executives never raised sufficient seed funding for the foundation and therefore never fully implemented its vision for assistance to black education within the Episcopal Church.

There is not much positive to be said about the resourcefulness of the ACIN during the latter era of the work of James Solomon Russell. Russell mostly likely considered Samuel Bishop an obstacle just as much as Bishop did Russell. Samuel H. Bishop died prematurely in 1914 and was succeeded by Robert W. Patton, a priest and a Southerner from Virginia. The ACIN did not operate in the same manner once Patton took over the reins. Patton was preoccupied with leading the Episcopal Church's moderately successful general fundraising effort known as the Nation-Wide Campaign.[53] It is what happened to Russell that is interesting. He never became merely the nominal principal of St. Paul's School that Samuel Bishop wanted. St. Paul's School grew in the coming years and Russell would eventually establish more than thirty African-American congregations on the Southside of Virginia.

CHAPTER SEVEN

Addressing Challenges

R USSELL HAD NO CONTROL OVER HISTORY and its development up to the time
he entered ordained ministry. We have learned about his strong convictions and purposeful manner of living. As a young man in his local church
he offered a resolution to improve the quality of its ordained clergy. Not a
shy person, Russell knew no strangers and knew how to work with people.
He always played the hand he was dealt regardless of its rightness or wrongness
for the situation. His years of preparation included his early participation in
the Zion Union Apostolic Church, followed by his seminary training in
Petersburg, and the first ten years of ordained ministry in the Episcopal Diocese of Virginia. Indeed, those latter ten years proved to be a remarkable
expansion of membership within the Diocese of Virginia, including its African
American membership.

There were obstacles to overcome. Primarily, the social structure of antebellum Southern life and thought had to be overcome in the decades following
the Civil War. Military occupation of the former Confederate States, the Freedmen's Bureau, Northern missionary societies, and federal laws could not and
did not wipe away totally the old ways of Southern living. Real change had
to be dealt with directly — person to person. With no smooth ride for anyone,
and seeing no quick solutions, most Southerners had to fend for themselves
while the mega-culture of the emerging new American society evolved. Every
man, woman, and child participated. But not all people were uniform nor
united in the way a new South would unfold. Russell, either intuitively or
intellectually, knew this. Former slaves were ready for this huge effort. Even
though oppressed and limited in their slavery, they had eyes and ears and
knew more than they let on. Their experience of slavery was a long-running
exercise of freedom-in-waiting. And finally, at the moment of emancipation,
freedom was theirs. In church life Russell prepared and dealt with all that
was thrown at him.

In the first year of the Diocese of Southern Virginia, its bishop, Alfred

135

Booker T. Washington (center right) visits St. Paul's College, year unknown. Archdeacon Russell is center left. Others are unidentified (Russell Memorial Library, Saint Paul's College, Lawrenceville, Virginia).

M. Randolph, appointed Russell as archdeacon. The undivided Diocese of Virginia created the Colored Convocation but never engaged it in its Annual Councils. It was left to the new southern diocese to carry on the work and the first step was for Randolph to make the archidiaconate appointment. As archdeacon Russell accepted a position that, in effect, accepted the failed proposal of the Sewanee Conference of 1883. He was the leader of all the colored churches and missions in the Diocese of Southern Virginia, inherited under the rules originally established by the Diocese of Virginia in 1890: Article II, Section 3 of the Constitution, and Canon XIII, the "Black Canon." Within this framework, which he had opposed in the Annual Councils of Virginia, he would continue to plant churches, attempt to affect attitudes of people, and build his school in the midst of a large number of African-American citizens.

The Negro Problem — the Southern Problem — the Church Problem

There is no doubt that Russell understood the meaning of the fertile ground for evangelization of the 700,000 African-Americans within his geography. This was the opening framework for Russell's ministry. Virginia Bishop F.M. Whittle, according to Russell, who had opened schools for colored people in many counties within his diocese, was known as the "Apostle to the Negro Work."[1] The match between Russell and Whittle seemed providential to Russell. Both men had similar goals in mind, but as noted, there were obstacles to overcome. For example, adverse social and political circumstances developed after the end of Reconstruction. Holdover negative attitudes of whites toward blacks still lingered in the subcultures of daily living. Blacks distrusted whites and whites resented losing their political power during the period known as Radical Reconstruction and sought to regain it. Soon the notion of the "Negro problem" was debated and acted on within civil/secular society; the parallel of that debate had a life of its own in the church, especially within the Episcopal Church. Russell had his work cut out for him.

As detailed in an earlier chapter, eighteen months after Russell's ordination to the diaconate, the Episcopal Bishop of Mississippi, W.M. Green, wrote on April 2, 1883, to his fellow "Bishops of the late Slave States" asking them to meet in a special Conference (prior to the General Convention of that same year) "for the purpose of conferring ... on a matter of such vital importance to the welfare of our country and the salvation of a race perishing in the midst of us for the want of right instruction."[2] Bishop Green was sure that one of the many subjects claiming attention at General Convention was to be the church's relationship to the former slaves. The wording of his letter was revealing. He first stated that the bishops needed to find the best means to be adopted for the "colored" peoples' religious benefit and he then added that this required the serious attention of both the "patriot and the Christian." He intimated that not only Southern but perhaps a few Northern bishops thought it a good idea to have the conference. But his use of "welfare of the country" and the "patriot and the Christian" perhaps best describes in summary the double-sided nature of the problem: what to do about the freedmen and what to do about their church. Perhaps the underlying concern of the Southern bishops was maintaining control of their dioceses in the face of other losses. Southern whites had lost much of their political leadership during Radical Reconstruction. A post–Reconstruction backlash mindset developed after 1877 and whites were again gaining control of state governments. The parallel side of this mindset was ecclesiastical. Perhaps the Southern bishops feared that as the national or Union government subdued the South, so too might the church's General Convention impose order on the Southern church. Whatever the true reasoning, Bishop Green issued invitations to Southern bishops, other clergy, and lay persons asking them to attend the conference at the University of the South in Sewanee, Tennessee. The conference convened during the last week in July 1883 in advance of the General Convention later that year.

Thirteen bishops attended the conference, as well as eighteen presbyters and 11 lay persons. Bishops of most of the dioceses of the South attended, but not Bishop Whittle. The reason for Whittle's absence is unclear, but two of his lieutenants, the Rev. T.G. [Grayson] Dashiell and the Rev. Pike Powers, were dispatched. The only Northerner on record attending the Sewanee Conference was the Rev. James Saul of Philadelphia, from a wealthy Pennsylvania family, rector of an Episcopal church, and a philanthropist and financial supporter of Southern black schools. No African-American Episcopalians were invited nor attended the conference. What resulted from the conference was a proposal to the General Convention of that year, known forever as the "Sewanee Canon."

With the exception of one dissent by the Bishop of Alabama, the "Sewanee bishops" proposed, in effect, the separation or "segregation in any diocese of the colored people under the direction and authority of the diocesan bishop, with such missionary organization as might be necessary for its purposes."[3] Although the General Convention rejected the proposal,[4] some Southern bishops implemented the scheme of "colored convocations"[5] anyway. There was no mechanism available to the General Convention to stop any bishop from implementing such an arrangement. The Sewanee Conference resulted in an ecclesiastical reflection of Southern white sentiment prevalent in secular life at that time. But why did the Bishop of Alabama dissent?

Richard Hooker Wilmer, a Virginian, was consecrated as Bishop of Alabama during the brief life of the separated Episcopal Church of the Confederate States of America. During the Civil War, the church within the Confederacy had no choice but to follow the political lead of the new Southern government. Wilmer was consecrated on March 6, 1862, in Richmond by William Meade, Bishop of Virginia, as well as the presiding bishop of the Confederate Episcopal Church. Meade died eight days after Wilmer's consecration. Meade, it should be mentioned, hesitated for some time before pulling his diocese into the Confederate church. He had no choice. By the time of the Sewanee Bishops' Conference of 1883 many social, political, and ecclesi-astical developments had taken place. But Wilmer objected to the resolution of the Sewanee bishops because he believed it would stratify society by creating social classes. As a Virginian and active in the Diocese of Virginia in antebellum days, Wilmer participated in some of the positive, if mea-ger, moves in bringing slaves into the church. "I say nothing in vindica-tion of slavery in its origin. It was a foul wrong, shared alike by North and South, and to be repented of both sections with works meet* for repen-tance."[6]

After the end of the Civil War the bishops of the Northern churches wel-comed the return of the Southern dioceses and their bishops, saying that there was only a brief separation during the war, not a schism. At the time of Wilmer's consecration and before the two sections of the church reunited, there was always a concern about the regularity and the validity of Wilmer's episcopal orders. But upon reunion the Northern bishops recognized Wilmer as a valid bishop with jurisdiction in Alabama. Politically, Wilmer espoused mixed positions regarding race. But he was one Southerner who opposed any limitation of colored clergy by the church, and that is probably the main rea-son for Wilmer's dissent. Less likely, Wilmer would have been grateful to Northern bishops for their recognition, almost twenty years earlier, of the regularity and validity of his episcopal office. For this, Wilmer's dissent could be seen as *quid pro quo*. More likely Wilmer wanted no class distinction in the church. His autobiography suggests as much.

The Sewanee Canon met its opposition at the Philadelphia General Con-vention. One month prior to the General Convention a group of African-Americans led by the Rev. Alexander Crummell met in New York. The elderly Crummell was the church's senior African-American clergyman and rector of St. Luke's Church in Washington, D.C. The group's purpose was to present a united front against the canon and "exert every means in their power to encompass the defeat of the proposed canon."[7] George Freeman Bragg, Jr., the historian of the "Afro-American Group"[8] within the Episcopal Church, subtly mentioned in his analysis of the situation that at the same time there was a movement in the Southern state legislatures to disfranchise African American citizens. In diplomatic fashion Bragg said that he did not mean to imply that the "two things had any connection."[9] Many prominent white state legislators, according to Bragg, were also laymen in the Episcopal Church.

"Meet" from the Old English "to settle" or "to conform to, especially with exactitude and precision." Merriam-Webster Collegiate Dictionary, *11th Edition, 772.*

Church Social Attitudes

Prior to the Civil War, at a confirmation service in May 1856 in Law-renceville, Virginia, in which he confirmed several colored people, Bishop William Meade apparently said things that later met with strong opposition. An article in the *Petersburg Democrat* charged Meade with anti–Negro senti-ments. Without reading the article but from hearsay, Meade responded that he said "that the larger portion of the human race had always been in some form of bondage to the other, being poor and dependent; that God, in His providence, had permitted a large number to come to this country from Africa, intending to make it a blessing to them, their posterity, and Africa itself, by bringing them to the light of the gospel and sending the gospel back to that country...." He went on to say that he "exhorted the servants [the Confirmands/slaves] to rejoice that they had been born in this Christian land, and not in a heathen land — to seek that liberty of soul from sin, which Christ alone could give, and which was infinitely better than any other liberty."[10] According to church historian (and Meade's successor) Bishop John Johns, Meade had no problem with the civil lawfulness of slavery and did not chal-lenge it. Early in Meade's life he freed or manumitted his servants to non-slaveholding states but over time saw that manumission was a failure, particularly if the freed person stayed within the United States.[11] Meade thought that a freed slave should return to Africa because his opportunities in America would be limited to nonexistent. Philip Slaughter, one-time his-toriographer of the Diocese of Virginia, portrays Meade as a man dedicated to freedom. But Slaughter said little to nothing about Meade's views on race. Meade's view of the conditions preceding the Civil War is as close as Slaughter gets to anything to do with slavery. Meade is said to oppose the separation of the North and the South into two separate nations, and therefore he delayed as long as possible separation within the Episcopal Church as the state of Vir-ginia delayed in separating itself from the Union until the last moment.[12]

Russell, in his *Autobiography*, inserted a quote from Meade's biography. It focused on one seemingly innocuous statement. Russell wrote that Bishop Meade, in trying to justify the affiliation of slave members in the Episcopal Church, "showed that they were in numbers large enough to become a prob-lem."[13] Bishop Johns in his biography of Meade said that Meade often preached without a prepared text and therefore may have said things that did not necessarily reflect what he meant. Meade obviously did recognize that the large number of slaves and later former slaves in that geography would present perhaps not a threat but a challenge to the controlling white people. This attitude was not unique in Southern thinking. It was this kind of think-ing that most likely prompted Bishop Green of Mississippi to call for a conference of Southern bishops at Sewanee in 1883. All of this was most likely ecclesiastical and political posturing whereby the South was telling the North how it intended to run its dioceses. Pass or fail in General Convention did not necessarily matter. For his part Alexander Crummell had no choice but to oppose the Sewanee proposal because its purpose would subordinate and separate African-Americans within their own church. At the time, African-American Episcopalians wanted full inclusion with no color line. As discussed in an earlier chapter, this was the time when a memorial to the General Convention of 1889 was submitted by the Church Workers among Colored People and Crummell which asked the national Church "to give an emphatic and unequivocal answer to this our earnest and almost despairing inquiry [about the position of colored men in the Church]."[14]

The importance of the Sewanee Conference is that it was probably the one most visible event in church life that clearly set the stage for fierce, internecine struggles within the Episcopal Church. It also formed the general framework in which Russell would navigate his career. Given this political kickoff at the time of Russell's entrance (he was ordained in 1882) into the vineyard, whatever the legislative outputs of diocesan councils and General Conventions or the edicts of diocesan bishops, none of these would frustrate the thinking and actions of the newly ordained deacon, future priest, and archdeacon. He had his vision, and no matter what obstacles lay before him he was not about to give in to current pressures. He knew that he had to create a long-term strategy imbedded with many short-term tactics to achieve his educational goals for the St. Paul School and the spreading of the gospel in planting colored congregations. Spiritually centered, politically astute, and diplomatically inclined, Russell proved adept at achieving his goals.

In 1889, one year after Russell had started his school and after seven years as a voting member of the Diocese of Virginia, Assistant Bishop A.M. Randolph gave his yearly address to the Annual Council regarding the "relations between ourselves and the colored race, in the affairs of the government of this Church." Russell was present. Randolph stated that it was this government of Christendom that made it a government of the people. In that address Randolph said, "The question, with reference to the negro as legislator in the Episcopal Church, is not a question of race, a question of color, but a question of faculty, of ability. It is a question of capacity of character."[15] Randolph was providing the groundwork at best to delay and at worst to prevent African-American Episcopalians from participating in the government of the church. The legislative result of Randolph's address was Canon XIII, referred to by Russell and others as the "Black Canon."[16] In that same year on a national level the Conference of Church Workers Among Colored People (CCWACP), in a protest memorial to the General Convention, argued in part that since

"Christian theology taught that race had no bearing on the powers of a priest," black clergy should be granted seats in the legislative assemblies of the dioceses. And although luminaries like Philips Brooks[17] condemned segregation and disfranchisement of black communicants, the General Convention's House of Deputies believed that the national church had no say in the representations in diocesan conventions.[18]

When the Diocese of Southern Virginia was created in 1892 out of the Diocese of Virginia, the "Black Canon" was included in its canons without modification. This canon stipulated that "grandfathered" colored clergy[19] could still have a vote in Annual Council but the Colored Convocation as a whole — and not any single colored, self-sustaining church — could have two lay and two clergy voting representatives. Russell himself was not affected due to the grandfathering provision. The secular politics of this period provide insight into the actions of the Diocese. For example, Peter G. Morgan, Russell's father-in-law and a delegate to the Constitutional Convention that created the post–Civil War Virginia Constitution, was one of 25 Negro delegates elected in 1867. From that point forward the number of African-American delegates to the state's General Assembly grew, peaked, and then disappeared. The first election under the new Virginia Constitution was held in 1869. In correspondence with Monroe N. Work, Virginia State Librarian H.R. McIlwain said that the journals of Virginia's General Assembly for years did not identify their members as black or white (possibly a result of Morgan's insistence that the new Constitution contain no reference to race or color). But from other documents McIlwain reported that in the 1869-70 session of the General Assembly there were no Negro Senators but 18 members of the House. In 1870, according to Russell, there were six Negro Senators and 21 Negro House Delegates.[20] By 1877, when Reconstruction had ended, there were only three black Senators and four black Delegates. In 1885 there was only one Negro Senator out of 39, and seven Negro Delegates out of 100 in the House. In 1892 there were no Negro Senators or Delegates in the Virginia legislature.[21] Any progress that African-Americans may have made immediately after the Civil War gradually began to disappear after the period of Radical Reconstruction. The prevention of black participation in civil government during this period reflected the attitudes and actions of Episcopal Church leaders in limiting or preventing black participation in the councils of the church. In an observation similar to that of George Freeman Bragg, Russell opined that it is "fair to say that one of the chief reasons for the survival of the 'Black Canon' is the fear on the part of the Southern Virginia laymen of an influx of lay delegates from the 28 active colored congregations of the diocese. The fear of the laity is undoubtedly greater than the fear of the white clergy."[22] If all of those obstacles were not enough, the United States Supreme Court, in an 1896 decision known as *Plessy v. Ferguson*, effectively and legally separated blacks and whites by validating segregation in public accommodations of "separate but equal."[23] The principle of "separate but equal" would not be overturned until the 1950s. History provides a record showing that young James Solomon Russell, aware of his environments, both secular and ecclesiastical, intended to pursue his ministries in spite of prevailing circumstances. How did Russell go about his work?

In the Councils of the New Diocese

The primary, and organizational, council of the Episcopal Diocese of Southern Virginia took place in St. Paul's Church, Lynchburg, on November 23 and 24, 1892. The First Annual Council took place in 1893 between June 7 and 10 at Christ Church in Norfolk. The journal of the council shows nine African-American ministers as clergy of the diocese: William Patterson Burke, missionary at Grace Church, Norfolk (George Freeman Bragg, Jr., was the former rector who resigned and left for Baltimore in 1892); Joseph W. Carroll, missionary in Mecklenburg County; John Thomas Harrison, missionary in Brunswick County; George E. Howell, missionary in Campbell County; William E. Howell, missionary in Mecklenburg County; Joseph Fenner Mitchell, missionary in charge of St. Stephen's Church, Petersburg; Lafayette Winfield, missionary in Nottoway and Lunenburg counties; Charles L. Simmons, missionary in Brunswick County; and James Solomon Russell, missionary in Brunswick County.[24] Of those, only Burke, Carroll, Harrison, Mitchell, Winfield, and Russell were entitled to seats in the Council. The carryover "grandfathering" clauses from Article II of the Constitution and Canon XIII allowed each of these ministers to a seat and a vote. The other colored clergy could have been voting delegates had the Colored Convocation voted them in. It was in this year that Russell was appointed archdeacon. Preceding the beginning of the First Annual Council, Russell wrote, "The Rev. Claudius R. Haines, rector of St. Paul's Church, Petersburg, whispered to me, 'Bishop Randolph has made up his mind to appoint you as archdeacon of the new diocese.' Shortly after, the Bishop threw his arms around me and told me of his decision and asked me to assume charge of the work at once...."[25] Russell, as principal of the St. Paul School, was under the direction of and salaried by the Colored Commission. An arrangement had to be made between the commission and the bishop in order for Russell to hold both positions. And so it was agreed, and Russell's official appointment date was October 11, 1893. The First Annual Council adopted Canon XIII, among others carried over from the old diocese.

It was in the Report of the Committee on the State of the Church that the impact of the new diocese's missionary work became clear. Accordingly the committee reported, "A heavy portion of real missionary work has fallen to us in our share in the Colored work; an element of alarm and anxiety to some among us."[26] The committee explicitly recognized the social attitudes of its day in their locale, but knew that their missionary efforts among the largest concentration of African-American population in Virginia could not and must not be ignored. In his address, Bishop Randolph told the delegates that he "cannot speak too highly of the work of my brother, the Rev. James S. Russell, of Lawrenceville. He has earned the respect and the confidence of all classes of people in Lawrenceville and the adjoining counties. He has, by his own efforts, aided by the confidence and commendation of his Bishops, built up an institution for the education of the negro [sic] race of both sexes, which for economical management, for sensible and practical methods of instruction, for faithful and genuine religious training and for successful results compares most favorably with any institution in the country."[27] Indeed, Russell had already established himself quite well in his community. He now had his platform as school entrepreneur and principal, and as archdeacon of colored churches. In the journal of the Second Annual Council, Russell's name in the "List of Clergy" was posted as "Archdeacon in charge of Colored Missions."[28] In the years afterward his name was listed as "Archdeacon in charge of Colored Missions and Principal of St. Paul's School, Lawrenceville."

A few years after being made Archdeacon for Colored Work in 1892 for the Diocese of Southern Virginia, Russell's reports and addresses regarding his work were published in the journals of the diocese's Annual Councils. It is in these reports, as well as in other addresses given by Russell, that the year-to-year details of colored work are presented and examined. Also in these reports are Russell's ongoing pleas, requests and expressions of gratitude. In 1905 Russell told the Council that the colored church was handicapped by both men and means and that the church needed to recognize and grapple with the opportunity so presented. He asked the white clergy to undertake some "colored work" in their parishes. Colored people, he said, yearn for an intelligent liturgy as found in the Book of Common Prayer (BCP), and he knew that the bishop was interested in colored work and urged him to influence others.[29] He continued his reports in 1906 by expanding his appeal to "those people of means" to help the colored congregations. Russell alluded to other churches in the area that were numerically larger and financially stronger than the colored churches in the Episcopal diocese. He was citing the growth and progress of the African Methodist Episcopal Churches, the Baptists and the spin-off Colored Methodist Episcopal Churches. Russell noted that many of his churches were without clergy and those with clergy had difficulty in supporting them and their families. With all of this he requested that the diocese provide funding of $10,000 to meet the demand.[30]

The source of the underlying demand was a large black population within the jurisdiction of the Diocese of Southern Virginia. To Russell this statistic meant that there was a large field to harvest for the Kingdom and that the church must move judiciously. Even when the diocese did not move quickly enough, Russell still went about his business. For Russell his work with St. Paul School and the Diocese of Southern Virginia were one and the same. It was difficult to separate the two strands of his ministry as if they were simply parallel ministries. In 1907 the diocese created a committee to research and then report on the state of the church.[31] Russell read the report of the work into the "state of the Negro." Even though the report of the committee stated, "The extent of the colored work in our bounds constituted another, if not the greatest, of our Diocesan responsibilities," it did not take it to be "within its province to discuss, or even to enumerate the plans which have been proposed," but recommended that the council give due consideration to its importance. Therefore, the committee extracted a portion of the annual archdeacon's report into its own document, and Archdeacon Russell read it in Council.

Although Russell reported that he was hopeful of the future of the colored work in Southern Virginia, the past ten years [1896–1906] had seen large numbers of colored people leave their rural country homes for the city. Since most of the "black belt" of Virginia was within the Diocese of Southern Virginia in the rural Southside region (Brunswick, Mecklenburg, Lunenburg, Greensville, Dinwiddie and other counties), this migration had a potential negative growth impact on the diocese. Added to that, some of the colored clergy left the diocese for other dioceses which paid higher salaries. The archdeacon reported that in his opinion if the diocese provided a living salary[32] there would be little to no trouble in securing colored clergy. Russell described his and the diocese's work as a "feeder" of clergy to other dioceses. Of particular note, and a continuing expression of Archdeacon Russell, is his gratitude to white clergy. He said in this report that there were nine colored and five white clergymen engaged in colored work. His litany of "men and means" was repeated annually.[33] In the year leading up to the 1906 Annual Council, Bishop Randolph confirmed 117 colored communicants from seventeen missions. The Committee on the State of the Church reported that although there were marked improvements in the condition of the colored work, much more needed to be done. But there were many reasons why the colored people within the boundaries of the diocese did not come to their church. It cited the fact that many of the colored congregations worshipped in halls, rented rooms, and in courthouses. "A very noticeable feature in the reports from the Colored Missions is that of more liberal giving of their own means for the support of Church and educational work generally."[34]

In the 1908 Council report Archdeacon Russell continued his request for "men and means." He reported that he visited every Negro mission and parish in the previous year and that without the help of fellow white and black clergy he would not have been able to do so.[35] Two new colored church buildings were erected with the help and the "considerable sacrifice by the white people of Houston and Hampton." He also reported signs of growth. Financially, Russell was asking the General Board of Missions (he was really asking his bishop) and prosperous individuals to appropriate $2,000 per year for the following five years to support black churches and clergy.[36] Russell's themes continued into future reports from the Colored Convocation to Annual Council. He gave evidence of growth where there was growth, and he asked for appropriations to pay clergy a living salary. He always gave expression of thanks to both black and white clergy in the support of colored work. In 1909 he reported, "When you take into consideration the very small number of white and colored clergy engaged in colored work in Southern Virginia, I think you will be willing to give due credit to those who are holding things together. Our great and most pressing need for men to do the work cannot be disputed."[37] Russell might have been showing his frustration because he was asked to begin work in a number of towns and counties where colored people were waiting for the coming of the Episcopal Church. He said that unless the diocese had a sufficient number of men to minister to those awaiting the arrival of the church it would be of no use to attempt the task. Again he said, "Men and means are necessary to successfully operate on such a scale."[38]

The Colored Convocation, certainly at the behest of Russell, submitted a memorial to the Annual Council of Virginia in 1909. In part it read, "Part of the burning questions of the Church to-day in all parts of the country is that of better salaries for the [colored] clergy.... From no quarter, however, does the cry for relief come so strongly as from the colored clergy of the Diocese of Southern Virginia, who are the poorest paid ministers in the American Church. The Diocese of Southern Virginia, by reason of its location in the black belt of Virginia, has an immense population of colored people who are dependent upon the Episcopal Church for their Christian and moral training. Of this number more than 1,600 have been gathered into the fold, and have become loyal and earnest adherents of the faith. The great body of the people however, has not as yet been touched, because while the harvest is indeed ripe the laborers are too few." The memorial provided statistics showing deacons in the Diocese of Florida salaried [annually] at $450, priests at $720.

Archdeacon Russell at Oak Grove Colored School in Brunswick County, Virginia. Patrons visiting the Brunswick County Exhibit (University of Virginia Archives, The Jackson Davis Collection, Charlottesville, Virginia).

Southern Virginia deacons' salaries ranged from $200 to $300 and priests from $300 to $400. The dioceses of Georgia, South Carolina, East Carolina, Arkansas and Tennessee fell into the middle of the Florida and Southern Virginia extremes.[39]

One year later, no change. Salaries remained the same. White clergy, reported Russell, still were in charge of some colored congregations and Bishop Payne Divinity School students of others. By 1910 there were 31 missions and parishes in the Colored Convocation.[40] Coadjutor Bishop Tucker asked Russell to provide this information to the Annual Council. On a piece of paper in the official records of the diocese, the bishop and everyone else could see the names of the missions and parishes in the Colored Convocation along with their numerical strength in numbers. It is well to keep in mind that the journals of the annual councils of the dioceses in the Episcopal Church were delivered to all the dioceses. Other areas of the Church could read what was going on in each diocese.

The two controversial canons—Canon XIII, limiting colored clergy and laypersons' participation in the councils of the church; and Canon XV, which would create separate colored missionary jurisdictions—were debated. As noted earlier, the Colored Convocation of Southern Virginia had not supported the creation of a separate colored jurisdiction. Russell and his Convocation supported the status quo in contrast to the Colored Convocation of the Diocese of North Carolina, which supported the idea of a missionary jurisdiction for colored people.

In a memorial dated May 13–15, 1913, at the annual diocesan convention, and addressed to North Carolina Bishop Joseph Blount Cheshire, the Colored Convocation requested that their "beloved Bishop, and fellow members of this Convention, both clergy and laity ... to favor this [missionary jurisdiction] movement and to use your kindly influences in the General Convention next October, to accomplish this purpose, which we do most sincerely believe will work great good for the growth of the church among our people."[41] Reasons in the memorial favoring the movement were (a) the salvation of 10 million negroes in the country; (b) the betterment of the race in moral, religious and educational standards; and (c) for the church herself to set forth her true position while maintaining her catholic spirit with respect to the apparently perplexed situation in dealing with colored people. But the memorial went on to assert that even though there had been cordial relations between blacks and whites at conventions and other gatherings, and that their bishop always defended blacks when they could not defend themselves, the Colored Convocation realized that even though they did not want to separate from the diocese, they knew that white churchmen preferred separation. The finger was pointing not just to the white churchmen of the North Carolina diocese, but all white churchmen in the "Southland." The North Carolina Convocation was positioning for a missionary jurisdiction for the Southland and provided statistics to justify it.

Using the term "department,"[42] the North Carolina Convocation provided regional statistics. According to their statistics the Third Department had a total of 6,034 colored communicants and the Fourth Department 6,432. The largest concentration of communicants from both departments was in the Diocese of Southern Virginia at 1,748. Of the total of 20 dioceses listed, only five had more than 1,000 communicants, all in the Third Department except for Georgia at 1,020. North Carolina's Colored Convocation concluded and thus promoted the creation of a missionary jurisdiction for the Fourth Department (Province Four). The "colored" communities within the Episcopal Church were split on this issue. James Solomon Russell and the Southern Virginia Colored Convocation opposed, at least at first, creation of missionary jurisdictions.[43] (Russell was not supporting any notion of separation — he was a person of reconciliation). North Carolina's Colored Convocation and the CCWACP called for "separation." Battles ensued over this issue in the local dioceses and through the triennial General Conventions from 1904 to 1917.

Russell, repetitious and consistent in his annual reports to his diocese, wrote on July 20, 1917, in the "Annual Report of the Archdeacon for Colored Work in the Diocese of Southern Virginia": "Ours is the largest rural work of any diocese in this Country and it is destined to become much larger provided we can secure the men and means to carry it on." He continued by saying, "At the present time we have but twelve colored clergymen in the Diocese, including the Archdeacon, and of these ten are devoting their whole time to the Church work among colored people, in addition to the valuable help rendered us by five white presbyters."[44] These concerns were typical of Russell, always telling his bishops and the diocese of the real needs of African-American communicants, exhorting people to support the ministry and recognizing publicly those who had been of great help. His mission was always clear.

Advancing the Kingdom

The appointment as Archdeacon for Colored Work changed Russell's ministry of evangelization. Although Russell possessed a catholic view of advancing the Kingdom, the appointment placed him in an official capacity that carried with it the responsibility for specially advancing the gospel with colored people. As archdeacon he was given no official guidelines on how to pursue his ministry except for the directive given in Canon XIII, which formed the Colored Convocation. Section 3 reads: "There may be appointed by the Bishop, one or more Presbyters who shall have general supervision of such colored churches and congregations as the Bishop may designate, and perform such duties as he may prescribe."[45] The earlier version of Canon XIII first presented to the undivided Diocese of Virginia used the title "archdeacon" as well as "presbyter." In this case, however, the designation "shall have general supervision" was operative, and the Bishop could appoint whomever he wished and provide a title, such as archdeacon. An archdeacon could be either a deacon or a presbyter (priest) in Anglican churches. It is not an order of ministry but a title usually designating some responsibility. In this case Russell was given the responsibility for supervising the colored mission in the Diocese of Southern Virginia. Given the large population of African-Americans within the boundaries of the diocese, Russell's field of evangelization was huge, and he knew it.

Another interesting aspect of Russell's appointment rests on Bishop Randolph's confidence in Russell's abilities. Although Randolph gave sermons and addresses in which he questioned the "capacity" of former slaves to be sufficiently experienced and knowledgeable to be elected a voting delegate in the councils of the church, the appointment of Russell betrays a shift in Randolph's thinking. There was never a bishop who was not fond of Russell, beginning with Bishop Francis M. Whittle and ending with Russell's career. Russell's upbringing certainly had to have been the foundation of this principled man. The encouragement and nurturing of his mother, Araminta, and the camaraderie between the youthful Russell and adults, had the effect of developing this smart and capable minister. As archdeacon, Russell would chair, along with the bishop, the annual convocation meetings of all of the colored churches, missions and stations. This annual gathering was another platform for Russell to display his leadership and speaking skills. The diocese's Annual Council was another venue where Russell would argue in behalf of the colored congregations, their needs, hopes, and desires. Russell provided a written annual report to the Annual Council which was included in the council's printed journal. In that "Archdeacon's Report" Russell chronicled the work of the Colored Convocation and his own visitation schedule, similar to what a bishop would write for the entire year's work.

In 1905, at the 13th Annual Council in Wytheville, Russell reported that the colored missions were handicapped for lack of men and means to further their work — a theme echoed at almost every Annual Council. But he challenged white clergy to consider ministering to colored churches without ministers. This petition was significant in that Russell's challenge was a marked departure from the historic attitude of the church. It may be recalled that when the undivided Diocese of Virginia called for the formation of a separate Colored Convocation, the then-current understanding was that colored people wanted separate churches from whites, and colored congregations would not worship with white ministers, and white congregations certainly could not subject themselves to colored ministers. This, then, was a sign of imminent change, with Russell leading the charge. Russell challenged the Council: "The colored people, as never before, are yearning for and welcoming an intelligent liturgy, such as is contained in the Book of Common Prayer. Will this Church withhold from the masses of the colored race these wonderful advantages for bettering their moral and spiritual condition? This remains to be seen by the future conduct of those who are in position to assist in spreading this great work."[46]

In 1908 Russell again thanked the white clergy of the diocese for their work in assisting with furthering the work among the colored people in Southern Virginia. Ever so vigilant in his attempts to involve more white laity and clergy in colored missionary work, Russell balanced his annual pleas between the good work in progress and the disappointing and discouraging features as well. In his 1909 report he identified the linchpin of colored churches with the wider diocese: "I think you will be willing to give due credit to those [white and colored clergy] who are holding things together."[47] Russell cited the fact that in addition to himself there were only six colored clergy in the diocese, three of whom served in cities and pastored only one church. The other three clergy and the archdeacon ministered to the remainder of the twelve colored churches, the archdeacon, with lay readers, overseeing almost half. Russell, asking for larger salaries and provision for more colored clergy, was careful not to drift into a call for black bishops. There were at that time many black clergy and laity calling for a separate national jurisdiction with a black bishop.

In his report in 1910 Russell included a list of thirty-one colored churches, missions, and church stations served by colored and white clergy. The footprint of colored churches had expanded greatly but the support needed to maintain those churches was lacking. The report of a year later simply addressed the positive work that had taken place over the past year, including a contract to build a chapel in Lynchburg and a fundraising effort on behalf of St. Mary's Church in LaCrosse. By 1912 there were more than 1,700 colored communicants in thirty-one churches ministered to by nine colored and four white ministers. And because there were now two bishops instead of one (the Rev. Beverly Dandridge Tucker was elected bishop coadjutor), each colored church had at least one visitation per year, some two. In terms of evangelization, church growth among the colored population was going quite well. The leadership of the diocese changed when on April 6, 1918, Bishop Alfred M. Randolph died. Bishop coadjutor Beverly D. Tucker then became bishop ordinary.

By 1919 there were 2,235 colored communicants; twelve colored presbyters (priests); 6 postulants for holy orders; four candidates for holy orders; two deacons; 27 catechists; and 17 lay readers. Twenty-two congregations were listed as churches; four congregations were chapels; and two were designated parishes. In all, organized missions numbered 36, with six parish houses, and 8 rectories. The Sunday school programs counted 2,295 students and 145 teachers in thirty-three Sunday Schools. A broadened or expanded set of ministries is found by the listing of 16 physicians, twelve nurses, and 17 women workers. Those positions were associated with ten mission schools with 15 teachers and 685 students.[48] The Colored Convocation of the Episcopal Diocese of Southern Virginia was a highly active ministry.

In what may have been one of his boldest observations, Russell said the colored clergy "realize that the harvest for the Episcopal Church in the Diocese of Southern Virginia is whiter than ever before, and that, in the face of the scarcity of the laborers." What did he mean? For years, certainly since his appointment as archdeacon, Russell had argued for means and men. He had watched how the number of colored clergy had risen and fallen. He watched clergy leave Southern Virginia for higher-paying salaries in other dioceses. But in this 1919 report Russell appears to be frustrated by the lack of sufficient assistance from the diocese as a whole. His clergy, especially those who had remained in the diocese under difficult circumstances and at some level of personal sacrifice, had remained at their posts while colored clergy in other dioceses had moved about. There are probably two points Russell was attempting to make. First, the reason for the explosive growth of the Colored Convocation in Southern Virginia is due primarily to the long-serving colored clergy and their sense of mission despite financial hardships on them and their families. Russell never discounted the help he received from white clergy. But secondly, by saying that the "harvest ... is whiter than ever before," he was perhaps making a quantitative comparison of black versus white evangelization numbers. In other words, if there are an insufficient number of colored clergy to keep up with the growth of the church in colored communities, the mathematical door widens for more new white communicants in white-led churches. Or Russell could have been saying that some of the black clergy were able to reach the souls of some white people who were open to the message of the gospel regardless of the race of messenger.

There are probably several ways to interpret Russell's statement, but it can be observed that the structure of the Colored Convocation within the diocese produced unintended as well as intended results. As Convocation, Russell and his cadre of black clergy evangelized the Southside and Tidewater areas of Virginia in what now could be said to be in rapid fashion. The growth rate of African American congregations was steady and positive. But diocesan support never achieved the level Russell deemed sufficient and just. So he kept hammering away at the issue of support. By 1922 another diocese had been created in Virginia, this time the western portion of the state. Although this reduced the size of the Diocese of Southern Virginia, it did not reduce the size of its African-American population. A decade after the formation of the Diocese of Southwestern Virginia, it and the Diocese of Virginia eliminated their Colored Convocations and removed all limitations imposed on its African-American membership. It made sense because their African-American communicants were not of large numbers. It was still in Southern Virginia where the social and spiritual challenge remained and where the Colored Convocation remained an entity or unit of the diocese for several more years.

A Bishop, Almost

Russell wrote in his Annual Report of the Archdeacon in 1917, "On the tenth day of May last, I was elected Suffragan Bishop of the Diocese of Arkansas, but after long and careful and prayerful consideration of every phase of the subject, I notified Bishop Winchester [of Arkansas] that I could not see my way clear to leave the Church and educational work in this

Diocese."[49] Word of Russell's election moved swiftly about the country. His refusal to accept election also hit the presses. The *Southern Workman* reported that "this son of Hampton" decided not to "accept the office of Suffragan Bishop of the Diocese of Arkansas" and that Arkansas's loss was Virginia's gain.[50] *The Crisis* reported Russell's election much as an after-thought in the last paragraph of an article in the "Men of the Month" section celebrating Russell's long career as archdeacon and educator.[51] What Russell did not mention in his report was the fact that he was elected on the first ballot.

Michael J. Beary, in his book *Black Bishop*, provides some interesting machinations among bishops of the church leading up to the election of Russell.[52] Behind the scenes the bishops of the Southwest, including the bishop of Arkansas, James R. Winchester, had decided on Edward Demby as a "safe" candidate for the position of suffragan bishop for colored work of Arkansas and the Southwest dioceses (today known as Province 7, earlier as Department Seven). Beary accurately stated that black clergy during this era were forced by circumstances to walk a fine line in trying to maintain the respect of both races. Black clergy could not be too accommodating to whites, thereby losing respect of the black community. Likewise, a too-assertive black priest would alienate the white community. Demby, apparently, was good at this middle road while at the same time developing self-reliant black churches. Like Russell he had been an archdeacon for colored work (in the Diocese of Tennessee) and had built schools. Probable negatives for Demby were that he was not a member of the CCWACP (neither was Russell) and he was an Anglo-Catholic. Most African-American congregations in the Southern Episcopal Churches were low-church or evangelical, liturgically.

But Demby declined the invitation to be a candidate and submitted three other names for consideration: George Freeman Bragg, Jr., the outspoken editor and secretary of the Conference of Church Workers Among Colored People; and Hutchins C. Bishop, rector of St. Philip's in Harlem, New York; and Russell. Eventually, however, the ballot listed three nominees: Demby, Bragg and Russell. Russell and Demby were considered the front-runners, primarily because of their similar work in church and in educational initiatives, and secondarily because the outspoken and controversial Bragg had been a vocal opponent of Jim Crow or anti-black social norms. White communicants would be voting. Russell was perceived to be the "voice of the Negro Clergy and congregations in the South."[53] Michael Beary attributes to Bragg the comment that Russell "has few peers in the art of accommodation and progress."[54] Bragg turned against Demby later, but never against Russell. Bragg and Russell were friends. Russell lived for a period of time with Bragg and his family in Petersburg when he was a student in seminary. Beary reports that Russell was a man "revered by one and all as an especially pious man, an educator, and a builder of churches."[55] So, with the candidates Bragg, Demby, and Russell the election was held.

Russell, and not the hand-picked "safe" choice of back-room bishops, was elected suffragan bishop for Arkansas and the Southwest. The results of the balloting[56] were the following:

	Russell	Demby	Bragg
Clergy	9	5	2
Laity	17	3	0

Two elections were held in Arkansas that day, and E.W. Saphore, a white priest, was elected a suffragan on the third ballot. Because Archdeacon Russell declined his election, a special election was held in Arkansas later that year, and Edward T. Demby won election. Why did Russell decline? Russell stated that instead of moving to Arkansas he preferred to stay with his educational project and his church convocation. No one can seriously doubt his sentiment; however, there may have been an experiential or psychological reason for not accepting election.

At an early stage in his life, it should be recalled, Russell lived through a few years of turmoil in the Zion Union Apostolic Church. We know that he was secretary to a Zion Union annual conference as a young man and not as an ordained person. In 1875, five years after their founding, the Zion Unions elected their president James R. Howell bishop for life. This election created a rift within the Zion Unions, causing its disarray for several years. Russell's attachment was to Zion Union Bishop Howell, and Russell probably witnessed firsthand the disrupting effects of dissention and separation resulting from that election. A person of reconciliation and highly principled even in that stage of his life, and probably in a powerless position to reconcile the factions, Russell perhaps recalled that situation as one factor in his decision to decline election as suffragan bishop of Arkansas. Clearly the Arkansas and Southwest powers-that-be intended for someone else to be their bishop, and Russell's election may have been an after-the-fact cause of dissention and separation in the Diocese of Arkansas.

Had Russell accepted election as a bishop he would have undergone a liturgical examination during his consecration in which he would have been asked whether or not he was persuaded to become a bishop. James Solomon Russell was not persuaded to accept this election.[57] What priest would turn down a significant place in history by saying no to election as bishop? He had to explain his decision. In an exchange of letters and telegrams between the Archdeacon of Southern Virginia and Bishop Winchester of Arkansas, Russell provided his explanation for declining election.

Russell, the priest and educator who founded a school for former slaves and their descendents, a missionary who formed at least thirty African American Episcopal congregations, the archdeacon who oversaw the development of Christian work among African Americans in his diocese, a speaker and fund-raiser who eloquently presented his case for supporting his school at General Conventions and other functions around the nation: how could such a tireless and faithful servant of the Church refuse to accept such high honor and recognition? After all, this election was not simply a local event in one region of the country; this election had national importance.

At the time of his election Russell was sixty years old and an accomplished and well-known person. Most men would covet the office of bishop since the position carries with it not only personal recognition of high honor but a certain level of power and authority. Bishop Winchester wrote to Russell on May 12, 1917, outlining all of the details surrounding the election and the responsibilities of the new appointment. Russell kindly responded that he would appreciate time to consider the impact of the election on him and his work. Russell did not say no immediately, but did so later in a letter to Winchester dated June 20, 1917.

Separate Black Jurisdiction, Again

In 1904 when the movement began for a black missionary jurisdiction for the wider Episcopal Church, Russell was a member of the national church's commission considering the plan, but he fought to defeat it and eventually the "suffragan plan" emerged as the acceptable alternative. Suffragans, like diocesans, had seats in the House of Bishops and would be considered equal but they had no right of succession. Suffragans worked under the authority and direction of the diocesan bishop. Russell believed that the suffragan arrangement would be protective of the first black bishops in the church, knowing certainly that pitfalls lay in wait for them. A "missionary" bishop, Russell figured, would be under constant attack from detractors, and for the bishop himself, a sudden thrust into the episcopate would be personally risky. But, as Russell writes in his book, he later came to change his mind about the "missionary plan." In his attempt to justify his change of heart Russell cites an "increase in black communicants and a greater number of trained priests. A "missionary" bishop would bring the scope and magnitude to existing efforts and representation of the Negro in the highest senate of the church — the House of Bishops."[58] At first reading, Russell seems to favor "separation" of the races within the church because he likened a "missionary" bishop to a "diocesan" bishop — one with power and authority. But this goes counter to Russell's career-long struggle for African-Americans in that he was a reconciler moving in a slow-paced, orderly direction to improve the lives of the people of his race. His apparent change of heart at this point in time was moot because the "suffragan plan" had been accepted and there would be no change in the church in the foreseeable future now that a black suffragan was elected. Why did Russell need to write about his change of heart when the timing of this subject was by then irrelevant?

It should be recalled that Russell wrote his *Autobiography* in 1935 after eighteen years of reflection on his election. He may have desired to interpret his past in a perspective more acceptable to those who opposed him on the "missionary plan," or he was simply voicing his frustration that his own Diocese of Southern Virginia had not advanced much, legislatively. As far as black bishops were concerned, Russell had favored the status quo in his diocese, but the "Black Canon" or equal representation was never settled. The Diocese of Virginia kept the "Black Canon" until 1936, the year following Russell's death. Southern Virginia tried to change the canon in 1933 but failed by just one vote.[59] Perhaps this disappointment was on Russell's mind as he penned his *Autobiography*.

In his letter to Bishop Winchester declining election, Russell wrote about his work at St. Paul School and his work as a missionary in the Southside of Virginia. In effect he provided Winchester with an historical sweep of his work in Lawrenceville over the years. One can interpret from this letter that Russell truly did not want to take up any new work at age 60. Simply put, Russell was not persuaded to accept his election. He even played down his election in his "Annual Report of the Archdeacon for Colored Work" by hiding the paragraph about the event exactly in the middle of his report.[60]

Russell continued his work both in the church and with his St. Paul's School. As suggested earlier, these dual ministries provided Russell a platform for discussing the issues of his day, both secular and religious. Russell, of course, delivered many sermons, but he also addressed religious societies, beneficial societies, and political associations. In all, regardless of the secular or religious setting, Russell's message was consistent.

CHAPTER EIGHT

International Forums and Ideological Differences

THE FINAL DECADE OF THE NINETEENTH CENTURY and the first two decades of the twentieth century experienced more change in lifestyles, social arrangements, and political ideologies than the years immediately following the end of the American Civil War. The beginnings of the breakdown in the old world order were emerging as competing ideologies sought followers in all corners of the earth. World-changing events occurred not only in the United States but in other nations from the time of Russell's birth to the First World War. In 1834 the British Empire abolished slavery, and when Russell was turning the age of two, John Brown and his followers seized the United States Armory and Arsenal at Harpers Ferry, Virginia. In 1860, soon after Abraham Lincoln's first election, South Carolina withdrew from the Union, followed by ten other Southern States in 1861. The Civil War produced a new state, West Virginia, from the western counties of Virginia who refused to be part of the Confederacy. In 1865 the General Convention of the Episcopal Church funded the Freedman's Commission to support Southern black education. During the time Russell was engaged with the Zion Union Apostolic Church, the nation went into an economic crisis in 1873. The impact of that depression lasted for more than five years. By 1910, shortly before the First World War, Queen Victoria had been dead for nine years; her successor and son Edward VII would die and the English throne would be passed on to King George V, as President William Howard Taft led the United States of America.

Worldwide Christian evangelization was active and competing with the current-day remnant of the Enlightenment. Science and Christianity were on a collision course at the same time European nations began to compete with each other over land and resources. It was a period of the excitement of new possibilities, socially, ideologically, and politically yielding organized

Archdeacon Russell, second from left, with unidentified Lawrenceville business-men (University of Virginia Archives).

efforts to change the world. Russell was not unaffected by all these happenings and entered into some of their deliberations.

Edinburgh Missionary Conference — 1910

Even before the beginning of the American Civil War, the missionary departments of American Protestant churches were quite active. After the Civil War the Episcopal Church, along with other churches, considered its work with colored people a missionary effort. At the time of Russell's ordination a world movement of Christian mission was in its ascendency. Mostly Protestant, the international movement was the calling together of mostly North American and northern European churches to come together to learn better how to implement the Great Commission. Russell, as a clergyman, was constantly involved in mission and his way of thinking was always guided by a sense of mission. It was not an uncommon phenomenon among churchmen of his time. But each denomination had its own separate and independent method of tactical missionary approaches. In 1888 the first attempt at an ecumenical assembly of worldwide church missionary groups gathered at Exeter Hall in London. That was followed by a second meeting in New York in 1900. By far the best-known gathering of missionary groups was the 1910 conference held in Edinburgh, Scotland. Edinburgh may have been the most famous, but the Exeter Hall conference was the largest.

This missionary movement was but one sign of competing movements attempting to attract the hearts and minds of people around the world. The modern age was present and an accepted reality since 1815,[1] and the move to worldwide thinking and worldwide association was in the making. Christianity — mostly that which is called "evangelical" Christianity — was moving toward global mission, guided by Christ and the Great Commission: it had a calling to fulfill. Concurrently, the movement known as progressivism found its beginning at around the same period of time. With all of its multiple areas of emphasis, progressivism's target was broad and deep. Christian mission, also broad and deep in scope, had but one center — a person, a saving person called Christ. Progressivism's program center was science, the product of the Enlightenment. Over time each movement absorbed accretions from the other: Christian evangelicalism fell victim to the Social Gospel; and progressivism, though it tolerated Christian activity, mostly shut it out. The two movements were incompatible. The Edinburgh Missionary Conference of 1910 was the last attempt at consolidating or solidifying a worldwide effort to understand for themselves the tactics and strategies that should be used in the modern age to evangelize the world. The topics discussed and debated in Edinburgh included the transport of the gospel to the whole non–Christian world, the church in the mission field, the place of education in national Christian life, missions and government, and the promotion of Christian unity.[2] There were other, lesser conferences in the years that followed, but none as notable as Edinburgh. The successor to Edinburgh, according to many, was the World Council of Churches, organized in 1945. By that time the World Council's goals were different.

The worldwide temperament of the times during the working life of James Solomon Russell is important to know. Russell's local environment was never unaffected by issues and movements around the world. Russell probably would have appreciated participating in the conference in Edinburgh because its agenda was more closely aligned to his evangelical purposes than any other movement. But he had his local issues that he was called to attend, a microcosm of a worldwide Christian spirituality.

The First Universal Races Congress — 1911

In an earlier chapter we mentioned that the executive director of the Episcopal Church's agency known as the American Church Institute for Negroes (ACIN) underwrote a trip to London for Russell and his son Alvin.

While in London, Russell attended a one-of-a-kind gathering of delegates from the world's racial or ethnic groups. His experience, as well as that of other African-Americans at that conference, is worth exploration.

Russell had traveled to London and Paris in 1907 thinking that he would never again return to these places, so he took in all that he could. On that trip Russell traveled with the Rev. N. Peterson Boyd[3]; this time he traveled with his young son, Alvin. What could Russell see and do in 1911 that he did not cover in 1907? Certainly Russell wanted to introduce Alvin to many sites of historic interest. It so happened that at the University of London during the week of July 26–29, 1911, there was a major international conference — the First Universal Races Congress. Many nations of the world sent representatives to this inaugural congress, one purpose of which was to begin seeking universal racial reconciliation.[4] After all, slavery and the slave trade had been legally abolished in most countries. Many American freedmen and their children had been living in freedom since 1863. Russell himself was of the age that made him part of the American transitional generation: a brief time in slavery but now much longer as a free person.

There is no evidence that this conference was the primary reason for Russell and his son to take the vacation. It is difficult to discern from reading Russell's *Autobiography*, except for a pithy clue which reads, "My 1911 journey to the Old World was more or less forced upon me."[5] By 1911 Russell had made a name for himself as the founder of St. Paul Normal and Industrial School, church planter of African-American missions, and community leader among blacks and whites. Indeed, Russell and his school were identified as one. Samuel H. Bishop, the first executive director of the American Church Institute for Negroes[6] (ACIN), is the person who suggested to Russell that he take an extended vacation. Perhaps this offer of an all-expenses-paid trip to Europe was a reward for Russell's work at St. Paul's. Neither Russell nor the school had the funds to underwrite such a trip, but the Rev. Mr. Bishop suggested that Russell take "a much needed rest and spend the summer in England."[7] In his 1912 annual report to his bishop and diocesan council, Russell reported, "Just after my last annual report [referring to his report to council in 1911] I was sent abroad by friends for a rest of two months. The trip was not so restful, however, as I had anticipated, and I returned home after two months feeling no better than when I left home, for the cares of my church and school work had followed me across the ocean."[8] Was Russell advising his bishop and the council in some subtle language that there were nefarious circumstances or conditions which led to his travel to London? Was Russell covering himself by confessing that he constantly worried about his churches and the school? The one thing that is clear is that Russell did not expect to visit the European continent at that time or ever again. Perhaps the vacation gift was not even a reward for excellent service on behalf of St. Paul's School. Bishop may have wanted Russell out of Lawrenceville in order to take over the operations of the college. That is probably the most likely reason. Another reason could have been the event taking place in London. Bishop, an educational and political progressive, more than likely knew about the Universal Races Congress in London. The lofty congress would have persons attending from all over the world who were to be mostly racial minorities. But those organizing and in control of the congress were white social progressives whose agenda called for papers written in an objective and "scientific" manner. With such an important congress to attend, it is interesting how the American delegates responded to its importance.

In the last days of July 1911, over 1,000 delegates representing more than fifty races from nations around the world gathered in Fishmonger's Hall at the University of London and convened the First Universal Races Congress. The overall purpose of the gathering, according to the Congress's organizer Gustav Spiller, was "to discuss, in the light of science and modern conscience, the general relations subsisting between the peoples of the West and those of the East, between so-called coloured peoples, with a view to encouraging between them a fuller understanding, the most friendly feelings, and a heartier co-operation."[9] It was, observed Felix Adler, a "theatre of humanity." The London press, according to Ralph Luker in his 1991 book on the social gospel and racial reform, reported that the Congress "was composed of 'long-haired men' and 'short-haired women,' 'soppy sentimentalists' and long-winded protagonists of every imaginable radical cause...."[10] The Congress met, adjourned, and produced a summary of its intended worldwide action plan. But there would be no Second Universal Races Congress and no rollout of its action plan.

Just one year earlier English monarch Edward VII had died, and leaders of the world had descended on London. The visual majesty of international royalty and political leaders in procession along the streets of London impressed many an onlooker. Ordinary folk standing curbside did not simply witness the largest regal funeral cortege in history; they unwittingly saw columns of the world's power players— players prefiguring sweeping changes in the political restructuring of the nations. According to Barbara Tuchman, "So gorgeous was the spectacle on the May morning of 1910 when nine kings rode in the funeral of Edward VII of England that the crowd, waiting in hushed and black-clad awe, could not keep back gasps of admiration."[11] Delaying his coronation for one year — to the week before the opening session of the Congress— Edward's successor, King George V, began his two-day public celebration. Three weeks before the Congress convened, the *Panther*[12] incident occurred, signaling a future European and worldwide political crisis.

One of the observers of the Congress was author and universal spiritualist

W.J. Colville. He called it one of the "remarkable epoch-making gatherings which have convened in London and other parts of England during the past summer [of 1911]...." In his "Mystic Light Essays" of 1913, Colville referenced the coronation ceremonies of George V as educational, especially when related to the purpose of the Congress. Colville wrote, "It is no idle pageant when persons of widely different appearance, habits and traditions are brought close together for the first time to unitedly celebrate a great event and rejoice together to acknowledge a common representative.... Peace Meetings do good, but they reach only comparatively few people, while processions catch the eye and ear, and hold the sustained interest and appeal successfully to the imagination of enormous multitudes."[13] Colville was one of those persons involved in a peace movement where the goal was absolute world peace found in racial harmony. He and many others held high hopes for the future as a result of the gathering labeled the First Universal Races Congress. It, too, was a large gathering of "widely different appearances ... and traditions" attempting to unite in a common purpose. But did it attract the eye and ear, and did it have the capacity to sustain an ongoing interest around the world? The Congress was either an epoch-making event, a footnote to world history, or irrelevant.

The Congress was the brainchild of Professor Felix Adler of Columbia University; England's Lord Weardale was its titular leader, and Gustav Spiller its organizer and secretary. The Ethical Culture Society financed the Congress and both Spiller and Adler promoted its promise. Spiller's planning efforts took two years. A circular, in advance of the Congress, was distributed widely. It contained the invitation, the object of the Congress, and a questionnaire. Approximately one month before the Congress, Spiller compiled, edited, and distributed the submitted papers in a document titled "Papers on Inter-Racial Problems Communicated to the First Universal Races Congress Held at the University of London July 26–29, 1911." Others also had high hopes for the Congress.

The Congress was endorsed by several American leaders of social Christianity. Many Black American intellectuals believed that the gospel could be applied to race relations with the right results. Although W.E.B. Du Bois believed more in the gospel of ideas than in the social gospel, he did not ignore the potential force the social gospel movement had for his own purposes. Du Bois and Adler co-chaired the American delegation, a delegation including several notable African-Americans. Du Bois recruited classicist scholar William Sanders Scarborough, president of Wilberforce University, as a delegate, telling him that he was hoping that the gathering of Negro Americans would receive full recognition. Du Bois envisioned African-Americans as stars of the Congress, receiving high honor and praise not experienced within the United States.[14] Also attending the Congress were R.R. Moton of Tuskegee Institute in Alabama and the Venerable James Solomon Russell of St. Paul Normal and Industrial School in Virginia.

The "Invitation for Papers" stated that all points of view in accord with the object of the Congress would be received and published as written. But papers of a political character should not be submitted. In the introduction to the published "Papers," Lord Weardale (Philip James Stanhope, 1st Baron Weardale) addressed those who wanted to further international goodwill and peace and professed that the Congress held "boundless promise." Because of the rise of the East in the world's balance of power, Weardale envisioned a new world order where racial prejudice would have vanished and whites and the "coloured races shall no longer merely meet in the glowing periods of missionary exposition, but, in very fact, regard one another as in truth men and brothers." Science, the child of the Enlightenment, took priority in terms of perspective. All writers were asked to maintain the "spirit of this object" in their papers. If these guidelines were not specific enough, it would be necessary to know more about the Congress's founder, its organizer, and the Ethical Culture Society.

In the preface to his book *Faith in Man*, published three years before the Congress, Gustav Spiller proclaimed that mighty and irresistible readjustments in men's beliefs and actions were taking place; that conscience has eclipsed the Scriptures; that science has destroyed the belief in divine interposition; and that democracy has become ethical, therefore ceasing to be supernatural. He went on to write that "the creeds and dogmas are practical moral helps whose truth is a matter of indifference and that the supreme test of a revival is the ethical result."[15] A new faith in moral endeavor was replacing faith in supernatural hopes and fears. Spiller went on to give account of Felix Adler's rise in the ethical movement. After earning his Ph.D., Adler was the heir apparent to his father's Jewish congregation in New York City. His maiden sermon was well received by the estimated 2,000 in attendance. All went well until the printed copy of his sermon became available. The aspiring rabbi never mentioned and made no allusion to the Deity — the God of Abraham, Isaac and Jacob. According to Spiller, the sermon was a shock of both surprise and horror to the congregation. Adler was still offered his father's pulpit but with the condition of acknowledging the Deity. Although he claimed not to be an atheist, the young Adler "preferred not to bind himself." In effect, Adler gave up his Jewish faith. Over time those who identified with Adler's non-theological "spirit" encouraged him to found a new religious organization, an organization that became the New York Society for Ethical Culture, in 1876.[16]

The ethical movement remained somewhat indefinite as to precise articulation except that the ethical test would be applied to all parts of a person's life, and that test would be superior to any other test. For example, there would be no belief in a deity, no dogma and therefore no authority deemed superior to living the ethical life. Those invited to join the movement had to give up their old beliefs and traditions, discard their older theological and nondemocratic views. The Old and New Testaments were to be irreconcilable with the new ethical views of the universe and of life. On the last page of his book Spiller wrote, "Men are turning from theology to science, the rule of social castes is being suspended by the rule of democracy...." This is the belief system or the foundation governing the First Universal Races Congress. Did its participants buy in to this Enlightenment-based foundation?

According to historian and Du Bois biographer David Levering Lewis, philanthropist John Milholland, a member of the Ethical Society and a supporter of the Congress, encouraged Du Bois to attend the Congress. He also offered to underwrite Du Bois's expenses. One could make an assumption from this that Du Bois may not have given serious consideration to attending the Congress. This was to be an interracial or multiracial Congress, led mostly by north Atlantic Anglos, which promised to bring benefits to all the races through peace and harmony of understanding.[17] Du Bois had participated in an initial Pan-African conference in 1900 led by Henry Sylvester-Williams. That was the first known meeting of leaders of the African *diaspora* who opposed colonialism and racism. An all-races Congress might not have fit into his overall vision. Du Bois would actually take over leadership of the Pan-Africanist congresses beginning in 1919. But what about his Congress?

Booker T. Washington had been in Great Britain in 1910, and Milholland wanted Du Bois to speak to two particular groups to "undo the harm" caused by Washington's visit. Milholland wanted these organizations, the Anti-Slavery and Aborigines Protection Society and the ladies of the Lyceum Club, to know the "true state of American race relations." Milholland himself told the secretary of the Anti-Slavery Society that Du Bois's visit was specifically intended to oppose Washington's view. Du Bois, feeling trapped, wanted to withdraw from the speaking engagement. However, in the end Du Bois gave his speech without controversy. But he did not write about it until 40 years later. For Du Bois the international atmosphere of London for those weeks and months in 1911 was possibly more appealing than the Congress.

Washington did not attend the Congress and probably never intended to, but other African-Americans were present. Robert Russa Moton attended at Washington's request. Washington's purpose was to have Moton watch Du Bois closely and to counter him publicly if necessary. But Moton reported to Washington that there was no need and Moton actually supported Du Bois's presentation.[18] Russell, judging from what he wrote in his *Autobiography* and in a report to his church council, was probably not a delegate, desired no rest, but was restless during his entire absence from the St. Paul School. Since he had visited London just four years earlier, what could he see?

An examination of biographies and autobiographies of Du Bois, Scarborough and Russell suggests that the short-term personal interests of these attendees were not necessarily aligned with the Congress's goals—their off-session stories were of more interest than the immediate workings of the Congress. For example, Scarborough seemed more interested in sightseeing than in the Congress; Du Bois enjoyed being in the presence of, and hobknobbing with, notable people from Europe, Africa and Haiti; and Russell "rested" by showing his son around town and taking in the sights. Scarborough's autobiography confirmed the presence of these other "prominent representatives of the race from the United States," namely Dr. and Mrs. Moton and Archdeacon Russell and his son, but went on to express his disappointment "that more of our leading people were not present."[19] On the day of his address, according to Scarborough's documentation, the former President of Hayti [Haiti], General Francois Denys Legitime, presided as Scarborough spoke about the "Color Question in the United States." That is all that Scarborough allowed in recalling his talk in his autobiography — nothing more, nothing less. The advance document distributed by Spiller did not list any Scarborough address nor display his name as a delegate. Perhaps his address was scheduled after the Congress began and was not documented in the pre–Congress mailing. Yet Archdeacon Russell, in his *Autobiography*, not only confirmed Scarborough's attendance but the theme of Scarborough's address, of which he disapproved.

Russell wrote in his *Autobiography*, "On the afternoon of the closing of the [C]ongress, a statement by Dr. W.S. Scarborough of Wilberforce University that the Negro in America was much better off in slavery brought a sudden rush to the platform and the sending in of cards from persons who wanted to rebut the speaker." Russell said that he and Dr. Moton quickly approached the platform asking for time to talk. Moton was allocated seven minutes, but in the end no opportunity to rebut was made available "due to the lateness of the hour."[20] What could have been Scarborough's motivation, particularly at a conference that condemned slavery? Neither Du Bois nor Moton mentioned Scarborough's speech in any of their future writings. Did Scarborough actually say what Russell recorded? Since the record is missing, we will never know the full content or intent of his address. One can only accept the description provided by Russell.

Scarborough, as a child in slavery, lived as if he were free. His mother's master was that rare slave-owner who compassionately took care of his chattel's family. Scarborough went on to secure an education (at Oberlin in

Ohio) of which most young blacks could never dream. Du Bois, educated at
Fisk, Harvard and Berlin, never lived under slavery. Russell and Moton, both
educated at Hampton as was Booker T. Washington, were not considered
black intellectual elites and certainly not of the "Talented Tenth" espoused
by Du Bois. Du Bois and Scarborough, however, placed themselves in the
African-American elite class. This would account, in part, for the differences
in the educational philosophies between the Du Boises and the Washingtons.
These vignettes are certainly intriguing and have some historical interest.
More interesting to the issue at hand is the fact that these men, all of them,
wrote very little of the important events of this Congress.

In his chapter "Second Trip to Europe," Scarborough bequeaths the
reader with less than two pages out of twelve about the Congress. Considering
the Congress's "boundless promise," one would have expected a more detailed
description of the conference's undertakings. Russell, likewise, spends few
words on the Congress— even fewer than Scarborough. After citing Scarborough's misstatement, Russell reminisces about his travels around England,
Continental Europe and Africa. Russell mixes his four trips to Europe in his
chapter on "Seeing Europe and Africa." Biographer David L. Lewis writes
that Du Bois enjoyed social acceptance in London, and feeling "at ease and
buoyant," he was seen on the arm of the beautiful daughter of the president
of Hayti [Haiti]. At a later time Mary Ovington and John Milholland saw
their friend "with another woman of remarkable beauty and culture."
Although the social setting was more than pleasant, it was Du Bois's conviction
that this 1911 gathering of the world's intellectuals would provide the leadership to break down the "color line."

At the Congress's end and after the completion of their European and
African excursions, delegates would return home to face a multitude of struggles.[21] Scarborough would return to Wilberforce University saddened by the
fact that while in Europe he was unable to meet the benefactress of Wilberforce. According to his autobiography, Miss E.J. Emery was sojourning on
the seashore. Emery died in 1913 and left her entire estate to the Salvation
Army. Perhaps Scarborough lamented the loss of a potential large endowment
for his university. Russell returned to Lawrenceville, Virginia, where the ACIN
was indeed trying to wrest control of St. Paul's away from him.[22] It was Du
Bois, however, who reveled in the promise of the Congress. David Lewis
writes that Du Bois was unable to speak of the Congress in less than hyperbolic
rhetoric for the rest of his life. For all who attended the Congress, it had to
be an exciting event, and it held out promise of a better future for the world's
minority populations. But the world in 1911 was on the precipice of catastro-
phe and plans for any future Congress would soon have to be placed on hold.
If there were to be a Second Universal Races Congress, where and when would

it take place? Lewis speculates that the assassination of an archduke in Sarajevo killed any hope for a 1914 Congress.

Was the Congress a failure, and if so, was it due to subsequent international events, to a lack of interest, or to something else? It was a failure because it could not deliver on its promises, it had no political power, and it displayed no worldwide influence. But it can also be seen as a success because it played itself out as a preliminary event foreshadowing organizational adjustments with institutions working for better race relations. The organizers and leaders of the First Universal Races Congress were social and political progressives, and by 1911 progressivism in the United States and Great Britain had achieved significant momentum mostly by providing participation of various groups seeking social justice and recognition not afforded by general society or governments. Many organizations played roles in one way or another in the birthing of the Universal Races Congress: the Ethical Culture Society (in the United States and its branch in Great Britain), founded by Felix Adler; the Niagara Movement and Du Bois; the social gospellers; the National Urban League[23]; and the National Association for the Advancement of Colored People (NAACP). The elevated role given to science at the Congress pre-empted the inclusion of faith and religion as viable inputs and guaranteed an outcome with a secular bias. The American Christian social gospel movement, with its roots in antebellum Northern missionary efforts in the South, evolved into a secular orientation by the end of the nineteenth century, in sympathy with progressivism. With a general acceptance of the belief that all mankind emerged from one source, and therefore of one blood, the Congress worked with great hope and anticipation that it could solve the world's racial problems. But in the end the foundation for the Congress was fatally flawed.

The English Jesuit and author, C.C. Martindale, provided a critique of the Congress that was neither unfair nor belligerent. He understood that the effort at organizing such a large gathering was no small feat; that the number of high-ranking international persons was unprecedented; and that the cross-sciences categories were many; therefore, the Congress seemed destined for greatness. But the underlying premise of the Congress asserted that participants had to give up any traditionally held beliefs in order that a greater good would emerge. In other words, the organizers of the Congress had already decided the rules by which universal unity would be achieved. Those who acquiesced to this new religion must relinquish their old faiths. For Christians, and for Martindale, this was totally unacceptable. Martindale wrote that "when *unity* is aimed at, at once the alternative of absorption or fusion presents itself.... No one will fail to see how the very ideals of the Catholic Church may here, in the working out of forces divorced from hers, be turned to her own disaster."[24]

Martindale's analysis of the Congress is summarized in his critique of a paper on Bahaism. That paper, plus a letter from the then-leader the Bahai faith, was the one presentation at the Congress that, according to Martindale, embodied its "spirit." If the unity that is professed to be the essence of Bahaism (and the Congress) is not and cannot be based on dogma but on an ephemeral identity of human aspiration, then such a unity is simply an oft-told tale of the ages. We have heard it before and we hear it again. The language of world unity is attractive and it deceives in every generation. Martindale said that Catholics or Christians should have attended the Congress if only to act as a counter to its untruth and to proclaim the truth that is Christianity. Father Bernard Vaughan, another English Jesuit, attended the Congress and was listed as one of its "officers." Vaughan, though acclaimed as a master preacher, was accused by fellow priest and friend Father Leonard Feeney that "when speaking in public, he tried to offer England a sociological Jesus, instead of the Jesus Who died to save our souls. He made Our Lord the ardent supporter, almost contributor, to all sorts of uplift enterprises, for better food, better living quarters, better hospital care. As a Catholic in the pulpit, Father Vaughan was edifying." Even here the language of social reform is seductive, to such a point that Christians forget their calling. Interestingly, another "officer" of the Congress was the Rev. F.B. Meyer, a friend and an associate of American evangelist D.L. Moody.

Some of the Americans mentioned in that essay could not have agreed to the Ethical Movement's foundational premise of this First Universal Races Congress. Perhaps that is why so little was chronicled about the Congress. Certainly James Solomon Russell, an evangelical Christian, a priest, and an ardent believer in the creeds of the Church, was not interested in a general unity of the world based on something or someone other than Jesus Christ. Nor could William Sanders Scarborough, a scholar and president of a university belonging to the African Methodist Episcopal Church, accede to such a secular and Godless premise. Even the intellectual elitism of W.E.B. Du Bois—a nominal Episcopalian and possibly a Congregationalist at heart—would not interfere with his understanding of true Christian theology in matters secular. Du Bois understood Christian theology and would not oppose its revealed truth. What he would have opposed would have been any ecclesiastical attempt to impose or force a false theological interpretation. The First (and only) Universal Races Congress, though significant in some ways, was not an epoch-making event. World War I might have played a role in quashing a second "all races" congress. But the requirement that people of faith abandon their traditions and belief systems in order to secure world unity stymied global acceptance and choked the future of the Congress and its secular-only ideals. At best the Congress was an historical footnote or a minor international political event that inadvertently prepared some of its participants to later rise to significance.

Russell's nemesis, Samuel Bishop, knowingly sent him to the Congress most likely for at least two reasons: first, simply to get Russell out of town while Bishop worked his planned takeover of the school; and second, to educate Russell in the "science" of progressivism. The great debate between industrial and liberal arts education in Southern black schools had its roots in progressivism and secular elitism. Had Russell tapped into progressivism in the final decades of the nineteenth century, then the Congress would have been an appropriate gathering for him in which to participate. But Russell never embraced a godless or "other-centered" philosophy of life, religion, and politics. A practical man and a minister of the gospel, Russell was a shadow player in the largely secular Washington-DuBois debate over education. In the shadows he built a Christian school and a large convocation of churches for his fellow African-Americans and his church.

The Washington Congress — 1919

The Congress in Washington was completely different in tone and foundation from the London Congress, but not in subject matter. The platform was unusual. On November 12, 1919, J. Stanley Durkee was inaugurated as president of Howard University, a secular university, in a day-long celebration that included a church-like procession of academics, international personalities, faculty members, U.S. senators and representatives, and a former chief justice of the United States. Included also in the procession were members or trustees of educational boards that funded African-American schools in the South, such as the GEB, the Slater Fund, the Jeans Fund and the Rockefeller and Carnegie foundations. The second day, November 13, 1919, was a conference of various leaders giving a wide range of addresses at the Readjustment and Reconstruction Congress, sponsored by Howard University. One of its speakers was James Solomon Russell. The name of the Congress was in response to World War I and its aftermath. In this same year the Paris peace talks took place from January to June, with American President Woodrow Wilson playing the role of the leading international statesman.

The contrast in the underlying foundations between the two congresses is striking. In his inaugural address, Durkee's opening sentences proclaim the educational undergirdings of his inaugural and the Congress: "The foundation on which American democracy rests is Christian education. If the superstructure shall abide, the foundation therefore must abide. The strength of that foundation, and, hence, democracy itself, inheres in the Christian education of all the citizens of America. I am using the world 'Christian' not in any narrowing or even in any special religious sense, but rather to connotate [*sic*] all that is best and noblest in all the outreaching of humanity."[25] In his welcoming address the next day to the Congress, Durkee in part asked rhetorically whether God made all men of one blood. He answered without waiting for an answer: "He did." He went on to say that "all these races of men, God's children, are of the same Divine family. The question today is—how shall this family live together in peace and harmony, mutually helpful, honoring each other? This Conference is to face the question from both the national and international standpoints, as it relates especially to the darker-skinned races."[26] So the stage was set for another conference in an effort to bring the world together. The London Congress preceded World War I, which probably preempted a succeeding conference. The Washington Congress convened after the war, and yet the need for worldwide racial reconciliation continued. The London Congress was dominated by a scientific motif and disallowed any alternative approach. The Washington gathering was "Christian" in tone but open to other views. Russell's address was not unlike many other speeches, sermons and addresses given elsewhere. Because Russell was speaking by invitation, his presence represented a high level of credibility and authority in not only his public work in education and religion, but in his Christian integrity. Russell and two other speakers, Dr. J.E. Moorland and Miss Eva D. Bowles, were asked to address the topic of "Social Uplift in the Church." (See Appendix E — Social Uplift Address 1919.)

CHAPTER NINE

Reconciliation and Russell's Legacy

DESPITE ATTEMPTS BY LEADERS in the American Church Institute for Negroes to replace him as principal of St. Paul's School, James Solomon Russell persevered as principal and enjoyed an unusually successful career as an educator. Despite attempts by the legislative councils of his own church to deprive African-American Episcopalians of voting privileges, and their denying requests for more black clergy and more money to support black clergy and new churches, Russell consistently evangelized his area of responsibility and created or assisted in the creation of more than thirty African-American congregations. He encouraged and received the support of white clergy in helping the African-American community in the Diocese of Southern Virginia in its worship and evangelical work. Russell consistently expressed his gratitude for assistance from white clergy, his bishops and his local political leaders for any assistance they may have provided.

In speeches and other addresses to various organizations he maintained that relations between whites and blacks in Brunswick County, Virginia, were good if not the best in Virginia. Russell carried with him the latest statistics showing the year-to-year progress of African-Americans, not only in his Southside Virginia region but in all of Virginia. Yet Russell knew that white people harbored certain attitudes isolating themselves from more intimate contact with blacks. At an early age Russell understood human nature; furthermore, he not only knew what African Americans thought, he knew whites just as well. He was influential among all people. Nothing in Russell's writings or speeches suggests any personal or racial animosity toward anyone. He appears to be a man who dealt with other men on a straightforward, eye-to-eye basis. In other words, race was not a category of human separation in Russell's mind.

Normal human reactions to sudden and radical life-changing conditions build up to such a point that explosive and unintended consequential actions emerge. To whites immediately after the Civil War, their social fabric was torn apart; their old order had died. To blacks an emerging new order became the launching pad to their future, or so they believed. As far as the church is concerned, the paternalism label either hides or ignores any attempt to see into the truly heartfelt and positive motivations in the actions among many whites. Several examples should provide evidence.

Giles Buckner Cooke founded a normal school for ex-slaves at his church, which eventually became the location of the all-black Bishop Payne Divinity School. One church historian insists that "Cooke was a *racial paternalist* [emphasis added] who envisioned a relationship between education, evangelism, and social control. He emphasized the importance of saving African Americans from the 'heathenish manifestation of wild religious feeling' into which preachers of their own race were carrying them...."[1] Cooke is identified as a person with an unchangeable attitude toward blacks, suggesting a mitigation of any earnest effort on Cooke's behalf to assist former slaves. The picture of Cooke presented by James Solomon Russell, however, nowhere approaches the perspective presented by some historians. If anything, Russell's and Cooke's relationship was filial, not suzerain. Certainly Russell took issue with some of Cooke's advice. As a student in seminary, Russell was scheduled to read lessons from the pulpit. This assignment was not unusual except insofar as Russell had never been in an Episcopal Church until then and did not know what to do. Cooke advised Russell to think of the people in the pews as "heads of cabbage," but Russell said that neither at that time nor later could he ever consider people as heads of cabbage. This short excerpt from Russell's book shows nothing significantly domineering about Cooke, just some advice. It also shows Russell's point of view about people. Russell wrote:

> Major Cooke was a very exact man and a stickler for punctuality, but he was very human and wholeheartedly devoted to the right and the worthy. The acquaintance which we gained as a teacher and student has followed us down the years and has ripened into a rich and deep friendship. He has seen me grow and apply myself to the task at hand, and he has shown no little interest in all that I tried to do. So strong are the bonds of friendship between us that Major Cooke on more than one occasion declared publicly that I am to officiate at his funeral if I survive him, and that he will perform the last rites over me "With Virginia's [Russell's wife's] permission," if I should die first.[2]

It should be recalled that Russell, in his *Autobiography*, reminisced that his slaveholder's family fretted over those plantation sons' safety as Confederate soldiers, "and concern for them also gripped the slaves."[3] This example is not cited to suggest that some or most of the Southern slaves were emotionally attached to their owners to such a degree that they appreciated their slave status. But the example provides insight into Russell's perspective about his slaveowner's humanity regardless of the circumstances of life.

An Episcopal Church historian writes that a "fateful evolution" took place in race relations in the period between the 1883 Sewanee bishops' conference and the loss of black civil rights by the end of the nineteenth century. Blacks had gained much during the Reconstruction periods (Presidential and Radical), but much was also lost after Reconstruction ended, through the backlash of Southern white governments retaking the legislatures. This fact is undeniable. This period is described as occurring "while outspoken racists vied with paternalists for political control of the South. Within this context, most Episcopal leaders occupied a middle ground between the few white Southerners who genuinely wished to assist African Americans and those who sought only to degrade them."[4] Never identified are those "few white Southerners who genuinely wished to assist," but he did label the Sewanee bishops and unnamed others as paternalists. The paternalists are seen as protectors of the old, antebellum order: experts at keeping "lower-class whites" and blacks in their place. Though one can agree with the probable truth of the intentions which the historian places on the Sewanee bishops, the label "paternalism" might overstate or preempt what the bishops personally understood. There were a couple of items that the Sewanee bishops had to work through.

First, the Sewanee bishops probably understood all too well that the old order was dead. Why then call a meeting to discuss alternatives? Black communicants, if still around, no longer sat in the rafters of the church. Even though the Thirteenth Amendment freed the slaves in 1865, by 1883 an underlying white political backlash was on the upswing, and nowhere near its full potential. Secondly, the Sewanee bishops launched a trial balloon which eventually came into being in the form of "colored convocations" in the Southern dioceses. It may not have been consciously thought a trial balloon, but in the end those bishops believed that they had to act, and that action had to be founded on the principle of the old order. Those bishops were conditioned by the long-running old order. They could not accept and implement an imposed order modeled on the secular precedent implemented during Reconstruction: they were bishops of the church and well-trained in the gospel, although co-opted to a large degree by centuries of colonial and Southern lifestyles. The Sewanee Conference's call for separation of the races within the church — though rejected by General Convention of 1883[5] — was historically natural for them, but it was a knee-jerk reaction also.

One church historian[6] described the overall racial situation best when he wrote, "The contours of this debate[7] reveal Episcopalians' *profound confusion* [emphasis added] about the role that race and racial differences ought to play with the church fellowship."[8] Confusion was widespread in the Episcopal Church, and the existence of paternalism was simply one element in the mix — an element that needed to pass away. Everyone, from the Sewanee bishops to the lay and clerical faithful, assumed that the old structure of church management or governance was at risk. Active church participants, whether black or white, franchised or not, were now necessarily set up to engage in debate, using the existing structure and process while creating a new. There were black communicants involved in both the laity and the clergy.

The facts seem to reveal that the Sewanee bishops (and most Southern Episcopalians) were co-opted by the reigning "plausibility structure,"[9] that is, the dying culture of the American South. What was considered plausible in the South, particularly to those not enslaved, was a way of life lived from the early colonial days and continuing up to the mid–19th century. The fundamental questions in colonial days were about freedom and education. Should the church educate the Negro? The French provinces in America were under the "Code Noir," which required slave masters to teach their slaves how to read the Bible. The Spanish practice of miscegenation clearly prevented objections to educating the slave. But to the English colonists there was an unwritten law that a Christian could not be held as a slave. This belief restrained colonists from educating or enlightening their slaves. Education might have led to Christian conversion of the Negro and conversion would have led to manumission. Indeed there were manumissions by some slave-owners during the colonial era and the early years of independence, but the church, through its clergy, sought out exemptions which equated manumission with Christian conversion of slaves. In 1727 the Bishop of London issued a formal declaration to colonial Anglican pastors that "conversion did not work manumission."[10] This structure persisted from early seventeenth-century colonial days to the mid–1800s.

Blacks knew that such a plausibility structure was not only unreasonable, it was ungodly. Black slaves attended Anglican churches and knew the gospel very well. Apparently unchallenged, the colonial church and the emergent Episcopal Church continued for years under the illusion that God sanctioned slavery. But the reigning plausibility structure of the British Empire and its agent, the church, trumped such reasoning. There is no particular charge made here about the British Empire other than that it and its church operated in a certain way regarding converted slaves. Whether the ecclesiastical unit of society was the colonial Church of England or the Episcopal Church in the United States, the die had been cast in colonial times and continued unquestioned after the American Revolution. Was the church confused or was it failing to live up to the gospel? The church chose the status quo. That had to change on December 6, 1865, when the Thirteenth Amendment was ratified.

There were several prominent African-American Episcopalians prior to the outbreak of the Civil War — Absalom Jones, to name the most famous of them. In the decades immediately following the war, many African-American leaders emerged within the Episcopal Church, challenging its status quo of the old order and the church of Southern culture; James Solomon Russell was the leader of a counterculture, as odd as it might first appear. Russell worked within the reigning plausibility structure, and because of his high sense of mission through his understanding of the catholicity[11] of the church, he marched through history making subtle but effective waves of change. In the wake of those changes emerged the hardly noticeable but ever-increasing countercultural movement led by former slaves and their children.

Russell and his clergy peers constituted a remarkable group of African-American leaders from the 1880s through the mid–1930s. Men like Alexander Crummell, George Freeman Bragg, Jr., Edward Demby, and Henry Beard Delany were all instrumental in redirecting and changing not only the canons of the church but the mindset of many of its communicants. But that change took a long time. Russell was prepared to work on two fronts: education and the church. He knew the educational shortcomings of the church when it came to teaching its young Negro slaves. Most slaves young and old believed that education was the key to their emancipated futures. By creating the St. Paul School within months of his arrival in Lawrenceville, Virginia, Russell and his wife Virginia began educating as many former slaves as they could. As their school grew larger they always found funds and continued expanding the school. It was clear that fundraising was a major obstacle but that did not stop him. Russell enlisted the help of his bishop and his diocese; he was able to persuade well-to-do local white men to assist in the expansion of the school. He became well-acquainted with the local legal systems and political office-holders. Not a shy person, James Solomon Russell knew his calling and would not relent. He understood human nature. Even during his short history as a child slave at Palmer Springs in Mecklenburg County, Virginia, young Russell learned how to deal with adult overseers and local merchants. In his adult life he sensed that despite the radical change in Southern living brought about by the Civil War, it would not be easy to change the hearts and minds, and eventually the laws, supporting white supremacy.

Russell's appointment as Archdeacon for Colored Work in the Diocese of Southern Virginia paralleled his obligations as principal of his St. Paul School. The appointment was actually a blessing not only to him but to the entire diocese. The Archidiaconate provided Russell with a platform to expand Christian ministry into his geographical section of Virginia. The Black Belt of Virginia was within the Diocese of Southern Virginia and presented him with a huge opportunity, not only for Christian evangelism to unchurched

African-Americans, but in avenues to expand and promote educational, agricultural and economic betterment. Together with his school, his ecclesiastical
appointment provided his *de facto* leadership in the community with *de jure*
credentials. Russell created the St. Paul's Farmers' Conference, thereby not
only leveraging his notoriety and influence, but also providing an avenue of
hope to many African-American farmers and their families in creating a successful lifetime of achievement. In speeches Russell provided year-to-year
statistics citing black progress not only across the Black Belt but Virginia in
general. He became adept at providing factual numbers to willing and unwill-
ing listeners which supported the positive results of African-Americans' work
and spirit. His annual reports[12] to the diocese provided statistics enumerating
positive results in the growing community of colored churches in his convocation. Those reports also documented Russell's personal achievements within
the environment of the church. St. Paul's College had at one time the largest
student population of any other school in the state of Virginia; it was the
center of activity for the annual farmers' conferences; and it was the leading
institution for industrial education within the Episcopal Church. And who
was stopping Russell from doing all of this? No one! At least not until a few
national church leaders wanted to intervene.

The Church of the North had it own problems. St. Philip's Church in
New York City is a good example. Before the beginning of the Civil War and
after the Northern states legally abolished slavery, the Episcopal Diocese of
New York held its annual council in September of 1853. Three black men,
delegates from St. Philip's Church, walked into the gathering on the second
day of the council meeting. Most of the delegates, 500 plus in all, from the
eastern half of New York State were powerful and wealthy white men. According to one researcher, New Yorkers at that time basked in a sense of self-right-
eousness that they had rid themselves of that "peculiar institution" of slavery,
even though they were obligated to enforce the Fugitive Slave Law, whereby
runaway Southern slaves caught in the North had to be returned to their
Southern slave owners. The white New York Episcopal Diocese delegates were
proud of the fact that they had a black congregation in their fold where they
could bring the gospel to the "unfortunates." St. Philip's was that congregation, and the three black men were duly admitted as delegates to council. It
was disturbing to the white delegates that they had to treat these black delegates as equals.[13] From this one example it can be assumed that the racial attitudes of Northern Episcopalians were not much different from their Southern
counterparts. This common white attitude indicts the entire church, not just
the Southern contingent. Northern money or Northern philanthropy, as discussed earlier, held these same attitudes.

Most of the general fundraising organizations like the Southern Education

Board, the General Education Board, and eventually the ACIN, were managed by persons propagating "progressive education." Additionally, a couple of the fund managers were theological graduates of the "social gospel movement." Thomas Jesse Jones, the author/editor of the *1913–1916 Black Education Report of the U.S. Education Bureau*, and Samuel H. Bishop both were graduates of New York City's Union Theological Seminary, the center of the social gospel movement. Paternalism, if it existed in the Southern church, most certainly existed in the church of the North and was perhaps even stronger. The influence of the North cannot be ignored as a major factor in the complicity of the entire Episcopal Church in its poor and inadequate response to the "Negro problem" after the Civil War. Yet despite the differences between the North and South as to how education for the former slave should be controlled, and despite his problems with the ACIN, James Solomon Russell conducted the vast majority of his fundraising campaigns in the North. It was the North and not the South that provided funding for the post–Civil War schools.[14]

Why did Russell care about what was happening in the church? Given the historical record, he cared a great deal. Whether in his dealings with the ACIN or the legislative wrangling of his annual diocesan councils, Russell persisted. Year-by-year he proclaimed the same message: more men and means. Year-by-year he argued for more help from well-to-do communicants. Year-by-year he also thanked his white clergy brethren for supporting colored convocation churches when in need. Russell worked within the structure in order to change that structure. Venue did not matter.

At an early age Russell developed his leadership skills and continued to hone them over the years. His association with the beginnings of the Zion Union Apostolic Church, its hopes and its shortcomings, affected his thinking and his interactions with other people. Historically, the Great Awakening, the advent of Methodism, the imperfect biracial churches in the South, the splitting of Methodism into separate black and white churches, and the ouster of black members from white churches after the end of the Civil War, played on Russell's sensitivities. He did not like separation, nor division, nor ostracism. Early on he saw the catholicity of the church. Recall that Russell thought that African-American's flight from the Episcopal Church after the war was a mistake, though understandable. Given all that happened during the years preceding the formation of the Zion Unions— the disestablishment of the Anglican Church after the American Revolution; its virtual demise in influence; and the splitting of the Methodists into multiple sects between the two wars— and the disintegration of the Zion Unions (a "Methodist" church) after a minor squabble five years after formation, Russell clearly saw the need for a reconciling force. It was Russell who reconciled his bishop, James R.

Howell, to the true gospel. It was Russell's work that allowed for a large number of Zion Union members to seek admission into the Episcopal Church — the only church that stayed intact organizationally and theologically in the anxious stresses of the post–Great Awakening new republic. Perhaps these are the reasons which guided Russell into his longer-term, and patient, role as a reconciler of men.

James Solomon Russell lived fully as a person engaged in an ongoing process of reconciliation. He did not confront others by seeking clarity: he confronted others seeking reconciliation, because he knew how the church worked in the days before and after Emancipation. And he knew the message of the gospel he lived and preached. Reconciliation can be slow. Each and every time Russell presented his annual reports to his diocese he confronted his bishops and fellow delegates with the facts of the church's shortcomings in relation to its African-American members, and he sought reconciliation by providing them with courses of action. Russell was a practical man who knew that confrontation (even though his style was mild or civil) did not always persuade. Scripture advises the Christian to instruct, warn and train, not just to rebuke.[15] Russell used as many tactics as he needed in order to engage in conversation those who could not see properly due to the specks in their own eyes. Through his reports as cited throughout this book, his sermons, his fundraising travels, and through his speeches, Russell continually employed his skills in seeking change and reconciliation. As bad as the situation came to be in the evolving South, Russell had to "engage" in dialogue with his adversaries, not "preach" to them.

Russell's reconciliation tactics had to include in the first instance personal and face-to-face confrontation. His dealings with landowners in Lawrenceville provide examples. He acknowledged that when he initially arrived in Lawrenceville, an air of suspicion or outright racial hostility lived. That did not bother Russell. When he dealt with those who wished to sell their land, Russell's face-to-face engagement with these white men may have been their first time doing business on such large a scale with a black man.[16] Certainly it was a learning experience for both. Such interactions were fundamentally private or personal transactions. Russell's *Autobiography* contains numerous one-on-one interactions like this. But for larger issues encompassing many persons or groups, Russell had to modify his tactics. His annual archdeacon reports on the colored convocation's work and the proposals of the convocation to the diocese required a steady, broader and more nuanced appeal.

Russell exhibited great personal restraint over the years toward Bishop A.M. Randolph. It will be recalled that Randolph, while still bishop coadjutor of the undivided Diocese of Virginia, provided the keynote address in its annual council of 1889 that led to the disfranchisement of the colored clergy and laity. Russell and two other clergy were exempt according to the Randolph plan. Limits were placed on black voter participation in future councils. This canon carried over to the newly created Diocese of Southern Virginia. Randolph became the diocesan bishop and quickly appointed Russell as Archdeacon for Colored Work. Russell could have confronted the bishop and the diocese on the wrongness of the canon but he knew he could not advance his argument, at least not directly. He had to take an indirect approach.

Russell's colored convocation always presented memorials which backed their bishop by refusing to endorse a black bishop for a black province. Russell, a realist, knew that he did not have the votes. His *tactics* embraced years of unrelenting reinforcement of his consistent message found in his annual archdeacon reports, sermons, speeches, and prayers. His *strategy* was catholicity.[17] It was Russell's theology of the universality of the church that guided his spiritual, social and political posturing. Russell knew that it was the church — the Body of Christ — that was most important. To be catholic, the church must be open to all. To be catholic, the unified Body of Christ of individuals and groups had to sacrifice whatever in their lives stood between them and Christ's bride in order to witness to the world. In earthly or practical terms this meant that both blacks and whites had to give up something while simultaneously emptying themselves to others for the cause of Christ. For Russell this meant that the white leadership of the Episcopal Church had to give up its old ways and break through their old order so that they could receive their African-American brothers and sisters as complete human beings and equal partners in the cause of Christ. It is reasonable to assume that Russell's insistence that his Colored Convocation reject the proposed separate ecclesiastical jurisdiction for African-Americans was the sacrifice necessary by blacks as an act contributing to the catholicity of the church. It was Russell's spiritual and theological understanding of the nature of the church that supported and transcended his earthly or practical activities.

Between groups (the convocation and the diocese) the process was negotiation through a long-term and long-suffering endurance run. Russell never lived to see the change in the canon whereby all references to race were eliminated, and African-American parishes and missions in the Diocese of Southern Virginia were granted equal voting participation. Because of his nonstop efforts change eventually came. It was not until the late 1940s that the Diocese of Southern Virginia[18] dropped all of its obstacles to African-American participation in its deliberative assembly. Russell was never a person to deny his racial identity or to stand idly by if an explanation of the reality of slavery were distorted.

Russell's lifetime achievements are noteworthy and it is curious that historians have for the most part passed over the work of this remarkable man.

Marker of James Solomon Russell, St. Paul's Cemetery, Lawrenceville, Virginia (photograph by Worth E. Norman, Jr.).

Episcopal Church historians Gardiner Shattuck, Harold T. Lewis, and Michael J. Beary mention Russell rarely in their books.[19] To be fair to these scholars, their books had different purposes. However, the extent to which Russell was a major church actor during his era seems to be overlooked if not ignored by church history writers. *Dangerous Donations* by Anderson and Moss provides extended, if not unflattering, analysis on a significant period in Russell's career. Honor was brought to Russell by the fact that over the years many students passed through the halls of St. Paul Normal and Industrial School and received the education they sought and the success in life of which they dreamed. Midway into his *Autobiography* he writes about several of those students by name and identifies their successes.[20]

In 1922 the president of the nation of Liberia conferred upon Russell the dignity of "Knight Commander"[21] of the Liberian Humane Order of African Redemption.[22] Russell was the first African-American member of the Episcopal Church's Department of Christian Social Service and served from January 1924 to September 1931.[23] In 1929 Russell was presented the famed African American Harmon Award.[24] In 1931 he was named an honorary trustee of the Yorktown [Virginia] Sesquicentennial Association. The trustees of Liberia College conferred the honorary degree of Doctor of Laws, and the

Virginia Theological Seminary honored Russell with the Doctor of Divinity Degree (1917).[25]

Russell retired in 1929 and his son James Alvin Russell succeeded him as principal.[26] In 1996 the Episcopal Diocese of Southern Virginia declared Russell a "local saint."[27] In the 2009 General Convention of the Episcopal Church a memorial was entered to place Russell in the church's prayer book calendar, thereby assigning him a Lesser Feasts and Fasts Day. As of this writing, the memorial is expected to be presented again during General Convention 2012.

Appendices

Containing **A.** *Colonial Statutory Recognition of Slavery;* **B.** *Colored Churches' Membership, 1900;* **C.** *Methodist Churches in the United States, 1900;* **D.** *Virginia Legislative Assembly African-American Membership, 1872–1892;* **E.** *Social Uplift Address, 1919;* **F.** *Summary of the Official Acts of the Archdeacon for Colored Work;* **G.** *Churches and Missions in the Colored Convocation, Episcopal Diocese of Southern Virginia, 1910;* **H.** *General Convention [of the Episcopal Church] Opening Session, Portland, Oregon, 1922;* **I.** *Southern Virginia Resolution, 2009;* **J.** *Secular Education Funds for Negro Schools in the South, 1860s–1920s;* **K.** *Conclusion of the Report of the Committee on the State of the Church, 1907;* **L.** *Statistics of the Two Episcopal Dioceses in Virginia, 1892;* **M.** *"A Tribute to Lewis Morris," a Poem by Goronwy Owens;* **N.** *Brief Biographies;* **O.** *Timeline of Significant Events Affecting the Life of Russell.*

A. Colonial Statutory Recognition of Slavery

Year	Colony
1641	Massachusetts
1659	Connecticut
1661	Virginia
1663	Maryland
1664	New York and New Jersey
1682	South Carolina
1700	Pennsylvania and Rhode Island
1715	North Carolina
1755	Georgia

Prior to the above dates the legal status of Negroes was that of indentured servant or free person.

Year	Colony
1778	The sovereign state of Virginia enacted the prohibition of slave importation

Source: Ballagh, James Curtis. *A History of Slavery in Virginia.* Baltimore: The Johns Hopkins Press, 1902.

B. Colored Churches' Membership, 1900

Denomination	Membership
1. African Methodist Episcopal	842,023
2. African Methodist Episcopal Zion	569,305
3. African Union Methodist Protestant	3,887
4. Colored Baptist	1,729,939
5. Colored Congregationalists	3,200
6. Colored Contingent of the Methodist Episcopal	105,978
7. Colored Free-will Baptist	20,000
8. Colored Methodist Episcopal	214,987
9. Colored Presbyterian	27,581
10. Colored Protestant Episcopal	18,400
11. Colored Roman Catholics	25,600
12. Union American Methodist Episcopal	18,500
13. Others	5,000
Total Negroes in churches	3,584,400
Total Whites in all denominations	26,495,026

Source: Henry T. Besse, *Church History* (Cleona, PA: Holzapfel Publishing, 1909).

C. Methodist Churches in the United States, 1900

Divisions	Ministers	Churches	Members
1. African Methodist Episcopal (AME)	6,190	5,321	842,023
2. African Methodist Episcopal Zion (AMEZ)	3,659	3,161	569,303
3. African Union Methodist Protestant	128	90	3,887
4. Colored Methodist Episcopal	2,299	2,376	214,987
5. Congregational Methodist	415	425	24,000
6. Congregation Methodist (Colored)	305	5	419
7. Free Methodist	1,044	1,068	30,271
8. Evangelist Missionary	72	47	3,014
9. Independent Methodist	8	15	2,569
10. Methodist Episcopal	17,109	27,340	1,910,779
11. Methodist Episcopal, South	6,616	15,209	1,595,014
12. Methodist Protestant	1,551	2,242	183,894
13. New Congregational Methodist	238	417	4,021
14. Primitive	74	100	6,976
15. Wesleyan Methodist	402	556	17,909

Divisions	Ministers	Churches	Members
16. Union American Methodist Episcopal	138	255	18,500
17. Zion Union Apostolic (ZUAC)*	30	32	2,346
Total Methodists	40,278	58,659	5,429,912

*The Zion Union Apostolic Church (ZUAC) was organized in 1870 at Boydton, Mecklenburg County, Virginia. Within five years the church virtually disintegrated due to an unsatisfactory episcopal election, as viewed by some members. Many followed their bishop and James Solomon Russell joining the Episcopal Church in 1878. Others reorganized in 1882 to become the Reformed Zion Union Apostolic Church (RZUA). The RZUA continues as a small but vibrant church located primarily on the Southside of Virginia and bordering North Carolina counties.

Source: Henry T. Besse, *Church History*, (Cleona, PA: Holzapfel Publishing, 1909), 230.

D. Virginia Legislative Assembly African-American Membership, 1872–1892

Legislative Session	Senators #/out of ##	House of Delegates	It is reasonable to assume that for these years the Virginia Senate about 40 Senators and 100 Delegates in the Commonwealth's General Assembly
1870–71* (1869 election)	6/??	21/??	*See quote below from autobiography of James Solomon Russell
1872–73	ND	ND	(ND) No Distinction of race made in State Almanac
1873–74	3/40	17/132	
1874–75	3/40	17/??	
1875–76	3/??	13/??	
1876–77	3/??	12/??	
1877–78	3/??	4/??	Note: scholars and historians generally agree that Radical Reconstruction ended in 1877
1878–79	3/??	4/??	
1879–80	ND	ND	
1880–81	ND	ND	
1881–82	ND	ND	
1882–83	ND	ND	
1883–84	3/??	8/??	
1884–85	1/??	7/100	
1885–86	1/39	1/100	
1886–87	1/?	1/?	
1887–88	1/?	7/??	
1888–89	1/??	3/??	

Legislative Session	Senators #/out of ##	House of Delegates
1889–90	1/??	3/??
1890–91	1/??	3/??
1891–92	0/??	0/??

Compiled by Worth E. Norman, Jr. (2010)

  *On page 29 of Russell's autobiography he writes (*emphasis added*), "Her [Russell's wife's] father [Peter G. Morgan of Petersburg, Virginia] was one of the *twenty-five Negroes who were delegates to the Constitutional Convention* which was convened on December 3, 1867, in Richmond, to reestablish civil government in Virginia (*eighty of the delegates were white*). Later he represented Petersburg in the first General Assembly after the State's reentry into the Union. Mr. Morgan was one of those who *fought to keep the words, "white" or "black" from appearing in the constitution,* and he was a member of the committee which made the report authorizing the establishment of a system of public free schools. The convention continued its labors until it had completed a constitution for the State. Incidentally this document lasted longer than any other Southern Reconstruction constitution, not falling victim to changes and amendments until 1902. On July 6, 1869, an election was held as ordered by President Grant. Gilbert Walker was elected Governor and the constitution ratified by a vote of 210,585 against 9,136. *In this same election, six Negroes were elected to the State Senate and twenty-one to the House of Delegates,* a total of twenty-seven Negro members of the First General Assembly following the War Between the States and the black man's emancipation."

  Sources: *The Journal of Negro History* 5, No. 1 (Jan. 1920): pp. 63, 118, 119 as found in http://www.jstor.org/stable/2713503, viewed on September 9, 2009; Russell, James Solomon, *Adventure in Faith,* New York: Morehouse, 1936.

  These data are taken from a letter to Dr. Monroe N. Work, Tuskegee, Alabama, dated September 26, 1916. Dr. Work was the editor of *The Journal of Negro History* at that time.

  The writer of the letter was H.R. McIlwaine, State Librarian for the Commonwealth of Virginia. The documentation used by McIlwaine was not the *Journals of the Senate and House of Delegates* but state almanacs, though he said they were unreliable. According to McIlwaine, 1869 "was the first year in which Negroes were allowed to hold office in Virginia."

  This particular *Journal of Negro History* (Vol. 5, No. 1: January 1920) contains similar information for other Southern states. The entry for the state of South Carolina is quite voluminous and interesting. But Virginia is cited here because of the environment lived in by James Solomon Russell and his fellow ex-slaves in the Southside of Virginia. The number of Negro state senators and representatives declined as the "Jim Crow" era took effect. Similarly, the Sewanee bishops' action regarding the creation of colored convocations in their dioceses could be seen as parallel in intent.

E. Social Uplift Address, 1919

  Given on November 13, 1919, at the Reconstruction and Readjustment Congress in Washington, D.C., on the day after the inauguration of J. Stanley Durkee as president of Howard University. Transcribed and edited by Worth E. Norman, Jr.

Social Uplift in the Church

Archdeacon J.S. Russell, Lawrenceville, Virginia; Principal, St. Paul's Normal and Industrial Institute

The Church has always exerted a dominating influence on Negro thoughts and ideals. His first concrete expression of race consciousness after emancipation, found its ideal in the building of Churches and the development of denominational activities. It would be strange indeed if the Church did not occupy the chief place in Negro life. Almost coincidentally with his landing on American soil the Church began its work of civilization and evangelization. Only four years after his advent at Jamestown, we read in the parish register of old Bruton Parish that, Anthony and Isabel, and William, their child, slaves of Capt. Wm. Tucker, were baptized in Jamestown. In 1671, we find the Bishop of London addressing an inquiry to clergy of those parishes, asking what steps were being taken to give religious instruction to the slaves and infidels (irreligious).

The Church was the Negro's first mentor. It is to her he owes his first baptism; his first Christian marriage and first burial, his first emancipation from the darkness of African fetishism and superstition into the marvelous light of the Gospel. The Church, through its teachings, secured for him, mitigation from rigors of slavery. Small wonder, then, that he should look to her for guidance and deliverance. To him the Church was all; it represented not only future hope of salvation, but present deliverance. Throughout all the long lark night of slavery his faith in the Church and in her teachings kept him buoyed up with the hope of the expected day, which his faith told him would come. His whole life centered around the Church.

About the only gatherings freely allowed him were Church and prayer meetings. Many Churches up to the Civil War had galleries for Negroes. On nearly every plantation there was a preacher or leader of the prayer meeting. These meetings, religious in character, provided also in many instances the only social opportunity and recreation. Under such circumstances and conditions it was natural and inevitable that the Church should become the dominating influence in Negro life, and happily so, too. The whole life of the Negro shows this influence. No where is it interpreted more freely than in his songs, which in most cases expressed the burden of his desires— ultimate freedom. This subtle religious vein is what gives Negro spirituals their chief charm, for in them was given articulation to the hopes, fears and joys of his life, both present and future. Never has there been the tragedy and yearnings of a people's very souls more faithfully portrayed than in the weirdly beautiful haunting and often pathetic music of Negro spirituals.

As the Church is the center around which the whole fabric of Negro life is built, it is pertinent to consider how this influence is exerted and how far the Church is actually realizing and making use of its opportunity. It was natural that only the spiritual side should have been considered at first. Home life, so

essential to a proper development of social life, was lacking in the life of the
Negro during slavery. Social pleasures were few. The great moments of his life
was Christmas, when he was allowed a holiday and to engage in the simple
diversions of his nature. Christmastide was the one oasis in his life, then he
was free to visit and to have unheard of feats in his cabin. The doors of the
"Great House" stood ajar and "Ole Marster" and "Ole Missis" distributed gifts.
Aside from Christmas, his only social opportunity was at Church. There he
could mingle with his fellows and after church exchange the small gossip of the
day. The preacher was looked up to as the prophet and oracle. To him they
went for advice and counsel. The Church was all to him. To no people, with
the possible exception of the Jews, has the Church meant more.

The Civil War left the Negro free, but he had neither home life not social
life. His perspective was bounded on all sides by the blight of slavery. Its practices and institutions still influenced him. It was necessary for him to develop
both home and social life of which he had none. Naturally he turned to the
Church as his teacher. Along with his little log cabin, he built a Church, often
of logs, but frequently frame when he could. Thus, Church and home life were
the first developments of freedom. Concrete expression of this was found in
the character of the Churches oftener than in the homes. The best and most
pretentious building in the community was always the Church and the Church
became the center of community activities, religious on Sunday and secular on
week days. Ministers became the natural leaders of the people. It was through
the Church that the first impulse for better home life and improved social conditions came. Improved home life brought the desire for better social conditions,
a more highly developed social order, the refinements and embellishments of
civilized life, and a society with a back ground of high morality, culture, intelligence, sobriety and pure religion.

Fifty years of freedom has seen steady progress toward the attainment of
this goal. Social uplift has made great strides in the last two decades. Our homes
have become a measure of our social progress. Our Churches are generally well
built and some of them will vie [with] some of the best in the land. Up until
the war period [World War I] we were enveloped in a cloak of complacency.
We thought we were getting along very well. Our Churches were splendid structures. Our children were in school, we were getting ahead in property and some
of us were gathering up some of this world's goods. We were not particularly
concerned as to the exact particulars, some things of course were going wrong,
but the main, all was well, and why worry? Then the war came and then the
revelation. Our cloak of complacency was torn rudely asunder and we saw ourselves revealed in our nakedness.

Illiteracy, infidelity, inefficiency, inertia and almost every other "in," "ism"
and "il" under the sun, stalked among us. We found that our Churches were
losing ground; that their leadership in social uplift was declining; that our educational, farming and business methods were wasteful; that as a people, we

were illy [sic] prepared to meet the new conditions brought about by the great war. As the war has revealed our nakedness, the next question is what are we going to do about it? Social uplift is the first problem. Only highly developed peoples with highly specialized ideas of social and material development and uplift can now hope to succeed. Old creeds, old ideas and old standards have been wiped out of existence. The present is the day of efficiency and accomplishment. The world is not particularly concerned now with the color of a man's skin or the kink of his hair, but rather with what he knows and what he can do. Nation, people, or individual must rise or fall by this standard.

Social uplift translated into terms of the present day means social efficiency. The pertinence of this term to the Church is that the Church is not only our largest religious, but also our chief social and business institution. The business, administrative, executive and financial ability of the Negro has been shown to a greater advantage in his Church work than in any other capacity. Our Church property is worth millions of dollars and the sums raised and expended annually in our churches amount to huge proportions. We may well inquire then, what is the Church doing for social efficiency or uplift? This inquiry naturally divides itself into two heads: First, the purely Negro Churches; second, Negro Churches organically and officially connected with White Churches. To this a third division must be added — the general church or church at large. The first group, Methodists and Baptists, is raising money for general Missionary and Church work. The scope is planned to take in their educational institutions and extension and social work. In many localities, their Churches are realizing the need of Church leadership, establishing social group work and through community houses and settlement projects, endeavoring to play their part in meeting new conditions. Of course, money is their handicap. And perhaps the sense of realization is not as great in all cases as it should be. But it must be remembered in this connection, that their membership represents in great part those who have to toil for their daily bread, and it is out of their earnings that sums must come for their work, and what they are doing most probably represents sacrifice to a commendable degree.

The second group comprises the Negro contingents of White Church organizations, Methodist Episcopal, Presbyterians, Episcopalians. These are all raising sums in connection with the parent Church, sums that are creditable alike to their generosity and spirit of sacrifice. For instance, the contribution of the Negro element in the Episcopal Church Nation-wide Campaign is planned to be large. Presbyterians and Methodists are also adding the quota.

The general group, the Methodist, Baptist, Presbyterians, Episcopalians, and other denominational parts of this group are raising over $100,000,000 to their Nationwide movements to be applied to Missionary and Church effort. The Negro is to be the beneficiary for educational and Church work to the extent of millions. One branch of the Presbyterian Church will spend over $400,000 alone of Negro education. The Methodists plan the expenditure of

Summary of Official Acts	1905	1906	1907	1908	1909	1910	1911	1912	1913	1917	1918	1919	1920	1921	1922	1923	1924
# Public services, not incl. daily services at School	106	117	123	111	101	121	154	123	156	113	102	92	115	131	110	81	112
# Sermons and addresses	92	80	112	135	108	134	158	132	164	130	122	116	119	167	132	91	165
# Public addresses out of the Diocese in the interest of our Church and educational work	19	16	7	10	23	18	11	35	11	19	38	31	26	21	15	53	73
# Catechisings of Sunday school			22	26	18	19	17	21	19	17	20	17	19	27	22	19	20
# Private services in sick rooms	10	24	33	2	4												
# Private celebrations of HC in sick rooms								3	4	3	2	1	1	3	1	2	2
# Visits to sick in hospital and private homes					69	59	54	58	56	21	27	16	45	85	48	21	48
# Public celebrations of HC	35	34	32	24	29	48	39	36	44	32	20	15	19	24	25	15	22
# Baptisms—adults & infants	9	41	11	22													
# Baptisms—adults					12	7	7	18	20	13	3	3	4	6	9	5	3
# Baptisms—infants					14	16	17	12	7	6	4	6	7	21	11	13	7
Presided at Church and educational meetings					55	49	57	50	80	55	57	55	40	66	41	27	83
Presented for confirmation at St. Paul's, Lawrenceville					31	31		24	21								
Number of marriages	5	4	3	3	6	3	3	3	7	5	3	4	4	6	5	2	3
# Funerals	6	3	4	5	9	5	4	6	10	3	5	5	7	10	7	3	11
Assisted at Consecration of Churches and Ordination Services								2		3	3	1	2	3			3
Attended Educational and religious meetings of importance												12	29	16	38	45	33

hundreds of thousands. The Episcopal Church will expend about $2,000,000 on its Negro Schools. The Baptists' expenditure calls for hundreds of thousands. All these amounts are for education; social work comes in for substantial sums in all the Churches. In addition, millions are to be spent in missions, home and foreign, and in special fields of work. It would certainly appear from the above that the Church in general has a realizing sense of the responsibility and duty placed upon her by present conditions and is making the effort, at least, to meet them.

The world for Christ and its social, material and religious uplift is the war-cry of the Church in answer to the challenge thrown down by the world. For each of us there is a duty and we should perform it faithfully, wholeheartedly and conscientiously. To each of us comes the summons, who will go? Shall the answer of each be "Here am I; send me! Send me!" Only by this personal devotion and consecration added to our common national effort can the world be saved for Christ and this earth made a fit place to live on.

F. Summary of the Official Acts of the Archdeacon for Colored Work

See table on the facing page.

Source: Compiled from "Reports of the Archdeacon for Colored Work" in the Journals of Annual Council of the Episcopal Diocese of Southern Virginia

G. Churches and Missions in the Colored Convocation, Episcopal Diocese of Southern Virginia, 1910ᵃ

1. *All Saints', McKenny[b]
2. *Ascension, Palmer Springs
3. Ascension, Ream's Station
4. Christ, City Point
5. Christ, Houston
6. *Christ, Red Lawn
7. *Epiphany, Blackstone
8. Good Shepherd, Lynchburg
9. *Grace, Diamond Grove
10. Grace, Norfolk
11. Hope Chapel, Manchester
12. Peyton Chapel, Skelton
13. St. Cyprian's, Hampton
14. St. James', Lunenburg C.H.
15. *St. James', Portsmouth
16. *St. James', Warfield
17. St. James the Less, Charlie Hope
18. St. John's New River
19. St. Luke's, Chatham
20. *St. Luke's Edgerton
21. *St. Mark's, Bracey
22. *St. Mary's, LaCrosse
23. *St. Matthew's, South Hill
24. *St. Paul's, Lawrenceville
25. St. Paul's, Newport News
26. *St. Paul's, Union Level
27. St. Phillip's, Bedford City
28. St. Stephen's, Petersburg
29. St. Thomas', Freeman
30. *Trinity, Boydton

31. Trinity, McFarland's
    Total Communicants   1,628
    Total Sunday School Pupils 1,968

[a]James S. Russell, "Annual Report of the Archdeacon for Colored Work," *Journal of Southern Virginia 1910*, 268–70.

[b]Ulysses Russell, "Churches Established by James Solomon Russell," master's thesis, 1926: Appendix A. All churches noted with an asterisk (*) were founded by James S. Russell. Those churches founded after 1910 are St. John's, Forksville; St. Thomas, Totaro; St. Philips', Dillard's Siding; St. James's, Emporia; St. Luke's, Kenbridge; and St. Mark's, Suffolk.

H. General Convention [of the Episcopal Church] Opening Session, Portland, Oregon, 1922

The General Convention opened with the dignity and stateliness characteristic of the Church. Two hundred and fifty vested choiristers [*sic*] led the long procession. After the choir came the long line of bishops led by Dr. Anstice, the venerable secretary, and Dr. Nelson and Dr. Mann with the Bishops marching in the order of their consecration. *A striking picture as they walked side by side in the procession were the Church's two Negro Suffragans, Bishops Demby and Delany, of Arkansas and North Carolina, preceded and followed by their white colleagues*, convincing proof of the catholicity of the Church that knows no distinction of race or creed in her ministrations.

Besides the American Bishops, dignataries [*sic*] of the Eastern Churches in their gorgeous vestments were the cynosure of all eyes. The venerated Presiding Bishop, Bishop Tuttle, brought up the rear of the procession. Fully 5,000 people filled the edifice and joined in singing the opening hymn, "Ancient of Days."

Article from *Southern Missioner* (October, 1922): 150–1.

From *Adventure in Faith* [emphasis added below]:

... I have addressed the General Convention and church organizations of all kinds, traveled in many states, and written thousands of letters, all in the effort to secure the wherewithal to build and maintain the Institution. It has been my good fortune to attend eleven General Conventions of the Church — from 1898–1928 — and on all these occasions, special mass meetings have been held in the interest of the colored schools. Other opportunities also have been afforded the delegates to hear of the work among the colored people. In *1901*, I spoke to the Missionary Mass Meeting in *San Francisco* and was invited by the Woman's Auxiliary of the Diocese of Pennsylvania, to repeat the address at Holy Trinity Church, Philadelphia, a month later. After the *Richmond Convention of 1907*, nearly one hundred of the delegates— bishops, clergymen, laymen and women visited the school. I followed a number of ten-minute speakers at the general mass meetings in the *Cathedral of St. John the Divine in 1913*, but, at the end of my allotted period, several persons in the congregation were on their feet asking an extension of my time for five minutes, and I was accordingly, called back to the pulpit.

In *St. Louis, in 1916,* a special St. Paul's meeting was held at which Francis L. Stetson, the leading layman of the Convention was the speaker. During that I preached at All Saints' Episcopal and at the A.M.E. Zion churches. I addressed several meetings at the *1919 Convention in Detroit,* and while in the Middle West, went to Toledo, Ohio, to preach for the Rev. R.W. Bagnall, Sr., formerly warden at the Bishop Payne Divinity School Petersburg, Va. At *Portland, Oregon, in 1922,* I preached at the colored mission on the first Sunday of the convention, held conferences with many delegates, and was in the audience at the mass meeting of the Woman's Auxiliary when it was announced that a gift made from the United Thank Offering Fund toward the new dormitory for girls at St. Paul's. In *1925, in New Orleans,* a Missionary Mass Meeting was conducted in the interest of the schools for Negroes, and the principals were called upon to make five-minute talks. The Convention in *1928,* the last I attended, was held at the *National Cathedral, Washington, D.C.*

Firing the imagination of the leaders of the Church who attended these Conventions and winning their good-will by bringing them, at first hand, the story of what St. Paul's was and what it hoped to be, was of untold benefit to the School and helped to make hundreds of white Church people better acquainted with the Negro race and to realize their opportunity in the field of human race relations" [pp. 43–44].

I. Southern Virginia Resolution, 2009

2009 RESOLUTION 2

Resolved that the Delegates of the 117th Diocesan Council for the Diocese of Southern Virginia meeting in Annual council on February 13 and 14 2009 in Williamsburg Virginia, reaffirm resolution 7A adopted at the 104th (October 12, 1996) Annual Council of the Diocese of Southern Virginia submitted by The Liturgical Commission of the Diocese and submit a version calling for commemoration of The Ven. James Solomon Russell in the book ***Lesser Feast and Fasts***; Resolution 7A—104th Annual Council

RESOLVED, that the Fall Session of the One Hundred Fourth Annual Council of the Diocese of Southern Virginia hereby adopts and designates James Solomon Russell (Priest and Archdeacon) as one to be commemorated as a child of God worthy of remembrance in the Episcopal Church;

BE IT FURTHER RESOLVED, that March 28 of each year (except when displaced by Sunday, the days of Holy Week, Easter Week, or other Feasts designated by the Episcopal Church) be designated as the Feast of James Solomon Russell, for observance by congregations throughout the Episcopal Church.

BE IT FURTHER RESOLVED, that the proper for the feast be designated as follows:

Traditional Collect

Almighty God, in thy wisdom thou gavest to thy servant James Solomon Russell the courage to establish a college in which the lives of many are enriched and the truth of thy word is heard: Help us, we pray, to know and trust the power of thy love and follow faithfully where thou dost lead; through Jesus Christ our Lord, who livest and reignest with thee and the Holy Ghost, one God, for ever and ever. Amen.

Contemporary Collect

Almighty God, in your wisdom you gave your servant James Solomon Russell the courage to establish a college in which the lives of many are enriched and the truth of your word is heard: Help us, we pray, to know and trust the power of your love and follow faithfully where you lead; through Jesus Christ our Lord, who lives and reigns with you and the Holy Spirit, one God, for ever and ever. Amen.

Prayer Book Proper

First Lesson: 1 Kings 5:1–12
Psalm 127
Gospel: John 14:8–14
Preface of a Saint 1

Rationale

James Solomon Russell, known as the father of St. Paul's College, Lawrenceville, VA (one of the three historically Black Episcopal Colleges) was the founder of numerous congregations, a missionary, writer, and unique figure in the Virginia Episcopal Church. He was the first student of the Bishop Payne Divinity School, located at St. Stephen's Petersburg, VA. For his 52 years of ordained ministry in the Diocese of Southern Virginia, he worked tirelessly to encourage black candidates to enter Holy Orders so that they could care for growing numbers of black Episcopalians. In 1893, Russell was named the first Archdeacon for Colored Work. Southern Virginia had the largest population of black Episcopalians in the United States, thanks in large measure to the evangelistic efforts of the Rev. James S. Russell. In 1900 there were 30 Black Congregations. In 1917, Dr. Russell was the first African American elected Bishop in the Episcopal Church; however, he declined election in both Dioceses of Arkansas and North Carolina as Suffragan Bishop of Colored Work, and was glad that his action helped to defeat the idea of subordinate racial bishops. Dr. Russell was the first African American to be elected a member of a Department of the National Council of the Episcopal Church. Near the end of his life, Virginia Seminary, which he was unable to attend in his early years, conferred an honorary degree on him. His ministry continued until his death on March 28, 1935. James Solomon Russell's devotion to Christ's ministry in times and circumstances far from ideal was an inspiration to thousands of lives he touched.

Prepared for the 76th General Convention [2009] of The Episcopal Church

RESOLVED, that the 76th General Convention include The Venerable Archdeacon James Solomon Russell in the book of ***Lesser Feasts and Fasts***, using the date of March 28, the end of his earthly life, to be a day to commemorate him as a child of God worthy of remembrance, and

BE IT FURTHER RESOLVED, That the following proper be considered for that feast day:

Traditional Collect
Almighty God, in thy wisdom thou gavest to thy servant James Solomon Russell the courage to establish a college in which the lives of many are enriched and the truth of thy word is heard: Help us, we pray to know and trust the power o they love and follow faithfully where thou dost lead; through Jesus Christ our Lord, who livest and reignest with thee and the Holy Ghost, one God, for ever and ever. Amen.

Contemporary Collect
Almighty God, in your wisdom you gave your servant James Solomon Russell the courage to establish a college in which the lives of many are enriched and the truth of your word is heard: Help us, we pray, to know and trust the power of your love and follow faithfully where you lead; through Jesus Christ our Lord, who lives and reigns with you and the Holy Spirit, one God, for ever and ever. Amen.

Prayer Book Proper
First Lesson: 1 Kings 5:1–12
Psalm 127
Gospel: John 14:8–14
Preface of a Saint 1

Submitted by The Diocese of Southern Virginia and The Union of Black Episcopalians Chapter of Southern Virginia, with edits by author.

J. Secular Education Funds for Negro Schools in the South, 1860s–1920s

American Church Institute for Negroes
   Established in 1906 (ACIN tried to emulate the GEB)
General Education Board (GEB)
   Established in 1902
Jeanes Fund
   Established in 1901
Ogden Movement
   A group of philanthropists who beginning around 1900 sought to impose an education strategy to change the South

Peabody Fund
  Established in 1867
Phelps-Stokes Fund
  Established 1911
Rosenwald Fund
  Organized in 1917
Slater Fund
  Established in 1881
Southern Education Board (SEB)
  Established in 1901

"The work of the missionary societies [Congregational, Methodist, Presbyterians, and Baptist] was at first supplemented, and then ultimately overshadowed, by secular foundations. The Peabody Fund (established in 1867) and the Slater Fund (created in 1881) promoted southern education as 'a patriotic duty that could not well be shirked without disaster,' in the words of the millionaire merchant John F. Slater. This more secular motivation for the educational philanthropy reached fuller elaboration, under more complex organization, in the early twentieth century. The establishment of the General Education Board in 1902 marked a new phase in foundation philanthropy. Endowed with $33 million in Rockefeller gifts during its first decade of operation, the GEB was committed to the ideal of 'scientific' and efficiently organized philanthropy significantly different from the goals and organization of earlier donor groups. Rejecting 'sentimental' giving that responded to mere symptoms, these 'new philanthropists' believed they could eliminate the root causes of social problems through research and the careful application of insights."

Dangerous Donations, 5.

"The new philanthropists recognized that black leaders would probably be disappointed with the slow pace of progress, as well as the new emphasis on white education, but considered their criticisms less important, under the circumstances, than the views of the 'best whites.' As Robert C. Ogden, one of the most influential northern friends of Negro education, put it, 'We cannot meet the views of our colored friends and must be content to be greatly misunderstood for the sake of the largest usefulness.'"

Dangerous Donations, 41

K. Conclusion of the Report of the Committee on the State of the Church, 1907

"The Archdeacon [J.S. Russell] states that the colored clergy and laity of the Diocese are entirely pleased, with their present Bishop [A.M. Randolph], and do not ask for missionary jurisdiction and colored Bishops to preside over the same. Southern Virginia has the largest colored Church and educational work of any other Southern Diocese, and it has on more than one occasion in its Convocation placed itself on record as opposing the memorial from the Conference of Church Workers to the General Convention so long as they receive the regular visitations and cordial consideration of the Bishop and Bishop-Coadjutor of the Diocese, they pray that the present tie which binds the white and colored Churchmen together in God's Church be not severed. They welcome the Counsel and advice of their white brethren, and they do not want any severance of this bond of union."

> Rev. Arthur C. Thomson
> Rev. J.F. Ribble
> Rev. Martin Johnson
> Rev. Reuben Meredith
> Rev. James S. Russell
> Mr. R.O. Egerton
> Mr. George H. Nash
> Mr. H.C. Page
> Mr. B.W. Stras
> Mr. Wm. M. Boyd

Journal of the Annual Council of the Episcopal Diocese of Southern Virginia, May 1907, 50.

L. Statistics of the Two Episcopal Dioceses in Virginia, 1892

	Proposed Diocese of Virginia (restructured 1892)	Proposed Diocese of Southern Virginia (new 1892)
Clergy, white	76	55
Clergy, colored	3	10
Communicants, white	9,464	9,120
Communicants, colored	148	1,156
Contingent fund	$6,880.47	$5,362.65
All funds	$163,762.79	$142,42.32
Contributed to Diocesan Missionary Society, white	6,748.50	5,086.80
Contributed to Diocesan Missionary Society, colored	———	31.77
Received from Diocesan Missionary Society, white	3,695.00	3,760.84
Received from Diocesan Missionary Society, colored	15.00	1,183.75
Parishes	72	68
Congregations, white	145	131

	Proposed Diocese of Virginia (restructured 1892)	Proposed Diocese of Southern Virginia (new 1892)
Congregations, colored	3	18
Charges, white	69	57
Charges, colored	3	9
Vacant, white	12	18
Self-supporting, white	34	27
Self-supporting, colored	—	1
Population 1890, white	365,701	648,979
Population 1890, colored	241,617	399,250
Population 1880, white	329,063	551,795
Population 1880, colored	245,199	386,117
Counties	42	58
Square miles	12,691	27,431
Clergy 1880, white	68	47
Clergy 1880, colored	1	1
Communicants 1880, white	7,085	5,875
Communicants 1880, colored	18	196
Increase in communicants, white	33%	55%
Increase in population, white	36,638	97,181
Decrease in population, colored	3,582	12,833
Dioceses with fewer communicants	35	37

Source: *Journal of the Annual Council of the Protestant Episcopal Church in the Diocese of Virginia, 1892,* 52.

M. "A Tribute to Lewis Morris," a Poem by Goronwy Owens

Though it is a long-protracted journey from this
country there [to Britain]
Across the white-foamed ocean
The wretchedness of bad tidings
Is not hindered by land or mitigated by waves.

Waves of flowing tears run over my face
For a noble, faithful friend;
I have grown grey with losses,
It has been a chilling journey to this land.

The land of woods and of wild hills, the forested land
Of every kind of heinous insect,
The ugly land of murderous people —
Indians, strange lot, I am sorry to say.

Goronwy Owens was an Anglican priest from Wales who lasted only six months in 1761 as rector of St. Andrew's Parish in Lawrenceville, Brunswick

County, Virginia. There were no bishops in Colonial Virginia to protect Anglican priests. Vestries controlled every manner of church life including hiring and firing of priests. There was no love lost between Owens, the vestry, and the congregation. When Owens received the news of the death of his friend and tutor, Lewis Morris, he wrote this ode. Although a memorial to Morris, Owens wrote of unfavorable sentiments about Brunswick. More than a century later, James Solomon Russell would be assigned as a new deacon to St. Andrew's Parish.

Owens is revered as one of the best writer in the Welsh language.

Source: Janet Gay Neale, *Brunswick County, Virginia 1720–1975: The History of a Southside County* (Lawrenceville: The Brunswick County Bicentennial Committee, 1975), 89–93.

N. Brief Biographies

Richard Allen. Founder of the African Methodist Episcopal Church.

Samuel Chapman Armstrong. The founder of Hampton Institute in Virginia. A former brevet general in the Union Army during the Civil War, he founded the school for former slaves with the aid of the American Missionary Society. Russell wrote that his college training was under the direction of this Union Army general and his seminary education under a Confederate Army major.

Joseph Atwell. St. Stephen's Church in Petersburg, Virginia, was one of the oldest churches in the United States for colored churchmen. Its first colored rector and the first colored priest in the Diocese of Virginia was Atwell, who came some years after the Civil War from the Church of Our Merciful Saviour, Louisville, Kentucky. (See Giles Buckner Cooke, below.)

John E. Baird. In 1898 two staunch churchmen and friends of Russell in Philadelphia, John E. Baird and T. Broom Belfield, contributed $1,000 each to purchase a large parcel of land for St. Paul's College.

David Batchelder. The first teacher in the Freedmen's Bureau School in 1866 in an old hotel in Lawrenceville. A native of Vermont, he taught for only one year. Russell cites in his *Autobiography* early attempts at education after the end of the Civil War.

T. Broom Belfield. In 1898 two staunch churchmen and friends of Russell in Philadelphia, John E. Baird and T. Broom Belfield, contributed $1,000 each to purchase a large parcel of land for St. Paul's College.

Mary Benson. It was at a meeting of the Women's Auxiliary of the Diocese of Long Island that Russell first met Miss Mary Benson of Brooklyn, New York. She was a financial contributor to St. Paul's starting in 1897. Her gifts provided for the construction of the Long Island Domestic Science Building and in 1914 had contributed toward the construction of the Long Island boys' dormitory. When the domestic science building was first opened in 1898, Miss Benson herself turned the keys in the door.

Samuel H. Bishop. The first executive director of the American Church Institute for Negroes (ACIN) of the Episcopal Church. At one point in his tenure he attempted to oust Russell as principal of the St. Paul School. One method used was to get Russell out of the country, so he sent Russell to England in 1911 (all expenses paid) to get a "much deserved rest."

James Blair. A Scotsman and member of the clergy who refused to recognize James II, the Catholic king, as sovereign. In 1685 the bishop of London, Henry Compton, sent Blair to the Virginia colony as his agent or commissary. Blair became a powerful political figure and founded the College of William and Mary. Blair's political exploits, both secular and religious, provide a backdrop for the future structure of the post-colonial Episcopal Church.

N. Peterson Boyd. Brooklyn, New York, rector of St. Philip's Episcopal Church. He was a native of Mecklenburg County, Virginia, and a friend of Russell. Mary Benson was responsible for getting Boyd the St. Philip's appointment.

George Freeman Bragg, Jr. An Episcopal priest in Virginia and author of many books including the *Afro-American in the Episcopal Church*. He was editor of a church magazine and rector of St. James–Baltimore. He was a proponent of an all-black jurisdiction within the Episcopal Church, an issue that Russell opposed.

Felix R. Brunot. Of Pittsburgh, Pennsylvania, Brunot contributed funds for land purchases for St. Paul's College after hearing of Russell's land purchase activities in 1898.

Corbin Braxton Bryan. Dean of the Branch Divinity School (Bishop Payne Divinity School) from June 1903 to March 1922.

John Stewart Bryan. Editor of the *Richmond News Leader* newspaper and covered Russell and the St. Paul School for many years.

Edward P. Buford. A former commonwealth's attorney and member of the Virginia House of Delegates. He said "For more than twenty-five years I was prosecuting attorney for this [Brunswick] county and, during all that time, I never had any charge to come up against any student or the management of St. Paul's School."

Francis Emmet Buford. Pattie Buford's husband. After serving as an officer in a Brunswick County regiment (Confederate) during the Civil War, he became an attorney and later a judge. He fully supported the work of his wife. He founded the *Brunswick Times* newspaper after his wife's death.

Martha "Pattie" Hicks Buford. From a wealthy Lawrenceville family, she maintained a hospital for colored people in Lawrenceville and introduced Russell to Bishop Whittle of the Episcopal Diocese of Virginia. She was often ridiculed by her white peers for her work with slaves and former slaves.

Oscar Bunting. Immediately preceding Dr. Bryan's election as first dean of the Branch Divinity School, Bunting was principal. Russell said that Dr. Bunting impressed everyone as being in the largest sense a priest in the Church of God, and a soldier in the Church Militant.

A.C. Burbank (Mr. & Mrs.). Succeeded David Batchelder as teachers in the

Freedmen's Bureau School in Lawrenceville. The Burbanks were from Maine. It appears that Russell wanted to make the point that, not only was there an earlier attempt at educating former slaves (before the founding of St. Paul's) in Lawrenceville, but the instructors came from the North.

Thomas W. Cain. At the time of Russell's ordination, Cain was placed in charge of St. Philip's Mission in Richmond. Cain and J.H.M. Pollard were the other two black clergymen in the Diocese of Virginia. Cain eventually went to Galveston, Texas, where he died in the flood of 1900, the storm surge of a great hurricane.

William E. Cameron. Thirty-ninth governor of Virginia from 1882 to 1886 and native of Petersburg. Russell and the Rev. John D. Keiley, one of Russell's former professors, together succeeded in getting Cameron to issue a stay of execution for a father-son duo falsely accused of murder.

Lott Carey. Born into slavery in 1780 near Richmond, Virginia, Carey purchased his freedom in 1813. He mobilized both white and black Baptists into the First Baptist Church of Richmond and he founded the Baptist Missionary Society. He and his family eventually conducted missionary work beginning in 1821 in what is now Liberia. On one of his trips to Africa, James Solomon Russell attended a colorful meeting of the Lott Carey Baptist Convention in Summerville, Liberia.

Mr. Cheeley. A rather distinguished educator, according to Russell, who was employed as tutor to Russell's master's children. On several occasions he would say to Russell's mother, "That boy will someday be a good preacher."

Giles Buckner Cooke. A former major in the Army of the Confederacy, this southern soldier was the rector of St. Stephen's Church, a builder of schools for the emancipated youth, and principal of the St. Stephen's Normal School, to which the Branch Theological Seminary was grafted, with Russell as its entire student body. Major Cooke, the last surviving member of General Robert E. Lee's staff, celebrated his 95th birthday in May 1933. Russell wrote that his college training was under the direction of a Union Army general and his seminary education under a Confederate Army major.

Alexander Crummell. A freeborn African-American, grandson of a west African tribal king, an Episcopal priest, and founder of the American Negro Academy. He served in Liberia for many years and then returned to the United States to rector St. Luke's Episcopal Church in Washington, D.C. He organized an opposition group to the proposed "Sewanee Canon" at the 1883 General Convention of the Episcopal Church. He was a proponent, along with George Freeman Bragg, Jr., of an all-black jurisdiction within the Episcopal Church. Russell opposed the all-black jurisdiction. Crummell was the first African-American to graduate from Cambridge University.

T. Grayson Dashiell. In 1878, in part due to connections with Miss Pattie Buford, Russell met with Dashiell and Alexander Weddell. In Bishop Whittle's (Episcopal Diocese of Virginia) absence these two clergymen examined Russell as a possible student at the newly planned Branch Divinity School (for black men only) in Petersburg. Dashiell was his bishop's intermediary in bringing into the Diocese of Virginia more than 2,000 members of the Zion Union Apostolic Church beginning in 1878. He was also an observer at the Southern bishops' conference in Sewanee, Tennessee, in 1883.

R.A. Deane. One of Russell's daughters, Otelia Virginia, was married to this one-time St. Paul school physician.

Katherine Van Rensselaer Delafield. Made a large donation to the St. Paul School, making it possible to build the school's chapel, the first brick building constructed on campus, in 1904. Mrs. Delafield was from the Episcopal Diocese of Long Island (New York).

Edward T. Demby. Elected bishop suffragan of the Episcopal Diocese of Arkansas and the Southwest. Russell was elected at the first election in 1917 on the first ballot. But Russell declined. Another election was held later in which Demby won, thus becoming the first African-American bishop elected to a continental diocese.

J.J. Dosen. Chief justice of the Liberian Supreme Court. Russell, while visiting Liberia, walked into a session of the court simply to observe. The chief justice stopped the proceedings and asked "the Archdeacon, our friend from the United States," to make a few remarks. Russell did. See Russell's *Autobiography*.

W.E.B. Du Bois. The great African-American leader headed the American delegation to the First Universal Races Congress in London, England, in 1911. Russell attended with his son Alvin. Russell gave no speech and may not have been a delegate. The great debate for African-American education between an industrial format favored by Booker T. Washington and a classical format preferred by Du Bois affected to some degree Russell and the St. Paul School's program.

George W. Edmonds. Followed Benjamin Hicks as a student at the Lawrenceville Freedmen's Bureau School immediately following the end of the Civil War. In his *Autobiography*, Russell conveys to the reader the voracious appetite for education held by former slaves.

Shepherd Randolph Edmonds. A Brunswick County youngster, according to Russell, who walked six miles every day for more than eight years to and from classes at the St. Paul School, at the end graduating as valedictorian of his class. In his *Autobiography*, Russell wrote several inspiring stories about graduates and their successes.

Julia C. Emery. The executive secretary of the Women's Auxiliary of the St. Augustine League. At a meeting of the league at St. Bartholomew's Church in New York City in 1898, Emery talked about the needs of the St. Paul School and, in particular, the importance of a brick chapel. Russell was late to this meeting as there had been a typhoid epidemic and he was sick. He made his own speech once he arrived.

Jennie Fain. Russell's aunt. She wanted him to enter the ministry of the African Methodist Episcopal Church and set up a meeting between Russell and her pastor in Warrenton, North Carolina. At the time Russell was a teenager and lived a few miles north in Palmer Springs, Virginia. But Russell had already made up his mind that he would enter the Episcopal Church.

W.A.R. Goodwin. Twice rector of Bruton Parish Church in Williamsburg, Virginia. He is also known as the "Grandfather of Restored Williamsburg." When serving as rector of St. Paul's Episcopal Church in Rochester, New York, Goodwin invited Russell to preach. From that point a long-term relationship developed between the two priests. Eventually, both Goodwin and Russell were fellow clergy in the Episcopal Diocese of Southern Virginia.

Zabriske Gray. When visiting Hampton Institute he saw Russell working and gave $10.00 to Russell's school work supervisor. When Russell learned the name of his benefactor he vowed to look him up one day. Forty years later Russell located another Zabriske Gray in New York City. At Gray's office Russell learned that the original Gray was a relative and had long since died.

William Mercer Green. The first Bishop of Mississippi in the Episcopal Church. He was chancellor of the University of the South from 1866 to 1887. In April of 1883 he convened a conference of Southern bishops of the Episcopal Church at Sewanee, Tennessee, to discuss "the relation of the Church to the coloured people." The conference produced a proposal to legally separate black Episcopalians into nongeographical dioceses. The proposed canon failed at the church's national, triennial General Convention later that year.

H.C. Greene. A one-time commissioner of revenue for the Commonwealth of Virginia and vice-president of the St. Paul's Farmers' Conference. The Conference was founded by Russell. Russell, in his speeches around the county, always cited statistical evidence of Negro progress in Virginia, using many reports published by Greene.

David H. Greer. One-time bishop of the Episcopal Diocese of New York from 1904 (coadjutor 1904–1908) to 1919 (diocesan 1908–1919) and founding chair in 1906 of the church's American Church Institute for Negroes. Greer, frustrated that many wealthy Episcopal industrialists funded John D. Rockefeller's General Education Board (GEB), founded the American Church Institute for Negroes (ACIN) to funnel off "Episcopal" money for Episcopal schools in the South.

Aaron Hendrick. In his *Autobiography*, Russell writes about visiting his relatives. Russell was raised on the Hendrick estate in Virginia just north of Warrenton, North Carolina. Russell's father Solomon lived on the Russell estate in Warrenton. Father and son had little interaction until the end of the Civil War. Slaves in many instances took the surnames of their owners.

Benjamin J. Hicks. The first student at the post–Civil War Freedmen's Bureau School in Lawrenceville, Virginia.

Judge D.S. Hicks. Of Robert Turnbull and Hicks, a local judge, Russell wrote that they were "both typical of white Virginians who have befriended every movement for the advancement of the Negro." Russell continued: "Judge D.S. Hicks and I became staunch friends and, notwithstanding the fact that he was considered an atheist, he frequently invited me to his residence to discuss religious and contemporary topics with him."

Ada Hogan. A donor from Duluth, Minnesota, who contributed to the St. Paul School after learning of Russell's first major land purchase. They never met.

James R. Howell. The first president, and later bishop, of the Zion Union Apostolic Church. In April 1869, the New Yorker traveled to the Southside of Virginia to help establish the Zion Unions. At that time he was an elder (minister) in the African Methodist Episcopal Zion Church.

General Thomas J. "Stonewall" Jackson. An instructor at Virginia Military Institute and Confederate general. Giles Buckner Cooke, Russell's first seminary professor, studied under Jackson at VMI.

Absalom Jones. The first black man to be ordained to the priesthood. Ordained in 1795 a deacon at St. Thomas African Episcopal Church (originally named St. Thomas the Apostle Church) in Philadelphia by Bishop White of Pennsylvania. Jones was ordained to the priesthood in 1804 by Bishop White. Jones and others struggled for many years with the Episcopal Diocese to gain full acceptance into the mostly white denomination.

John D. Keiley. An instructor at the Branch Divinity School (later Bishop Payne Divinity School). He taught Russell Hebrew, Greek and Latin. Russell wrote that Keiley spoke seventeen different tongues. A Roman Catholic, Keiley tagged Russell "James the Just."

Charles R. King. One of the members of the first Board of Trustees of St. Paul's College. The first meeting was held in 1893 at the bishop's residence in Richmond, Virginia.

Robert E. Lee. A West Point Military Academy graduate and the famous Virginia and Confederate General of the Army of Northern Virginia. Giles Buckner Cooke, and Confederate Army major and then the first principal of Branch Seminary, served on Lee's staff during the American Civil War.

B.A. Lewis. A former Virginia commonwealth's attorney who spoke at St. Paul's College on March 9, 1931— the first Founder's Day celebration. He honored Russell by saying, "I value the advice of Archdeacon Russell so highly that I do not hesitate to call on him for advice when members of his race are brought to court. I discuss with him whether leniency should be shown or to what extent the full penalty of the law should be imposed and I never fail to act on his counsel."

Dr. N.C. Lewis. A long-time school physician at St. Paul's School and large landowner. Sold Russell a large tract of land for the school in 1890. See Russell's *Autobiography*.

Arthur Selden Lloyd. A bishop of the Episcopal Church during Russell's career. Once when giving a speech in Lawrenceville he referred to the town as "Russellville." Most listeners thought he made a mistake, but Lloyd said that he made no mistake. It was a salute to James Solomon Russell and his accomplishments and service to the town.

Mary Fletcher Mackie. At Hampton Institute, Mackie conducted entrance examinations to both Russell and Booker T. Washington. Stern, but well-beloved, she multi-tasked many duties at the school. According to Russell she was that rare person who, though professional, showed a human heart. That observation is more indicative of Russell than of Mackie.

William Meade. The third bishop of the Episcopal Diocese of Virginia. Often misunderstood, he preached without notes. In his *Autobiography*, Russell wrote that Meade did understand that the large number of Negroes in south central Virginia presented a "problem" to the church. Much of Meade's attitude on race in his era reflected the generally-held white belief. Meade believed that the church was universal and there was a full place in it for all races, but whites were the superior race. As a priest he was the last person ordained by Bishop James Madison (second cousin to the president), the first bishop of Virginia. Meade, as a priest, was an agent for the American Colonization Society, a position he eventually rejected. Ironically, during the Civil War, Meade, as the senior bishop in the separated Episcopal Church of the Confederate States (along with bishops Johns and Davis), irregularly consecrated Richard Hooker Wilmer as bishop of Alabama. Eight days later Meade died.

Armistead Miller. Owned and operated a small private school in Palmer Springs, Virginia. Russell was admitted in 1868. This was one of several educational experiences in Russell's young life that he summarizes with fondness in his *Autobiography*.

J.P. Morgan. In 1912 the St. Paul School had an $80,000 debt and the ACIN threatened closure of the school. Russell, learning that the philanthropist J.P. Morgan was in London, wrote to the industrialist asking for financial help. Morgan provided the last $10,000 if the other funds were raised.

Peter G. Morgan. Russell's father-in-law. A former slave who bought himself out of slavery in installments, became one of 25 delegates to the Commonwealth of Virginia's state constitutional convention after the end of the Civil War. He was later elected to a seat in the state's legislative assembly. According to Russell, Morgan fought to keep any mention of race or color out of the new Virginia Constitution. He succeeded.

Virginia Michigan Morgan. The wife of James Solomon Russell. They were married in the same year of his ordination to the diaconate. An accomplished organist, she and Russell developed what is now St. Paul's College.

Robert Russa Moton. Like Russell and Booker T. Washington, he was a native of Virginia and attended Hampton Institute. Moton succeeded Washington at Tuskegee Institute in Alabama and became president of Hampton Institute later in life. He founded the Negro Organization Society in 1912 at Hampton, a program for the state of Virginia similar to Russell's St. Paul's Farmers' Conference in Brunswick County. He and Russell attended the First Universal Races Congress in London in 1911.

Robert C. Ogden. The titular leader of the movement that bears his name. The Ogden Movement was a small group of Northern white philanthropists who proposed and enacted a secularly oriented program for Southern education in the early decade of the twentieth century. The central and most dominant organization in the movement was the General Education Board.

W.H. Overs. Bishop of Liberia when Russell made his last trip overseas in 1922. Bishop Overs was Russell's host and made sure that Russell's stay was pleasant. Russell wrote that Liberia was created by America as a possible solution to slavery but that Liberia was its own equal nation under the protection of America.

Goronwy Owens. He is revered in Wales as one of the best poets of the Welsh language. An Anglican priest, he survived only six months in 1761 as rector of St. Andrew's Parish in Lawrenceville, Virginia. He and another priest were recommended for the position by Virginia Governor Francis Fauquier. The other priest lasted only on 10 weeks. The church vestry and congregation were hard to please. Owens disliked Brunswick and Lawrenceville so much that he wrote an unflattering ode. (See Appendix M.)

Robert Treat Paine. Of Boston, Massachusetts, and a relative and namesake of the signer of the Declaration of Independence, Paine often contributed financial support to the St. Paul School.

Robert W. Patton. The second executive director of the American Church Institute for Negroes. In the national church office of the Episcopal Church, in addition to his ACIN duties Patton was responsible for a nationwide fundraising campaign. That campaign took up most of Patton's time. Unlike his predecessor Samuel Bishop, Patton held no animosity against Russell and assisted the St. Paul School in many ways.

John Payne. A white American, Payne was the first Bishop of Liberia. The church in Liberia was a province of the American Episcopal Church. The Branch Divinity School in Petersburg, Virginia (a branch of the Virginia Theological Seminary in Alexandria), was renamed as Bishop Payne Divinity School.

George Foster Peabody. A former investment banker, the philanthropist was a member of the initial Board of Trustees of the American Church Institute for Negroes. Peabody was also active in the Southern Education Board and the Rockefeller's General Education Board (GEB). All of the organizations were founded to assist in the funding of schools in the South for former slaves and their children.

J.H.M. Pollard. At the time Russell was ordained, Pollard and Thomas Cain were the only other colored clergymen in the Episcopal Diocese of Virginia. Both Pollard and Cain attended Russell's ordination to the diaconate in 1882.

Later that year Russell attended his first diocesan convention — Russell, Cain and Pollard were the only African-American clergy.

Frank J. Pope. The nephew of Czarina Russell (no relation to James Solomon Russell). When in Great Barrington, Massachusetts, on a preaching mission, Russell met Pope. W.E.B. Du Bois lived in Great Barrington as a young boy.

Alfred M. Randolph. The first bishop of the newly organized Episcopal Diocese of Southern Virginia in 1892. He appointed James Solomon Russell to the position of Archdeacon for Colored Work.

Julius Rosenwald. The Sears-Roebuck magnate who founded the Rosenwald Fund. The foundation provided funding in support of building projects at St. Paul's.

Czarina Russell. Not a relative of James Solomon Russell, but a regular contributor to the St. Paul School, she lived in Great Barrington, Massachusetts. James Solomon Russell did, however, name one of his daughters Czarina.

Macklin Russell. A minister of the Zion Union Apostolic Church and uncle of James Solomon Russell. Macklin accompanied James on their visit with the Rev. Grayson Dashiell in July 1878 in Lawrenceville.

James Saul. An Episcopal priest and member of a wealthy Philadelphia family. He formed a foundation which provided funds for schools in the South for former slaves and their families. Saul funded a building at the St. Paul School.

Williams Sanders Scarborough. The first African-American scholar of the classics, professor and one-time president of Wilberforce University in Ohio. Along with Du Bois, Moton and Russell, he attended the 1911 First Universal Races Congress in London.

J. Green Shackleford. An Episcopal priest and rector of St. Andrew's Parish in Lawrenceville, Virginia. Shackleford, though still himself a deacon in charge of St. Andrew's, petitioned Bishop Whittle to assign the newly ordained deacon, Russell, to his parish because there was a significant number of African-American congregants.

Thomas Spencer. An Englishman by birth, he was Russell's professor of theology at the Branch Divinity School. According to a report found in the Eighty-seventh Annual Council of the Episcopal Diocese of Virginia in 1882, Spencer instructed and examined Russell in systematic divinity, Greek Testament, church polity, and the Prayer Book, with daily recitations. Spencer also named five seminarians from the Zion Union connection whom he instructed in the Prayer Book and Shinn's Manual.

Francis L. Stetson. A leading layman in the Episcopal Church in the early twentieth century; a member of the first Board of Trustees of the American Church Institute for Negroes; J.P. Morgan's personal attorney, general counsel to J.P. Morgan & Co., and an acquaintance of James Solomon Russell.

Junius L. Taylor. An alumnus of the St. Paul School and one-time rector of St. Philip's Church in Richmond, Virginia. Russell tells the story of Taylor coming to St. Paul's as an illiterate person and rising to a leadership position in the church.

A.C. Thomson. The third bishop of the Episcopal Diocese of Southern Virginia. A bishop suffragan from 1917 to 1919, coadjutor from 1919 to 1930, and diocesan from 1930 to 1937. He presided over several diocesan conventions where resolutions to defeat the "Black Canon" failed.

Robert Turnbull. The first treasurer of the St. Paul School, an attorney-at-law, and later representative from the Fourth Congressional District of Virginia.

A.H. Turner. At one time the business manager of the St. Paul School and husband to Araminta, one of Russell's daughters.

A.T. Twing. General Secretary to the Domestic Missions Department of the Episcopal Church in the 1870s. Miss Pattie Buford wrote letters asking for funds for her schools.

Thomas Wade. The overseer of the Henrick estate when Russell was a boy slave. Wade took a liking to Russell and rode horseback with him, teaching the young and inquisitive boy how the farm operated.

John Walmsley. An Englishman and the ninth Bishop of Sierra Leone hosted Russell on a 1922 trip to Africa.

Booker T. Washington. Founder of Tuskegee Institute in Alabama. Washington and Russell were at Hampton Institute late in Washington's studies and early in Russell's. Both men were influenced by Samuel Chapman Armstrong's model for industrial schools for former slaves. Both men met infrequently during their careers; Washington, as an agent of the Slater Fund, provided financial resources for St. Paul's.

William Watkins. A Lawrenceville landowner whom Russell dealt with to acquire land for the St. Paul School.

Alexander Weddell. He and Grayson Dashiell were the two Episcopal clergymen who met with Russell in 1878 to discern Russell's calling to the priesthood. They met at St. Andrew's Parish in Lawrenceville, which turned out to be Russell's assignment after his diaconal ordination in March 1882.

William White. A former chaplain to the Continental Congress and rector of Christ Church, Philadelphia, in 1782 he wrote and presented *The Case of the Episcopal Churches in the United States Considered*. In that document he set out the potential structure for the new Episcopal Church in the United States. Central to his *Case* were that (a) there would be the three historic orders of clergy — bishops, priests and deacons; and (b) that the church would be democratic in its governance, meaning that both clergy and laity would participate in all church councils. This governance ideal mirrored that of the new United States of America.

Genevieve C. Whitehead. The head of the Training School at the St. Paul School during Russell's tenure.

J. Lyman Whitehead. According to Russell, "the present chief bookkeeper and accountant at St. Paul's is J. Lyman Whitehead, an alumnus, and a graduate of Yale Business College, whose work has won the commendation of the

Church, the General Education Board, and other bodies whose officers have right of way to inspect the books."

Francis McNeese (F.M.) Whittle. The fifth and last bishop of the undivided Episcopal Diocese of Virginia. Like Russell, Whittle was native to Mecklenburg County, Virginia. He was primarily responsible for bringing the Branch Divinity School into existence, and he was the bishop who sent the first colored missionary from the Virginia diocese.

Richard Hooker Wilmer. A Virginian, the only bishop consecrated in the Episcopal Church in the Confederate States in 1863 during the Civil War. His chief consecrator was William Meade, Bishop of Virginia and the senior and presiding bishop of the separated Confederate States church. Later, Wilmer attended the Sewanee Conference of Southern Bishops in 1883 and was the only bishop to dissent from the conclusions and recommendations of that conference.

James R. Winchester. The Bishop of the Episcopal Diocese of Arkansas at the time of Russell's election as bishop suffragan for that same diocese.

Osborne Wingfield. A prominent person of the Reconstruction era, according to Russell, and one of many African-Americans who owned substantial acreage throughout Virginia. Russell in his speeches always provided statistics on the success of the post–Civil War African-American. Winfield owned 250 acres of land. One thousand acres seemed to be the upper limit at that point in history. See Russell's *Autobiography.*

O. Timeline of Significant Events Affecting the Life of Russell

1607   Jamestown settled.

1619   Colonial law becomes operative with creation of Virginia House of Burgesses.

August — twenty Negroes sold to Virginia colonists by pirates. The cargo ship claimed to be under the Duke of Orange, but was not; therefore, as a pirate under international law, its cargo had a protected status as captives, not slaves.

September — one female Negro landed in Jamestown, others rejected by governor.

Church of England becomes established (but no bishops in the colony).

1634   The Virginia Colony is divided into counties by Governor John Harvey.

1649   Negro population in Virginia is 300 — natural growth, not from importation.

Negroes are either indentured servants or free blacks.

No slavery exists, *de facto* nor *de jure.*

1650   Approximate beginning of the Enlightenment or Age of Reason in Europe.

1659   Virginia's colonial assembly legislates in favor of Negro labor; some planters receive large estates through headrights of imported Negroes and whites.

1661   Legislative enactment in Virginia legally recognizes practice of Negro slavery.

1662   An English proprietary company forms solely for the purpose of bringing Negro slaves to Virginia.

1676   Virginia enacts laws to enslave Indians; passed again in 1682.
       Bacon's Rebellion in Virginia Colony.
              Bacon and followers not pleased with colony's friendly Indian policies.

1682   Virginia enacts statute to free slaves born of Christian parents in England, Spain or any other Christian nation.

1683   Royal African Company forces importation of Negroes on Virginia.
       King Charles II and Duke of York cut off supply of indentured servants.

1688   Glorious Revolution in England: James II overthrown; William and Mary reign.

1689   Edict of (religious) Toleration passed by Parliament in England.

1691   Virginia abolishes Indian (Native American) slavery.

1699   Virginia allows religious tolerance, but favors the established (Anglican) church.

1700   French Huguenots arrive in Virginia from England and Ireland.

1706   Virginia enacts statute to encourage baptism of Negro, Indian and mulatto slaves.

1701   Society for the Propagation of the Gospel (SPG) in the Anglican Church organized.

1720   Brunswick County, Virginia, forms.
              Designated as the Parish of St. Andrew also.
              In the colonial legislation that created Brunswick is the first written reference to freedom of religion within the Church of England–dominated colony of Virginia.

1732   The first legal documentation of a slave in Brunswick County found in July court records.

1734   The First Great Awakening (1734–1750).
              The rise of the concepts of individualism and republicanism begins.

1740   Movement of Dissenters from the Church of England begins.

1758   First black congregation organizes in Mecklenburg County, Virginia.
       On Plantation of William Byrd II.
       Part of Separate Baptist Church.

1772   The Virginia assembly petitions the British crown to stop the slave traffic.

1775   800 adherents in Brunswick County circuit of Methodism, but still operating within the established church of the colony — the Anglican Church, Church of England, or Church of Virginia.

1776   1,611 adherents in Brunswick County circuit of Methodism, a remarkable increase, far greater than any other circuit in the colonies.

American Declaration of Independence signed July 4.

Many Virginia slaves are freed by their masters on condition that they take their place fighting in the American Revolutionary War.

1777   Other than Massachusetts, Virginia recruits the most number of free blacks for its militia.

1778   The sovereign Commonwealth of Virginia enacts prohibition of slave importation.

1779   The Commonwealth of Virginia disestablishes the Church of England.

1784   Virginia Methodists, at the Baltimore Christmas Conference, lead all Methodists in the new United States of America; declare their separation and independence from the Anglican Church.

1785   The first quarterly meeting of the entire (new) Methodist Episcopal Church held in Brunswick County, Virginia, in May.

1785   Church of England (or Episcopal Church) lose exclusive right to perform marriage ceremonies and its vestries no longer administer relief to the poor (previously supported by taxes).

1786   The Commonwealth of Virginia establishes freedom of religion.

1789   French Revolution; storming of Bastille, July 14.

1790   The Age of Reason (Enlightenment) at its peak (1790–1800).

Thomas Lundie, rector of St. Andrew's Church at Lawrenceville, in Brunswick County, Virginia, resigns his commission and becomes a Methodist.

In Brunswick County the population of blacks and whites is equal. Over time the number of whites holds at 6,000 while the black population grows at a slow rate.

1800   The Second Great Awakening (1800–1840).

1808   United States ends slave trafficking per Constitutional provision.

1814   The Episcopal Church Convention attended by only seven clergymen and eighteen laymen from the entire state of Virginia.

The Episcopal Church struggles after the Great Awakening due to its perceived attachment to the old colonial government and the English Crown.

1820   In Brunswick County there are 10,000 slaves and 717 free men of color.

1830   Brunswick County initiates a Register of Free Blacks. Free or freed black men and women must register annually and prove they are free and not runaways. Prior to this time free blacks lived with a high degree of independence.

The largest slaveholder in Virginia owns seventy-one bondsmen. The number grows from this point forward.

1831   Nat Turner rebellion in Southampton County, Virginia.

1840   The population of Brunswick County slaves drops to 9,000 and remains at that level until Emancipation.

1857 James Solomon Russell born on December 20, 1857,
          Palmer Springs, Mecklenburg County, Virginia
          Hendrick estate (plantation).
       Second Dred Scott decision by U.S. Supreme Court denies his freedom.
1860s An economic inflationary profit boom occurs.
          Ends in 1873; economy spirals downward.
          Bottom of depression hits in 1879.
       In Brunswick County there are 392 farms with fewer than 5 slaves each;
          251 farms from 5 to 20 slaves each; and 126 slaveholders. Only one-
          fourth of all families utilize and maintain the slave system.
1861 Civil War.
 –65 The Episcopal Church of the Confederate States of America forms.
1865 U.S. Congress creates Freedman's Bureau in March
          (officially the Bureau of Refugees, Freedmen and Abandoned Lands).
       General Robert E. Lee surrenders at Appomattox Court House on April 9.
       The Episcopal Church reunites.
1866 Virginia Constitutional Convention.
          Virginia under military rule/occupation.
          General John M. Schofield is commander in Virginia.
       All southern, and previously separated, dioceses have returned to the
          Episcopal Church.
1867 Peter G. Morgan, Russell's future father-in-law, is one of twenty-five
          Negro delegates elected to the Virginia Constitutional Convention. He
          fights to keep the words "black" or "white" out of the new state con-
          stitution.
       Article IV of the Virginia Constitution proposes free public school for
          all people.
1869 Zion Union Apostolic Church organizes in Boydton (Mecklenburg
          County), Virginia, by Elder James R. Howell.
1871 Public education begins in Brunswick County with 17 white teachers
          and 8 black.
1873 The first Great Depression:
          The banking system collapses—Jay Cooke & Company fails.
          The beginning of 65 months of uninterrupted economic contrac-
          tion.
1874 Russell enters Hampton Institute.
       Zion Union Apostolic Church falls into disarray after one of its founders
          elected bishop for life.
1875 Russell present at Booker T. Washington's graduation from Hampton
          Institute.
1877 Russell as a Sunday school teacher again.
       Radical Reconstruction ends.
          State of Virginia avoids Radical Reconstruction.

Miss Pattie Buford of Lawrenceville ministers to local former slaves, mostly Zion Union churchgoers.

1878   Episcopal Diocese of Virginia becomes interested in work of Pattie Buford and the Zion Union people.

Bishop Whittle of Virginia sends commission to interview Russell.

Russell enters Branch Divinity School in Petersburg, Virginia on October 1.

Economically, the Great Depression at its worst: more than 10,000 failed businesses.

1879   The Readjusters elected to state offices in Virginia. They:

    Provide large funding of newly formed public schools.

    Abolish poll tax.

    Raise taxes on corporations, lower tax on small farmers.

    Reinforce civil and political rights for blacks.

Pattie Buford's School of the Good Shepherd, next to her hospital in Brunswick County, educate black children up to the 6th grade level; at this time there are 60 males and 100 females.

1880   The Third Great Awakening (1880–1910).

Pattie Buford's school enrolls 90 males and 135 female black children.

1882   Russell ordained to the Diaconate in Petersburg.

    Moves to Lawrenceville, Virginia.

    Assists at St. Andrew's Church; oversees two "colored" churches.

    Writes letter to *The Churchman* journal.

    Attends his first diocesan council meeting and becomes instant hit.

    Organizes a benevolent society.

    Marries Virginia Michigan Morgan of Petersburg.

1883   Russell opens parish school — predecessor to the St. Paul School.

Sewanee (Southern) Bishops' Conference convenes in August to deal with its "Negro Problem."

Philadelphia General Convention of the Episcopal Church in October.

Russell's first child born — daughter Czarina.

1885   Brunswick County public schools: 52 percent of the black children are enrolled as legally required but only 23 percent attend; the white attendance is 32 percent.

1888   Establishes the St. Paul Normal School; the Saul building; a dozen students.

1890   Peter G. Morgan, Russell's father-in-law, dies on March 15.

Period of American and European "progressivism" begins (1890s–1920s).

1892   Episcopal Diocese of Southern Virginia created.

Primary Council of the Diocese of Southern Virginia convenes in Lynchburg.

Church canons from the previous "undivided" Diocese of Virginia carried over:

"Black Canon" permits full diocesan membership of colored clergy transferring to new diocese, but restricts rights of new black clergy and black congregations.

1893   First meeting of St. Paul's Board of Trustees in Richmond.
       Russell appointed Archdeacon for Colored Work in the Episcopal Diocese of Southern Virginia by Bishop A.M. Randolph.
1895   Booker T. Washington gives famous Atlanta Exposition Speech.
1896   Supreme Court rules on *Plessy v. Ferguson*, virtually endorsing "separate but equal" access or Jim Crowism.
       Compare with action of Southern church dioceses, re: Sewanee Conference.
1898   Biggest day of land purchasing for the St. Paul School.
       Washington, D.C., General Convention of the Episcopal Church.
       Russell attends first of eleven consecutive triennial conventions.
1900   Russell speaking engagements in Hartford, Connecticut, and Syracuse, New York.
1901   Queen Victoria dies.
       San Francisco General Convention of the Episcopal Church.
1902   St. Paul's Farmers' Conferences organizes in Brunswick County.
       General Education Board (GEB) of the Rockefeller Foundation forms.
       GEB becomes, over time, the model for funding Southern black schools.
       Virginia State Constitution modified for the first time; removes the vote from all except educated blacks, those who own property, and those who fought in the Civil War.
1904   Many southern dioceses create Colored Convocations by this time.
       Archdeacon Russell and Sewanee Bishops' output, converge in a long-term debate.
       Boston General Convention of the Episcopal Church.
       Movement to create missionary (black) bishops begins.
1905   Russell plays key role in electing first bishop coadjutor of Southern Virginia.
1906   The American Church Institute for Negroes (ACIN) forms.
       Russell receives personal threats from both whites and blacks.
1907   Richmond General Convention of the Episcopal Church.
       Delegates visit St. Paul School following convention.
       Russell takes first trip to Europe.
1910   Edinburgh Missionary Conference convenes in Scotland.
       King Edward VII dies; George V succeeds.
1911   Russell's second trip to Europe:
       Underwritten by ACIN executive director Samuel Bishop.
       Russell travels with son Alvin.
       Russell attends First Universal Races Congress at University of London.

Samuel Bishop and ACIN attempt to take control of St. Paul School.

1912 Critical time in funding for the St. Paul School.

Bishop David Greer, president of ACIN, tells Russell the school will soon become extinct.

1913 New York General Convention of the Episcopal Church.

1914 The first Rosenwald Foundation–funded school building erected in Brunswick County.

1916 St. Louis General Convention of the Episcopal Church.

Russell preaches at several African Methodist Episcopal Zion churches.

1917 Russell elected suffragan bishop of the Episcopal Diocese of Arkansas.

Declines election.

Honorary Doctor of Divinity degree conferred on Russell by the Theological Seminary of Virginia in Alexandria.

1919 Detroit General Convention of the Episcopal Church.

1920 Virginia Michigan Morgan Russell dies on July 2.

1921 The last illegal hanging or "lynching" in Virginia occurs in Brunswick County on August 3.

1922 Portland, Oregon, General Convention of the Episcopal Church.

Russell preaches to colored mission and delivers speech at "mass meeting" for fundraising purposes.

"Black Canon" reversal fails in Council of Diocese of Southern Virginia.

Russell takes third international trip — London, Liberia, other West African nations.

1923 "Black Canon" reversal memorial voted down at Council of the Episcopal Diocese of Southern Virginia.

1924– Russell serves on Episcopal Church's Department of Christian Social
1931 Service.

Serves on Board of Missions.

1925 New Orleans General Convention of the Episcopal Church.

Russell addresses "mass meeting" for fund-raising purposes.

Russell attends 50th anniversary of founding of Hampton Institute, honorary alumnus.

Russell honored with a place on platform.

1926 Russell makes final (fourth) trip to Europe — London.

1928 Washington, D.C., General Convention of the Episcopal Church.

Russell's final General Convention.

1929 Russell resigns position of principal at St. Paul's School; son Alvin succeeds.

1930 Brunswick County school board initiated a policy of underwriting housing for county high school students traveling great distances; county uses facilities at the St. Paul school.

1931   Diocese of Virginia rescinds its racial limitation canons.
       Yorktown Sesquicentennial Association celebration.
           The Rev. W.A.R. Goodwin, Rector of Bruton Parish Church, President.
           R.R. Moton and James Solomon Russell honorary trustees.
           President Herbert Hoover makes brief address.
       First Founder's Day inaugurated at St. Paul School in March.
           Faculty, staff, students and local community honor Russell.
           Russell receives Harmon Foundation Award of 1929 in a reenactment.
           Bishop A.C. Thompson "orders" Russell to write *Autobiography*.
1933   Colored Convocation of Southern Virginia meets in Ascension Church
       in Palmer Springs (Russell's birthplace), and creates a memorial to
       present in 1934 to the annual council of the Diocese of Southern Virginia to rescind its limitations on black clergy (a compromise proposal).
1934   Annual Council of the Episcopal Diocese of Southern Virginia in Petersburg ratifies memorial on black clergy.
           The compromise proposal asked for seat and vote for entire black
           clergy and two lay seats and votes for the (one and only) colored
           convocation of black churches and missions.
1935   Annual Council of the Episcopal Diocese of Southern Virginia ratifies
       memorial from 1934 on black clergy and black convocation.
       James Solomon Russell dies on March 29; funeral attended by three
       bishops, many clergy, and over 3,000 other mourners.
       U.S. Supreme Court rules Scottsboro (Alabama) boys' trial irregular.
1936   Morehouse Publishing Co. publishes James Solomon Russell's *Autobiography*.
1950   All dioceses of the Episcopal Church operate without any restrictions
       or limitations on black clergy and black convocations. Black convocations disappear.
1996   The Episcopal Diocese of Southern Virginia honors James Solomon Russell, posthumously, as a "local saint."
2009   The General Convention of the Episcopal Church fails to designate James
       Solomon Russell a place on its liturgical calendar in the Book of Common Prayer; another attempt is to be made at the 2012 General Convention.
2012   General Convention of the Episcopal Church, Indianapolis, Indiana (July).

Chapter Notes

Chapter One

1. *Virginia: A Guide to the Old Dominion* (Richmond: Virginia Conservation Commission, 1940), 475. In 1875 Miss Pattie used a building on her family plantation as a refuge for Negroes. She eventually exhausted her own funds and the Protestant Episcopal Church Institute for Negroes financed the home, which was then known as "Mrs. Buford's Hospital."

2. *The Churchman*, Saturday, March 1, 1879, 241–245; *The Journal of the Annual Council of the Diocese of Virginia — the 84th session, 1879*, 37–8.

3. The point of view of held by Miss Pattie was not unusual for white people. From the time of the beginnings of American slavery until decades following the end of the Civil War, most whites— including educated clergy — did not understand African religion and therefore considered much of African spirituality as heathen.

4. *The Churchman*, September 7, 1878, 289; *The Churchman*, September 21, 1878, 345; *The Churchman*, August 31, 1878, 257.

5. *Bureau of the Census, 1910*, 483. This document for the year 1906 cites the Reformed Zion Union Apostolic Church and its history from 1869. It is this documentation that suggests that colored Methodists in southeastern Virginia, especially those in Mecklenburg, Lunenburg, and Brunswick Counties, "found themselves in a peculiar situation" after they were no longer permitted to gather for worship in the white churches.

6. Estrelda Y. Alexander, *Black Fire: One Hundred Years of African American Pentecostalism* (Downers Grove, IL: InterVarsity Press, 2011), 90–92.

7. The General Education Board of the RZUA, ed., *History of the Reformed Zion Union Churches of America* (Lawrenceville, VA: Brunswick Publishing Corporation, 1998), 11.

8. *History of the Reformed Zion Union Apostolic Churches of America*, 12.

9. Carl N. Degler, *Neither Black nor White: Slavery and Race Relations in Brazil and the United States* (Madison, WI: University of Wisconsin Press, 1971), 101–11.

10. Peter Berger, *The Sacred Canopy: Elements of a Sociological Theory of Religion* (New York: Anchor Books, 1967), 45.

11. Berger, *Sacred Canopy*, 3–4.

12. David Robertson, *Denmark Vesey: The Buried Story of America's Largest Slave Rebellion and the Man Who Led It* (New York: Vintage Books, 1999), 3–10, 27–40.

13. Janet Gay Neale, *Brunswick County, Virginia 1720–1975: The History of a Southside Virginia County* (Brunswick County: The Brunswick County Bicentennial Committee, 1975), 202.

14. Berger, *Sacred Canopy*, 156.

Chapter Two

1. Betty Wood, *Slavery in Colonial America 1619–1776* (Lanham, MD: Rowman & Littlefield, 2005), 1–3.

2. Edmund S. Morgan, *American Slavery, American Freedom* (New York: W.W. Norton, 1975), 157. This quote ends a discussion beginning on page 154, wherein Morgan was explaining that a black man, Tony Longo, in Northampton County, Virginia (on its eastern shore), reacted to a court

subpoena similar to that of a white (English) settler. It was an attempt in seventeenth-century colonial Virginia to integrate all its settlers. An Englishman held a natural disdain for authority and so did Longo. In either case, any man of such temperament was held in contempt of court.

3. Carl N. Degler, *Out of the Past: The Forces that Shaped Modern America* (New York: Harper & Row, 1984), 51–2.

4. James L. Bugg Jr., "The French Huguenot Frontier Settlement in Manakin Town," *Virginia Magazine of History and Biography* 61, no. 4 (October 1953): 359–92.

5. Degler, *Out of the Past*, 55.

6. T.H. Breen and Stephen Innes, *Myne Owne Ground: Race and Freedom on Virginia's Eastern Shore, 1640–1676* (New York: Oxford University Press, 1980), 111.

7. James Curtis Ballagh, *A History of Slavery in Virginia* (Baltimore: Johns Hopkins University Press, 1902), 3–5.

8. Ballagh, 23.

9. Ballagh, 14.

10. Ballagh, 7–11.

11. Ballagh, 34.

12. The term "episcopal" in lower case refers to churches with bishops. Anglican, Roman Catholic, and Eastern Orthodox churches maintain bishops to lead dioceses, clergy and laity. In Colonial America the Anglican churches were denied bishops; vestries assumed local parish leadership, leaving the clergy dependent upon the lay vestry and without legal or ecclesiastical protections. This arrangement was just one factor having a longer-term negative effect on the successor Episcopal Church after the Revolutionary War.

13. Derris L. Raper and Constance M. Jones, *A Goodly Heritage: The Episcopal Diocese of Southern Virginia 1892–1992* (Norfolk: Pictorial Heritage Publishing Company, 1992), 11. "In 1642 the General Assembly [known as the House of Burgesses until 1776] instituted the vestry system so vital to local government in colonial times. Vestries were elected from among the most respected landowners in the parish, a geographical designation. The vestries, though, soon became self-perpetuating bodies. They performed civil functions as well as religious: they levied a tithe for parish expenses, cared for orphans and other dependents.... Colonial vestries have been accused of being well nigh tyrannical — of keeping the clergy in virtual thrall to their wishes, and even of keeping the pulpit vacant when they chose."

14. David L. Holmes, *A Brief History of the Episcopal Church* (Harrisburg, PA: Trinity Press International, 1993), 21.

15. Morgan, *American Slavery, American Freedom*, 348–49.

16. Holmes, *A Brief History of the Episcopal Church*, 44. Not only did James Blair found the College of William and Mary, he was "rector of Jamestown and Bruton parishes, first commissary to Virginia, member and president of the governor's council, acting governor of Virginia for one year, ambitious and imperative both for the church and for himself, [and] he dominated the religious scene in colonial Virginia."

17. Philip Slaughter, "Historiographer's Report," *Journal of the Proceedings of the Episcopal Church in the Diocese of Virginia 1883*, 46.

18. Holmes, 37–8; Prichard, 27–32.

19. Holmes, 33.

20. Ibid.

21. Holmes, 78.

22. Holmes, 79.

23. Holmes, 79–80.

24. Prichard, 43–60.

25. Charles F. Irons, *The Origins of Proslavery Christianity: White and Black Evangelicals in Colonial and Antebellum Virginia* (Chapel Hill: University of North Carolina Press, 2008), 18.

26. Irons, 34–35.

27. Irons, 39–40.

28. Neale, *Brunswick County*, 100.

29. Neale, 93–4.

30. Neale, 98.

31. Irons, 67.

32. Neale, 104.

33. Irons, 213, 217.

34. Neale, 159, 160.

35. Neale, 164–70.

36. Irons, 248–50.

37. Irons, 257.
38. H.T. Besse, *Church History* (Cleona, PA: Holzapfel Publishing, 1908), 215–18, 230; Frank Moore Colby, ed., *The International Year Book: A Compendium of the World's Progress* (New York: Dodd, Mead and Company, 1910), 176; Oliver S. Baketel, ed., *The Methodist Year Book* (New York: The Methodist Book Concern, 1918), 235–36; E. Dana Durand, director, *Religious Bodies — 1906: Separate Denominations — History, Description, and Statistics*, part 2 (Washington, D.C.: U.S. Bureau of the Census, 1910), 483–84.

Chapter Three

1. James S. Russell, *Adventure in Faith: An Autobiographic Story of St. Paul Normal and Industrial School, Lawrenceville, Virginia* (New York: Morehouse Publishing Company, 1936), 1.
2. Russell, *Adventure*, 2.
3. The terms "African-American," "black" and "colored" are used by the writer. However, historical documents cited herein, from the 18th to the early 20th centuries, are replete with various terminologies for African-Americans (for example, Negro, Africans, Afro-American, colored people), and are quoted as originally written.
4. Russell, *Adventure*, 2.
5. W.A.R. Goodwin, "The Church's Mission in Christendom: A Speech Given on Race Problems in America," special issue, *Pan-Anglican Congress 1908* 6, Section E (1908): 123–25.
6. Eric Foner, *Reconstruction: America's Unfinished Revolution 1863–1877* (New York: Perennial Classics, 1989), 142. The official name for this agency was the Bureau of Refugees, Freedmen, and Abandoned Lands. The scope of the bureau's charge is best understood if it is seen as an experiment in American social policy. Among the many tasks it was assigned were creating a free labor society; establishing schools for freedmen; providing aid to the destitute, aged, and insane; adjudicating disputes among blacks and between the races; and securing equal justice for blacks and Southern white Unionists.
7. Foner, *Reconstruction*, 35. The Civil War historian claims that Reconstruction began in 1863 and ended in 1877. There were two attempts at Reconstruction. The first was Presidential Reconstruction, in which President Abraham Lincoln "Issued on December 8, 1863, his Proclamation of Amnesty and Reconstruction," offering full pardon and the restoration of all rights to former southern Confederates who resumed their allegiance to the Union by taking an oath. The full rights of former slaves were understood to already be in effect since January 1863. The second Reconstruction was known as Radical Reconstruction, led by the Radical Republicans.
8. Russell, *Adventure*, 3.
9. Russell, *Adventure*, 60. Russell writes that others have said that St. Paul's is his monument.
10. Russell, *Adventure*, 15; Neale, *Brunswick County*, 210. "Most poor people got by as well as they could with the help of their friends, the people in their churches, and such individual kindness on the part of white people as those of Mrs. Pattie Buford (who was lauded by her Northern friends and practically ostracized by the upper class whites of Brunswick County)."
11. Russell, *Adventure*, 15–16.
12. Russell, *Adventure*, 14.
13. Neale, *Brunswick County*, 200.
14. Russell, *Adventure*, 63.
15. Harold T. Lewis, *Yet with a Steady Beat* (Valley Forge: Trinity Press International, 1996), 40.
16. Romans 12:2 (English Standard Version): "Do not be conformed to this world, but be transformed by the renewal of your mind, that by testing you may discern what is the will of God, what is good and acceptable and perfect."
17. Galatians 3:28 (ESV): "There is neither Jew nor Greek, there is neither slave nor free, there is no male and female, for you are all one in Christ Jesus."
18. Lewis, *Steady Beat*, 45.
19. Russell, *Adventure*, 62–3.
20. Russell, *Adventure*, 3.
21. Russell, *Adventure*, 4.
22. Russell, *Adventure*, 5.
23. Edith Armstrong Talbot, *Samuel Chapman Armstrong: A Biographical Study* (New York: Doubleday, Page & Company, 1904), 159.
24. Talbot, *Armstrong*, 137.

25. Talbot, *Armstrong*, 166.
26. Craig D. Townsend, *Faith in Their Own Color* (New York: Columbia University Press, 2005), 1, 5, 153, 168.There were two Fugitive Slave Laws or Acts; the first in 1793 and the second in 1850. It was not until 1864 that the 1850 law was repealed.
27. Benjamin Butler, *Butler's Book: Autobiography and Personal Reminiscences of Major General Benjamin Butler* (Boston: A.M. Thayer & Co, 1892), 256–65.; Talbot, *Armstrong*, 154–55.
28. Talbot, *Armstrong*, 138.
29. Talbot, *Armstrong*, 158–9.
30. R.R. Moton, A Virginia native and Hampton graduate, eventually became principal at Tuskegee Institute in Alabama and later at his alma mater. Moton attended the First Universal Races Congress in 1911 in London, as did Russell.
31. Robert J. Norrell, *Up From History: The Life of Booker T. Washington* (Cambridge, MA: Belknap Press of Harvard University Press, 2009), 31.
32. Russell, *Adventure*, 16.
33. Booker T. Washington, *The Booker T. Washington Papers*, ed. Louis R. Harlan and Raymond Smock (Champagne-Urbana: University of Illinois Press, 1981), 146.
34. *Journal of the Eighty-Third Annual Council of the Protestant Episcopal Church in Virginia*, Report of the Committee On the State of the Church, 1878, 103.
35. Russell, *Adventure*, 27.
36. Russell, *Adventure*, 28.
37. Russell, *Adventure*, 30.
38. Russell, *Adventure*, 28.
39. Russell, *Adventure*, 29.
40. James S. Russell, "Communications," *The Journal of Negro History* 8, no. 3 (July 1923): 341–44.
41. Russell, *Adventure*, 63.
42. George Freeman Bragg Jr., *History of the Afro-American Group of the Episcopal Church* (Baltimore: Church Advocate Press, 1922), 133–34. Russell lived with the Bragg family while at seminary. Bragg followed Russell to seminary a few years later.

Chapter Four

1. *Journal of the Eighty-Third Annual Council of the Protestant Episcopal Church in the Diocese of Virginia*, 1878.
2. *Journal of the Eighty-Fourth Annual Council of the Protestant Episcopal Church in the Diocese of Virginia*, 1879.
3. *Journal of the Eighty-Fifth Annual Council of the Protestant Episcopal Church in the Diocese of Virginia*, 1880.
4. *Journal of the Eighty-Sixth Annual Council of the Protestant Episcopal Church in the Diocese of Virginia*, 1881.
5. *Journal of the Eighty-Seventh Annual Council of the Protestant Episcopal Church in the Diocese of Virginia*, 1882.
6. *Journal of the Eighty-Eighth Annual Council of the Protestant Episcopal Church in the Diocese of Virginia*, 1883.
7. *Journal of the Eighty-Ninth Annual Council of the Protestant Episcopal Church in the Diocese of Virginia* 1884.
8. *Journal of the Ninetieth Annual Council of the Protestant Episcopal Church in the Diocese of Virginia*, 1885.
9. "A Wonderful Work Among the Plantation Negroes," *The Churchman*, March 1, 1879, 242.
10. http://www.rzua.org/history/address.php. Viewed last on December 14, 2011.
11. *Journal of the Proceedings of General Convention of the Episcopal Church 1889*, "Memorial" presented by Dr. Huntington of New York and signed by William V. Tunnell, Chairman, and George F. Bragg Jr., Secretary, 266.

Chapter Five

1. *Journal of the Ninety-First Annual Council of the Protestant Episcopal Church in the Diocese of Virginia*, 1886.
2. *Journal of the Ninety-Second Annual Council of the Protestant Episcopal Church in the Diocese of Virginia*, 1887.

3. *Journal of the Ninety-Third Annual Council of the Protestant Episcopal Church in the Diocese of Virginia*, 1888.

4. *Journal of the Ninety-Fourth Annual Council of the Protestant Episcopal Church in the Diocese of Virginia*, 1889.

5. *Journal of the Ninety-Fifth Annual Council of the Protestant Episcopal Church in the Diocese of Virginia*, 1890.

6. *Journal of the Ninety-Sixth Annual Council of the Protestant Episcopal Church in the Diocese of Virginia*, 1891.

7. *Journal of the Ninety-Seventh Annual Council of the Protestant Episcopal Church in the Diocese of Virginia*, 1892.

8. *Journal of the Primary Council of the Protestant Episcopal Church in the Diocese of Southern Virginia*, 1892.

Chapter Six

1. Foner, *Reconstruction*, 96.

2. James D. Anderson, *The Education of Blacks in the South 1860–1935*. (Chapel Hill: University of North Carolina Press, 1988), 4–5.

3. Anderson, 17.

4. Foner, 98.

5. Russell, *Adventure*, 84. Russell writes that in 1902 when he started the Farmers' Conference there were 12,000 Negroes out of a total of 20,000 people in Brunswick County; Thomas Jesse Jones, *Negro Education: A Study of the Private and Higher Schools for Colored People in the United States*, vol. 2, Bulletin 1916, No. 39 (Washington, D.C.: United States Bureau of Education, 1916), 614. According to this study, Brunswick County, Virginia, had 11,366 Negroes and 7,878 whites in 1910. If these two sets of numbers are correct, one assumption has to be that blacks migrated to urban areas over the 8-year period. Brunswick County is but one county making up Virginia's "black belt."

6. Russell refers to the "undivided" Diocese of Virginia several times in his book. The Diocese of Southern Virginia was created in 1892.

7. In Russell's account of this offer, the first layman referred to Russell as "Brother." The presumption here is that the layman was a white man and had sufficient leadership or clout to ask council for money and that the "Brother" reference meant either that Russell's personal and oratorical demeanor was "acceptable" to the white delegates or that this layman truly befriended Russell. Likewise Russell, a "colored" deacon ordained for less than 100 days, fearlessly showed his sense of equality and leadership by asking for the horse and "building funds."

8. Russell, *Adventure*, 27–28.

9. Russell, *Adventure*, 83.

10. Russell, *Adventure*, 31; Diocese of Virginia, *Journal of the Seventy-Ninth Annual Council of the Protestant Episcopal Church in Virginia Held in Christ Church, Charlottesville, on the 20th, 21st, 22nd & 23rd of May 1874* (Richmond: Clemmitt and Jones, 1874), 104; Diocese of Louisiana, *Thirty-Third Annual Council of the Protestant Episcopal Church in the Diocese of Louisiana, 1874* (New Orleans: James A. Gresham Booksellers and Stationer, 1874), 81; *James Holly vs. The Domestic and Foreign Missionary Society* [DFMS], No. 138 of October Term, 1900, in the Supreme Court of the United States, Record No. 17,523, Brief for Appellant, p. 1, and Brief for Appellees, p 41. Russell gives the reader no idea how he received money from Saul or who Saul was; the Diocese of Virginia shows a gift of $100.00 from Saul; the Diocese of Louisiana shows a gift of $100.00; but briefs from U.S. Supreme Court records show that Saul was a wealthy man having bequeathed his estate to the DFMS (⅓ to domestic missions, ⅓ to foreign missions, and ⅓ to the benefit of colored people in the former slaves states for the support of schools and missions).

11. A "normal" school was a high school and a teacher-training school for former slaves in the South. Many of the now famous African-American colleges and universities in the South began as "Normal and Industrial" or "Normal and Agricultural" schools.

12. Russell, *Adventure*, 33.

13. Russell, *Adventure*, 38.

14. Neale, *Brunswick County*, 233–34.

15. Russell, *Adventure*, 84.

16. Russell, *Adventure*, 83.

17. "St. Paul's Farmers' Conference," *Southern Workman* 35, no. 9 (September 1906): 468–69.The article went on to report that Negroes in Brunswick County, Virginia, paid real property

taxes of $250,000 that year. It also reported: "Archdeacon Russell and the Lawrenceville school have accomplished much toward the improvement of the black belt of Virginia...." The article also cited the Tuskegee Institute's farmers' and workers' conference in the black belt of Alabama; the Atlanta Conference — controlled by W.E.B. DuBois of Atlanta University, according to the article — which published studies in a series of reports regarding the condition of blacks; and the conferences at Hampton Institute which brought together "leading colored men" who presented reports on insurance, agriculture and criminal conditions.

18. Robert Strange, *Church Work Among the Negroes in the South* (Chicago: Western Theological Seminary, 1907), 17. This address was part of the seminary's Hale Memorial Sermon series.

19. Russell, *Adventure*, 83.

20. Fred D. Banks, "The St. Paul's Farmers' Conference," *Southern Workman* 37, no. 10 (October 1908): 571.

21. "The St. Paul's Farmers' Conference," *Southern Workman* 35, no. 9 (September 1906): 468–9.

22. *The Southern Missioner* (April 1913): 45.

23. Russell, *Adventure*, 44–5.

24. The correct spellings should be noted: the U.S. government's "Freedmen's Bureau" and the Episcopal Church's "Freedman's Commission."

25. Lewis, *Steady Beat*, 125. Immediately after the Civil War the agency created was named the Protestant Episcopal Freedman's Commission to the Colored People; it later was changed to the Commission on Work among Colored People, then simply the Commission on Negro Work. This work was dissolved in 1904, and the American Church Institute for Negroes was formed in 1906.

26. The "special mass meetings" of the General Conventions were provided to update delegates on missionary endeavors within the Church. Speakers were allowed five to ten minutes to make their pitches. The Women's Auxiliaries of the many dioceses usually made up the majority of the listeners. Mass meetings were excellent platforms for making contacts and for appealing for funds.

27. Russell, *Adventure*.

28. Strange, *Church Work Among Negroes*, 10. According to Bishop Robert Strange of East Carolina, there were 9,000 African-American communicants in the entire Episcopal Church in 1907. There were in the same year nine million African-Americans in the South. Of the 9,000 African-American communicants there were one in 7,961 in Mississippi and one in 381 in Virginia.

29. John W. Wood, "The Missionary Story of the General Convention," *The Spirit of Missions: An Illustrated Monthly Review of Christian Missions* 78, no. 11 (November 1913): 769. Though Wood edited this article he was actually paraphrasing Russell's presentation. Russell, not Wood, claimed that St. Paul was the largest school of its type in the country.

30. Lewis, *Steady Beat*, 125–26. The document cited by Lewis is Samuel H. Bishop's report in 1907 titled "The Church among the Negroes." Bishop, a white man, was the first executive director of the American Church Institute for Negroes, the successor in 1906 to the church's previous funding agencies.

31. Eric Anderson and Alfred A. Moss Jr., *Dangerous Donations: Northern Philanthropy and Southern Black Education, 1902–1930* (Columbia: University of Missouri Press, 1999), 3–4.

32. Norrell, *Up From History*, 194–6. Robert Ogden was a New York department store executive who had been working with Hampton Institute since its founding at the end of the Civil War.

33. Norrell, *Up From History*, 196.

34. GEB funds were given to secular schools like Hampton and Tuskegee and not to Episcopal Church–related schools like St. Paul, St. Augustine and Bishop Payne Divinity School. Though Rockefeller was a Baptist, most of the other seed money for GEB came from Episcopalians like Andrew Carnegie.

35. *Dangerous Donations*, 113.

36. *Dangerous Donations*, 117. S.H. Bishop was also an assistant editor of a journal called *Charities: A Weekly Review of Local and General Philanthropy*.

37. Bishop wrote to W.E.B. DuBois. Out of that contact Bishop became an original member of the National Association for the Advancement of Colored People and was prominent in the founding of the National Urban League.

38. St. Augustine's Normal and Collegiate School was founded immediately after the Civil War by the Episcopal Church's Freedman's Commission.

39. *Dangerous Donations*, 121.

40. *Dangerous Donations*, 122. Between 1906 and 1914 four more schools were affiliated: St. Mary's Industrial School in Vicksburg, Mississippi; St. Mark's Industrial School in Birmingham, Alabama; St. Athanasius Industrial School in Brunswick, Georgia; and St. Paul's Industrial School in Atlanta, Georgia.

41. *Dangerous Donations*, 136.
42. Russell, *Adventure*, 64.
43. *Dangerous Donations*, 139.
44. *Dangerous Donations*, 86–91.
45. "St. Paul School," *Southern Workman* 41, no. 9 (September 1912): 502. The article reads in part: "Many of the best buildings in the town of Lawrenceville have been constructed by his [James Solomon Russell's] students; its streets are lighted by electricity generated by his school plant."
46. *Dangerous Donations*, 143.
47. *Dangerous Donations*, 10. The authors explain that "progressive education" dealt in educational experiments alien to traditional education. For example, progressive education was new and innovative, proposed eliminating "dead languages," was socially oriented, encouraged diversity instead of uniformity, and promoted a curriculum of "life adjustment." It was never popular. But this "[e]ducational innovation was easier to carry out in weak and underfunded black schools than in more secure white schools."
48. A "memorial" could be a letter, or statement of fact preceding a motion or proposal. For example, in the Annual Councils of an Episcopal Church Diocese, a group or person may offer a motion to be voted on but preceded by a "memorial" of explanation; or a memorial could be simply a statement by a constituent group, e.g., a Convocation of Colored People, supporting a position of a bishop on a certain item prior to vote counting.
49. *Dangerous Donations*, 143.
50. The GEB and many other funds, such as the Phelps-Stokes Fund, the Rosenwald Fund, and the Jeanes Fund, shared common board members. These "interlocking" board memberships hardly rendered the Northern philanthropists independent and unbiased in their decision-making. Though the audit by Phelps-Stokes may have contained some truthful elements, because of the interlocking board memberships the audit should have been considered with qualification.
51. *Dangerous Donations*, 145–6.
52. *Dangerous Donations*, 153. The contributions were extracted from a report authored by U.S. Bureau of Education agent Thomas Jesse Jones titled *Negro Education: A Study of the Private and Higher Schools for Colored People in the United States*, vol. 2 (1916): 444, 615.
53. *Dangerous Donations*, 159–60.

Chapter Seven

1. Russell, *Adventure*, 23.
2. *Relation of the Church to the Colored People: An Account of a Conference Held at Sewanee, Tennessee, July 25 to 28, 1883* (Sewanee: Wm. M. Harlow, University Printer, 1883), 3–4; Gardiner Shattuck, *Episcopalians and Race: Civil War to Civil Rights* (Lexington: University of Kentucky Press, 2000), 13.
3. Bragg, *Afro-American Group*, 151.
4. The "Sewanee Canon" was adopted in the House of Bishops but failed in the House of Deputies at the Philadelphia General Convention.
5. Shattuck, *Episcopalians and Race*, 15.
6. Richard Hooker Wilmer, *From a Southern Standpoint: Reminiscences of a Grandfather* (New York: Thomas Whittaker,1887), 48. Hooker is also remembered for one of the first post–Civil War confrontations between church and state. The military commander overseeing Alabama ordered all Episcopal churches in Alabama closed until they changed their prayers for the Confederate president to the United States president. Hooker challenged the general, saying that the military had no right in managing ecclesiastical affairs, especially its liturgy.
7. Bragg, *Afro-American Group*, 152.
8. Bragg coined the term "Afro-American Group" in his book on the history of black Episcopalians.
9. Bragg, *Afro-American Group*, 152.
10. John Johns, *A Memoir of the Life of the Right Rev. William Meade, D.D. Bishop of the Protestant Episcopal Church in the Diocese of Virginia* (Baltimore: Innes & Company, 1867), 474, 476, 477.
11. Russell, *Adventure*, 62.
12. Philip Slaughter, *A Memoir of the Life of the Rt. Rev. William Meade, D.D.* (Boston: New England Genealogical Society, 1885), 27–30. Slaughter was historiographer for the Diocese of Virginia.
13. Russell, *Adventure*, 62.
14. *Journal of the Proceedings of the Bishops, Clergy, and Laity of the Protestant Episcopal Church*

in the United States of America Assembled in a General Convention, Held in the City of New York, 1889, 266.

15. *Journal of the Ninety-Fourth Annual Council of the Protestant Episcopal Church in the Diocese of Virginia,* 1889, 43–4.

16. Russell, *Adventure,* 66.

17. Philips Brooks, the famous preacher, it should be noted, also composed the hymn "O Little Town of Bethlehem."

18. Shattuck, *Episcopalians and Race,* 17.

19. The 95th Annual Council of the [undivided] Diocese of Virginia settled not only on Canon XIII but Section 3, Article II of its Constitution: "The Council shall also be composed of the Colored Ministers having a seat and voice in the Council on the 17th day of May of May, 1889, and two clerical and two lay delegates from the Colored Missionary Jurisdiction of the Diocese, as the same is now or may hereafter be constituted by Canon." See *Journal of the Proceedings of the Protestant Episcopal Church in the Diocese of Virginia,* 1890, 272.

20. Russell, *Adventure,* 29.

21. Monroe N. Work, "Some Negro Members of Reconstruction Conventions and Legislatures and of Congress," *The Journal of Negro History* 5, no. 1 (January 1920): 63, 118–19.

22. Russell, *Adventure,* 66–7.

23. Norrell, *Up From History,* 143.

24. *Journal of the First Annual Council of the Protestant Episcopal Church in the Diocese of Southern Virginia,* 1893, 7–8.

25. Russell, *Adventure,* 64.

26. *Journal of the First Annual Council of the Protestant Episcopal Church in the Diocese of Southern Virginia,* 1893, 82–3.

27. Ibid., 87.

28. *Journal of the Second Annual Council of the Protestant Episcopal Church in the Diocese of Southern Virginia,* 1894, 9.

29. James S. Russell, "Annual Report of the Archdeacon for Colored Work in the Diocese," *Journal of the Thirteenth Annual Council of the Protestant Episcopal Church in the Diocese of Southern Virginia Held in St. John's Church, Wytheville, Virginia May 30th, 31st, June 1st, 1905* (1905): 269–70.

30. James S. Russell, "Annual Report of the Archdeacon for Colored Work in the Diocese," *Journal of the Fourteenth Annual Council of the Protestant Episcopal Church in the Diocese of Southern Virginia Held in Trinity Church, Portsmouth, Virginia, May 29th–31st, 1906* (1906): 309–10.

31. "Report of the Committee of the State of the Church," *Journal of the Fifteenth Annual Council of the Protestant Episcopal Church in the Diocese of Southern Virginia 1907* (1907):46–47. What Russell read was his "Annual Report of the Archdeacon for Colored Work."

32. Self-sustaining parishes pay the salaries of their clergy. Missions, which are not self-sustaining, are funded through the diocese. At the time of this report there were only two self-sustaining "colored" parishes. All of the others were missions, which were funded through the diocese from the General Board of Missions. Therefore Russell argued that the Bishop should increase the pay from his appropriations from the General Board of Missions.

33. "Report of the Committee of the State of the Church," *Journal of the Fifteenth Annual Council of the Protestant Episcopal Church in the Diocese of Southern Virginia 1907* (1907): 47–50.

34. "Report of the Committee of the State of the Church," *Journal of the Fourteenth Annual Council of the Protestant Episcopal Church in the Diocese of Southern Virginia 1906* (1906): 85–6.

35. As Archdeacon for Colored Work Russell not only chaired its annual Convocation meeting but he traveled each year to the missions or churches in his charge. This visitation work was not unlike that of a bishop or a suffragan bishop assigned to a specific ministry. On these visitations that Russell made, the only two ecclesiastical functions that he could not perform were confirmation and ordination.

36. James S. Russell, "Annual Report of the Archdeacon for Colored Work in the Diocese," *Journal of the Sixteenth Annual Council of the Protestant Episcopal Church in the Diocese of Southern Virginia Held in Church of the Epiphany, Danville, Virginia, June 11th and 12th, 1908* (1908): 299–301.

37. James S. Russell, "Annual Report of the Archdeacon for Colored Work in the Diocease [sic]," *Journal of the Seventeen Annual Council of the Protestant Episcopal Church in the Diocese of Southern Virginia Held in St. Paul's Church, Newport News, Virginia, May 25th to 27th, 1909* (1909): 275.

38. *Journal of Southern Virginia, 1909* (1909): 276.

39. "Memorial from Colored Convocation to the Council of Southern Virginia," *Journal of Southern Virginia, 1909* (1909): 42–43. Salaries are presumed to be annual — no frequency was annotated in the document.

40. James S. Russell, "Annual Report of the Archdeacon for Colored Work in the Diocese of Southern Virginia," *Journal of the Eighteenth Annual Council of the Protestant Episcopal Church in the Diocese of Southern Virginia Held in St. Paul's Church, Lynchburg, Virginia, May 31st to June 2nd, 1910* (1920): 268–70; Ulysses W. Russell, "James Solomon Russell: Priest, Educator, Humanitarian" (master's thesis, Virginia State College, 1962), 53–4.

41. *A Memorial to the Bishop and Convention of the Diocese of North Carolina: By the Colored Convocation Asking for a Missionary Jurisdiction for the Colored People — May 13–15, 1913* (Tarboro: Diocese of North Carolina, 1913), 1–6.

42. "Departments" appear to be equivalent to current "provinces" with the Episcopal Church. For example, the "Fourth Department" is equivalent to "Province Four," which includes dioceses from North Carolina to Mississippi.

43. "The Coming Episcopal Convention," *The Independent* 63, no. 3068 (1907): 703. Written one month prior to General Convention in Richmond the editorial read "In the diocese of Southern Virginia, where the organized work of the Church among the negroes is oldest, where two of her strongest and best known institutions of learning [Bishop Payne Divinity School and St. Paul Normal and Industrial School] for them are located, and where there are over 1,520 negro communicants, they have earnestly protested against the proposed separation, and have, in convocation assembled, petitioned the council of the Church to oppose it."

44. James S. Russell, "Annual Report of the Archdeacon for Colored Work in the Diocese of Southern Virginia," *Journal of the Twenty-Fifth Annual Council of the Protestant Episcopal Church in the Diocese of Southern Virginia Held in Epiphany Church, Danville, Virginia, May 29th–30th, 1917* (1917): 238.

45. *Journal of the First Annual Council of the Protestant Episcopal Church in the Diocese of Southern Virginia Held in Christ Church, Norfolk, Virginia, 1893,* 76.

46. *Journal of the Thirteenth Annual Council of the Protestant Episcopal Church in the Diocese of Southern Virginia Held in St. John's Church, Wytheville, 1905,* 269.

47. James S. Russell, "Annual Report of the Archdeacon for Colored Work in the Diocese of Southern Virginia," *Journal of the Seventeenth Annual Council of the Protestant Episcopal Church in the Diocese of Southern Virginia Held in St. Paul's, Newport News, Virginia* (1909): 275.

48. "Annual Report of the Archdeacon for Colored Work in the Diocese of Southern Virginia," *Journal of the Twenty-Seventh Annual Council of the Protestant Episcopal Church in the Diocese of Southern Virginia Held in Trinity Church, South Boston, Virginia* (1919), 241–43.

49. James S. Russell, "Annual Report of the Archdeacon for Colored Work in the Diocese of Southern Virginia," *Journal of the Twenty-Fifth Annual Council of the Protestant Episcopal Church in the Diocese of Southern Virginia Held in Epiphany Church, Danville, Virginia, May 29th–30th, 1917* (1917): 238.

50. "Archdeacon Russell Remains in Virginia," *The Southern Workman* 46, no. 8 (1917): 424.

51. "Man of the Month: An Archdeacon and Educator," *The Crisis* 14, no. 4 (August 1917): 189.

52. Michael J. Beary, *Black Bishop: Edward T. Demby and the Struggle for Racial Equality in the Episcopal Church* (Urbana: University of Illinois Press, 2001), 106–9.

53. Beary, *Black Bishop,* 107. Beary cites a letter between Harry Rahming and Thomas S. Logan Sr. on May 10, 1978, from the private correspondence of the Reverend Canon Thomas S. Logan.

54. Ibid. Beary footnotes his comment using Bragg, *History of Afro-American Group,* 174, and Roberta Arnold's essay written in 1938 in tribute to Russell. Neither document uses the phrase "the art of accommodation" as it might apply to Russell. Indeed, one can surmise from examining Russell's adventures that he may have perfected the art.

55. Ibid..

56. *The Living Church Annual and Churchman's Almanac, 1918* (Milwaukee: The Young Churchman Company, 1918), 69.

57. Several church documents and correspondence of this era use the word "bishopric" instead of "episcopate." Chapter IX of Russell's book is titled "I Decline Calls to the Bishopric."

58. Russell, *Adventure,* 77–8.

59. Russell, *Adventure,* 66–7; Derris L. Raper and Constance M. Jones, *A Goodly Heritage: The Episcopal Diocese of Southern Virginia 1892–1992* (Norfolk: Pictorial Heritage Publishing Company, 1992), 42–3.

60. "Report of the Archdeacon for Colored Work," *Journal of Southern Virginia* (1917): 238.

Chapter Eight

1. Paul Johnson, *The Birth of the Modern: World Society 1815–1830* (New York: HarperCollins, 1991), xvii–xix, 1.

2. Mark A. Noll, *Turning Points: Decisive Moments in the History of Christianity* (Grand Rapids: Baker Books, 1997), 270.

3. William S. Pelletreau, *Historic Homes and Institutions and Genealogy and Family History of New York*, vol. 4 (New York: The Lewis Publishing Company, 1907), 65–67; Lewis, *Steady Beat*, 209; Bragg, *Afro-American Group* 286. N. Peterson Boyd, like Russell, was a native of Mecklenburg County, Virginia. Born in 1876, Boyd attended St. Mark's Parish School in Bracey, Virginia; St. Paul's School in Lawrenceville; and St. Andrew's Divinity School in Syracuse, New York. Russell mentions Boyd several times in his book; in one chapter as an outstanding alumnus of St. Paul's and in another as a valuable contact in the Northern states which helped in fund-raising efforts.

4. Gustav Spiller, *Papers on Inter-Racial Problems Communicated to the First Universal Races Congress Held at the University of London, July 26–29, 1911* (London: P.S. King & Son, 1911), v. The document's preface states in part: "The object of the Congress is 'to discuss, in the light of science and the modern conscience, the general relations subsisting between the peoples of the West and those of the East, between so-called white and so-called coloured peoples, with a view to encouraging between them a fuller understanding, the most friendly feelings, and a heartier co-operation.'"

5. Russell, *Adventure*, 94.

6. The American Church Institute for Negroes (ACIN) was a fundraising agency of the Episcopal Church formed in 1906. One of its purposes was to fund Episcopal schools educating former slaves in the South.

7. Russell, *Adventure*, 94–95.

8. James S. Russell, "Report of the Archdeacon for Colored Work," *Journal of the Twentieth Annual Council of the Protestant Episcopal Church in the Diocese of Southern Virginia Held in St. Paul's Church, Petersburg, Virginia, May 28th to 30th 1912* (1912): 316.

9. Spiller, *Papers*, "Preface," v.

10. Ralph E. Luker, *The Social Gospel in Black and White: American Racial Reform 1885–1912* (Chapel Hill: University of North Carolina Press, 1991), 313.

11. Barbara W. Tuchman, *The Guns of August* (New York: Ballantine Books, 1962), 1.

12. The *Panther* or Agadir (Morocco) incident occurred July 1911, weeks before the Race Congress. The German government sent their gunboat *Panther* to challenge the French government's rights in Morocco.

13. John Colville, *Mystic Light Essays* (New York: Macoy Publishing and Masonic Supply Company, 1913), 255–57.

14. David Levering Lewis, *W.E.B. Du Bois: Biography of a Race* (New York: Henry Holt, 1993), 438–440.

15. Gustav Spiller, *Faith in Man: The Religion of the Twentieth Century* (New York: The McMillan Company, 1908), 9–12.

16. Spiller, *Faith in Man*, 182–85.

17. David L. Lewis, 438–40.

18. Ibid.

19. William Sanders Scarborough, *The Autobiography of William Sanders Scarborough: An American Journey from Slavery to Scholarship*, Michelle Valerie Ronnick, ed. (Detroit: Wayne State University Press, 2005), 218.

20. Russell, *Adventure*, 95.

21. Scarborough, 218.

22. *Dangerous Donations*, 142–146.

23. Samuel Bishop, the first executive director of the ACIN, was an early member of the National Urban League.

24. C.C. Martindale, "Inter-Racial Problems," *The Month: A Catholic Magazine* (UK) 118, no. 568 (October 1911): 353–63.

25. The preamble to the "Inaugural Address of President [J. Stanley] Durkee" given on November 12, 1919, at Howard University, *Inauguration Program Bulletin* (Washington, D.C.: Howard University, 1919), 14.

26. President J. Stanley Durkee's "Welcoming Address" on November 13, 1919, at the Reconstruction and Readjustment Congress, as part of the two-day inaugural ceremonies. *Inauguration Program Bulletin* (Washington, D.C.: Howard University, 1919), 39.

Chapter Nine

1. Shattuck, *Episcopalians and Race*, 12.

2. Russell, *Adventure*, 18.

3. Russell, *Adventure*, 2.

4. Shattuck, *Episcopalians and Race*, 14.

5. Recall that the House of Bishops passed the proposal but the House of Deputies rejected it.

6. The writer of this book understands fully that Gardiner Shattuck's and Harold T. Lewis's books referenced herein are primarily about the struggles of African-American Episcopalians in the twentieth century. Attention paid to the late nineteenth century is minor in their books. This book places it focus or emphasis on the personal interactions or personal transactions between James Solomon Russell and other people. Extended emphasis is placed upon transactions involving numerous types of relationships: black and white; black and black; and white and white. The term "paternalism," used as a broad brush, potentially ignores personal transactions in which blacks and whites cooperated for the common good, and as such modifies the term's traditional definition.

7. The "debate" refers not only to black participation in the church and their separation; it refers to the germinating ideas of separate black missionary districts and black bishops.

8. Shattuck, *Episcopalians and Race*, 28.

9. The concept of a socially dominant or reigning plausibility structure was introduced in Chapter 1.

10. Loretta Funke, "The Negro in Education," *The Journal of Negro History* 5, no. 1 (1920): 2; Craig D. Townsend, *Faith in Their Own Color* (New York: Columbia University Press, 2005), 15–16. Funke cites Carter G. Woodson's book *The Education of the Negro Prior to 1861* as one of her sources. In his index Woodson clearly states, "Bishop of London, declared that the conversion of slaves did not work manumission," but no year was listed. The website known as Dinsmore Documentation (see http://www.dinsdoc.com/jernegan-1.htm; viewed on March 6, 2010) features an article by Marcus W. Jernegan titled "Slavery and Conversion in the American Colonies" from *American Historical Review* 21 (April 1916), wherein he writes on page 511: "Indeed the Bishop of London had declared, in 1727, that Christianity did not make 'the least Alteration in Civil Property; that the Freedom which Christianity gives, is a Freedom from the Bondage of Sin and Satan, and from the Dominion of those Lusts and Passions and inordinate Desires; but as to their outward condition they remained as before even after baptism.'"

11. Russell, *Adventure*, 60; Lewis, *Steady Beat*, 45–46, 176; Bragg, *Afro-American Group*, 43.

12. See the Appendix for a year-to-year summary of the "Report of the Archdeacon for Colored Work."

13. Townsend, *Faith in Their Own Color*, 1–2.

14. Booker T. Washington raised his funds from the North also. But unlike Russell, Washington eventually became a decision-maker and distributor of funds (foundations) to black colleges including St. Paul's.

15. See Rom. 15:14; Gal. 5:21; Eph. 6:4; 1 Thess. 5:14, 21; 1 Tim. 4:6; 2 Tim. 3:16.

16. Russell, *Adventure*, 35–36.

17. See Appendix C below.

18. Raper and Jones, *A Goodly Heritage*, 42–3.

19. Shattuck, *Episcopalians and Race*, 24; Lewis, *Steady Beat*, 97; Beary, *Black Bishop*, 106–9, 118, 128.

20. Russell, *Adventure*, 49–59, Chapter VII "The Living, The Real St. Paul's."

21. The Liberian Humane Order of African Redemption was founded on January 13, 1879, during the presidency of Anthony W. Gardiner. It is awarded for humanitarian work in Liberia, for acts supporting and assisting the Liberian nation, and to individuals who have played a prominent role in the emancipation of African-Americans and the pursuit of equal rights. The Order replaced the older Liberian Lone Star Medal. The three grades of the Order are: *Grand Commander* — The Grand Commander wears a wide ribbon on the right shoulder and the star of the Order on the left; *Knight Commander* — The Knight Commander wears a ribbon around the neck and a smaller but otherwise identical star; *Officer* — The Officer wears a narrow ribbon with rosette on the left.

22. Russell, *Adventure*, 101.

23. Russell, *Adventure*, 115, Appendix; "James Solomon Russell Day Celebrated at St. Paul's," *The Jamestown Cross: The Episcopal Diocese of Southern Virginia* 73, no. 3 (May 2009): 3.

24. Russell, *Adventure*, 108; "2 State Negroes Will Be Honored: J.M. Gandy and J.S. Russell to Receive Awards for Service to Race," *Richmond News-Leader*, January 3, 1929.

25. Russell, *Adventure*, 106.

26. Russell, *Adventure*, 30.

27. Archives of The Episcopal Church; see http://www.episcopalarchives.org/Afro-Anglican_history/exhibit/leadership/russell.php, viewed February 19, 2010.

Bibliography

Books

Alexander, Estrelda Y. *Black Fire: One Hundred Years of African American Pentecostalism.* Downers Grove, IL: InterVarsity Press, 2011.

Alford, Terry. *Prince Among Slaves: The True Story of an African Prince Sold into Slavery in the American South.* New York: Oxford University Press, 1977.

Anderson, Eric, and Alfred A. Moss, Jr. *Dangerous Donations: Northern Philanthropy and Southern Black Education, 1902–1930.* Columbia: University of Missouri Press, 1999.

Anderson, James D. *The Education of Blacks in the South, 1860–1935.* Chapel Hill: University of North Carolina Press, 1988.

Armentrout, Don S., and Robert Boak Slocum. *Documents of Witness: A History of the Episcopal Church 1782–1985.* New York: Church Hymnal Corporation, 1994.

Baketel, Oliver S., ed. *The Methodist Year Book: 1918.* Cincinnati: Methodist Year Book Concern, 1918.

Ballagh, James Curtis. *A History of Slavery in Virginia.* Baltimore: Johns Hopkins Press, 1902.

Beary, Michael J. *Black Bishop: Edward T. Demby and the Struggle for Racial Equality in the Episcopal Church.* Urbana: University of Illinois Press, 2001.

Berger, Peter. *The Sacred Canopy: Elements of a Sociological Theory of Religion.* New York: Anchor Books, 1967.

Besse, H.T. *Church History.* Cleona, PA: Holzapfel, 1908.

Blackmon, Douglas A. *Slavery by Another Name: The Re-Enslavement of Black Americans from the Civil War to World War II.* New York: Anchor Books, 2008.

Bloom, Harold. *The American Religion: The Emergence of the Post-Christian Nation.* New York: Simon & Schuster, 1992.

Booty, John. *The Episcopal Church in Crisis.* Cambridge: Cowley Publications, 1988.

Bracey, Susan. *Life by the Roaring Roanoke: A History of Mecklenburg County, Virginia.* South Hill, VA: The Mecklenburg County Bicentennial Commission, 1977.

Bragg, George Freeman, Jr. *History of the Afro-American Group of the Episcopal Church.* Baltimore: Church Advocate Press, 1922.

Bratton, Theodore DuBose. *Wanted — Leaders: A Study of Negro Development.* New York: Department of Missions and Church Extensions, 1922.

Breen, T.H., and Stephen Innes. *Myne Owne Ground: Race and Freedom on Virginia's Eastern Shore, 1640–1676.* New York: Oxford University Press, 1980.

Bruggeman, Walter. *A Social Reading of the Old Testament: Prophetic Approaches to Israel's Communal Life.* Edited by Patrick D. Miller. Minneapolis: Fortress Press, 1994.

Butler, Benjamin F. *Butler's Book: Autobiography and Personal Reminisces of a Major General*. Boston: A.M. Thayer, 1892.

Caldwell, A.B., ed. "James Solomon Russell." In *History of the American Negro and His Institutions: Virginia Edition*. Vol. 5. Atlanta: A.B. Caldwell, 1921.

Cheshire, Joseph Blount. *The Church in the Confederate States: A History of the Protestant Episcopal Church in the Confederate States*. New York: Longmans, Green, 1912.

Colby, Frank Moore, and Allen Leon Churchill, eds. *The New International Year Book: A Compendium of the World's Progress for the Year 1909*. New York: Dodd, Meade, 1910.

Cromwell, John Wesley. *The Negro in American History: Men and Women Eminent in the Evolution of the American of African Descent*. Washington, D.C.: American Negro Academy, 1914.

Cusic, Don. *The Trials of Henry Flipper, First Black Graduate of West Point*. Jefferson, NC: McFarland, 2009.

Dashiell, T. Grayson. *A Digest of the Proceedings of the Conventions and Councils in the Diocese of Virginia*. Richmond: Wm. Ellis Jones, 1883.

Degler, Carl N. *Neither Black nor White: Slavery and Race Relations in Brazil and the United States*. Madison: University of Wisconsin Press, 1971.

_____. *Out of Our Past: The Forces That Shaped Modern America*. 3rd ed. New York: Harper & Row, 1984.

De Tocqueville, Alexis. *Democracy in America*. New York: Alfred A. Knopf, 1994.

Douglass, Frederick. *Narrative of the Life of Frederick Douglass: An American Slave*. ed. David W. Blight. Boston: Bedford Books, 1993.

Douglass, Harlan Paul. *Christian Reconstruction in the South*. Boston: Pilgrim Press, 1909.

Du Bois, W.E.B. *Black Reconstruction in America*. New York: Oxford University Press, 2007.

_____. *The Souls of Black Folk*. New York: Barnes & Noble Classics, 1903/2003.

Flanagan, Maureen A. *America Reformed: Progressives and Progressivism 1890s–1920s*. New York: Oxford University Press, 2007.

Frazier, E. Franklin. *Black Bourgeoisie*. New York: Free Press Paperbacks, 1957/1985.

Elliott, Mark. *Color-Blind Justice: Albion Tourgee and the Quest for Racial Equality from the Civil War to Plessy v. Ferguson*. Oxford: Oxford University Press, 2006.

Ellison, Ralph. *Invisible Man*. New York: Vintage International, 1990.

Ferguson, Niall. *Empire: The Rise and Demise of the British World Order and the Lessons for Global Power*. New York: Basic Books, 2004.

Foner, Eric. *Reconstruction: America's Unfinished Revolution 1863–1877*. New York: Perennial Classics, 1989.

Fukuyama, Francis. *The Origins of Political Order: From Prehuman Times to the French Revolution*. New York: Farrar, Straus and Giroux, 2011.

Fulton, John. "The Church in the Confederate States." Chapter 8 of *The History of the American Episcopal Church 1587–1883*. Edited by William Stevens Perry. Boston: James R. Osgood, 1885.

Gates, Henry Louis, Jr. *Tradition and the Black Atlantic: Critical Theory in the African Diaspora*. New York: Basic Books, 2010.

Hahn, Steven. *A Nation Under Our Feet: Black Political Struggles in the Rural South from Slavery to the Great Migration*. Cambridge: Harvard University Press, 2003.

Harris, Odell Greenleaf. *The Bishop Payne Divinity School: A History of the Seminary to Prepare Black Men for the Ministry of the Protestant Episcopal Church*. Alexandria: Protestant Episcopal Theological Seminary, 1980.

Heidelberg, Andrew I. *The Norfolk 17: A Personal Narrative on Desegregation in Norfolk, Virginia 1958–1962*. Pittsburgh: Rose Dog Books, 2007.

Holmes, David L. *A Brief History of the Episcopal Church*. Harrisburg, PA: Trinity Press International, 1993.

Innes, Stephen, ed. *Work and Labor in Early America*. Chapel Hill: University of North Carolina Press, 1988.

Irons, Charles F. *The Origins of Proslavery Christianity: White and Black Evangelicals in Colonial and Antebellum Virginia*. Chapel Hill: University of North Carolina Press, 2008.

Isaac, Rhys. *Transformation of Virginia, 1740–1790*. Chapel Hill: University of North Carolina Press, 1982.

Johns, John. *A Memoir of the Life of the Right Rev. William Meade, D.D. Bishop of the Protestant Episcopal Church in the Diocese of Virginia*. Baltimore: Innes, 1867.

Johnson, Paul. *The Birth of the Modern: World Society 1815–1830*. New York: Harper-Collins, 1991.

_____. *Intellectuals*. New York: Harper Perennial, 1988.

_____. *Modern Times: The World from the Twenties to the Nineties*. New York: Harper Perennial, 1983.

Jones, Thomas Jesse. *Negro Education: A Study of the Private and Higher Schools for Colored People in the United States*. Vol. 2, Bulletin 1916, No. 39. Washington, D.C.: United States Bureau of Education, 1916.

Jordan, Winthrop D. *The White Man's Burden: Historical Origins of Racism in the United States*. London: Oxford University Press, 1974.

Koger, Larry. *Black Slave Owners: Free Black Slave Masters in South Carolina, 1790–1860*. Columbia: University of South Carolina Press, 1985.

Lewis, David Levering. *W.E.B. Du Bois: Biography of a Race 1868–1919*. New York: Henry Holt, 1993.

Lewis, Harold T. *Yet with a Steady Beat*. Valley Forge, PA: Trinity Press International, 1996.

Luker, Ralph E. *The Social Gospel in Black and White: American Radical Reform, 1885–1912*. Chapel Hill: University of North Carolina Press, 1991.

McConnell, John Preston. *Negroes and Their Treatment in Virginia from 1865 to 1867*. Pulaski, VA: B.D. Smith, 1910.

Miller, Kelly. "Progress in Education." In *Progress and Achievements of the Colored People*, by Kelly Miller and Joseph R. Gay. Washington, D.C.: Austin Jenkins, 1917.

Morgan, Edmund S. *American Slavery, American Freedom*. New York: W.W. Norton, 1975.

Morgan, Philip D. *Slave Counterpoint: Black Culture in the Eighteen-Century Chesapeake & Lowcountry*. Chapel Hill: University of North Carolina Press, 1998.

Moses, Wilson Jeremiah. *Alexander Crummell: A Study of Civilization and Discontent*. London: Oxford University Press, 1989.

_____. *Creative Conflict in African American Thought*. Cambridge, UK: Cambridge University Press, 2004.

Neale, Gay. *Brunswick County, Virginia, 1720–1975: The History of a Southside Virginia County*. Brunswick County, VA: Brunswick County Bicentennial Committee, 1975.

Noll, Mark A. *The Scandal of the Evangelical Mind*. Grand Rapids, MI: William B. Eerdmans, 1994.

_____. *Turning Points: Decisive Moments in the History of Christianity*. Grand Rapids: Baker Books, 1997.

Norrell, Robert J. *Up from History: The Life of Booker T. Washington*. Cambridge, MA: Belknap Press of Harvard University Press, 2009.

Pelletreau, William S. *Historic Homes and Institutions and Genealogy and Family History of New York*, vol. 4. New York: Lewis, 1907.

Pritchard, Robert. *A History of the Episcopal Church*. Revised edition. Harrisburg, PA: Morehouse, 1999.

Raper, Derris L., and Constance M. Jones. *A Goodly Heritage: The Episcopal Diocese of Southern Virginia 1892–1992.* Norfolk: Pictorial Heritage, 1992.

Richings, G.F. *Evidences of Progress Among Colored People.* 12th ed. Philadelphia: Geo. S. Ferguson, 1905.

Robertson, David. *Denmark Vesey: The Buried Story of America's Largest Slave Rebellion and the Man Who Led It.* New York: Vintage Books, 1999.

Russell, James S. *Adventure in Faith: An Autobiographic Story of St. Paul Normal and Industrial School, Lawrenceville, Virginia.* New York: Morehouse, 1936.

Scarborough, William Sanders. *Williams Sanders Scarborough: An American Journey from Slavery to Scholarship.* Edited by Michele Valerie Ronnick. Detroit: Wayne State University Press, 2005.

Scarisbrick, J.J. *The Reformation and the English People.* Oxford, UK: Blackwell, 1993.

Schofield, J.M. "Doc. No. I. Communication from Major General Schofield." In *Documents of the Constitutional Convention of the State of Virginia.* Richmond: New Nation, 1867.

Shattuck, Gardiner. *Episcopalians and Race: Civil War to Civil Rights.* Lexington: University of Kentucky Press, 2000.

Slaughter, Philip. *A Memoir of the Life of the Right Rev. William Meade, D.D.* Boston: New England Genealogical Society, 1885.

_____. *A Virginian History of African Colonization.* Richmond: MacFarlane & Fergusson, 1855.

Sowell, Thomas. *A Conflict of Visions: Ideological Origins of Political Struggles,* revised edition. New York: Basic Books, 2007.

Spiller, Gustav. *Papers on Inter-Racial Problems Communicated to the First Universal Races Congress Held at the University of London, July 26–29, 1911.* London: P.S. King, 1911.

Steele, Shelby. *White Guilt: How Blacks and Whites Together Destroyed the Promise of the Civil Rights Era.* New York: Harper Perennial, 2007.

Strange, Robert. *Church Work Among the Negroes in the South.* Chicago: Western Theological Seminary, 1907.

Strictland, W.P. *Pioneer Bishop: The Life and Times of Francis Asbury.* New York: Carlton & Porter, 1858.

Talbot, Edith Armstrong. *Samuel Chapman Armstrong: A Biographical Study.* New York: Doubleday, Page, 1904

Townsend, Craig D. *Faith in Their Own Color.* New York: Columbia University Press, 2005.

Tuchman, Barbara W. *The Guns of August.* New York: Ballantine, 1994.

Venerable Bede. *A History of the English Church and People.* Revised by R.E. Latham. Translated by Leo Sherley-Price. New York: Dorset Press, 1968.

Washington, Booker T. *The Booker T. Washington Papers.* Edited by Louis R. Harlan and Raymond Smock. Champagne-Urbana: University of Illinois Press, 1981.

_____. *Up from Slavery.* Garden City, NJ: Double, Page, 1919.

Wilmore, Gayraud S. *Black Religion and Black Radicalism: An Interpretation of the Religious History of Afro-American People.* Maryknoll, NY: Orbis Press, 1986.

Wood, Betty. *Slavery in Colonial America, 1619–1776.* Lanham, MD: Rowman & Littlefield, 2005.

Woodson, Carter G. *The History of the Negro Church.* Washington, D.C.: Associated, 1921.

Work, Monroe N. *Negro Year Book: An Encyclopedia of the Negroes 1914–1915.* Tuskegee: Institute Press, 1914.

Diocesan Journals of Annual Councils

"Bishop's Report." *Journal of the Eighty-Fourth Annual Council in Virginia Held in St. George's Church, Fredericksburg, on the 21st, 22d, 23d, and 24th May, 1879* (1879): 36–37.

Journal of the Fifteenth Annual Council of the Protestant Episcopal Church in the Diocese of Southern Virginia 1907. Report of the Committee of the State of the Church. 1907.

Louisiana, Diocese of. *Thirty-Third Annual Council of the Protestant Episcopal Church in the Diocese of Louisiana, 1874.* New Orleans: James A. Gresham Booksellers and Stationer, 1874

Randolph, A.M. "Address of Bishop Randolph." *Journal of the Ninety-Fourth Annual Council of the Protestant Episcopal Church in Virginia Held in St. Paul's Church, Lynchburg, May 15–17, 1889.*

"Report on Diocesan Colored Work." *Journal of the Eighty-Seventh Annual Council of the Protestant Episcopal Church in Virginia Held in Christ Church, Norfolk, Virginia, May 17, 1882* (1882): 70.

Russell, James S. "Annual Report of the Archdeacon for Colored Work in the Diocese." *Journal of the Thirteenth Annual Council of the Protestant Episcopal Church in the Diocese of Southern Virginia Held in St. John's Church, Wytheville, Virginia, May 30th, 31st, June 1st, 1905,* 1905.

_____. "Annual Report of the Archdeacon for Colored Work in the Diocese." *Journal of the Fourteenth Annual Council of the Protestant Episcopal Church in the Diocese of Southern Virginia Held in Trinity Church, Portsmouth, Virginia, May 29th–31st, 1906,* 1906.

_____. "Annual Report of the Archdeacon for Colored Work in the Diocese." *Journal of the Sixteenth Annual Council of the Protestant Episcopal Church in the Diocese of Southern Virginia Held in Church of the Epiphany, Danville, Virginia, June 11th and 12th, 1908,* 1908.

_____. "Annual Report of the Archdeacon for Colored Work in the Diocease [sic]." *Journal of the Seventeenth Annual Council of the Protestant Episcopal Church in the Diocese of Southern Virginia Held in St. Paul's Church, Newport News, Virginia, May 25th to 27th, 1909,* 1909.

_____. "Annual Report of the Archdeacon for Colored Work in the Diocese of Southern Virginia." *Journal of the Eighteenth Annual Council of the Protestant Episcopal Church in the Diocese of Southern Virginia Held in St. Paul's Church, Lynchburg, Virginia, May 31st to June 2nd, 1910,* 1910.

_____. "Annual Report of the Archdeacon for Colored Work in the Diocese of Southern Virginia." *Journal of the Twenty-Fifth Annual Council of the Protestant Episcopal Church in the Diocese of Southern Virginia Held in Epiphany Church, Danville, Virginia, May 29th–30th, 1917,* 1917.

_____. "Report of the Archdeacon for Colored Work." *Journal of the Twentieth Annual Council of the Protestant Episcopal Church in the Diocese of Southern Virginia, Held in St. Paul's Church, Petersburg, Virginia, May 28th to 30th 1912,* 1912.

"St. Paul's Farmers' Conference." *Southern Workman* 35, no. 9 (September, 1906): 468–69.

Virginia, Diocese of. *Journal of the Seventy-Ninth Annual Council of the Protestant Episcopal Church in Virginia Held in Christ Church, Charlottesville, on the 20th, 21st 22nd & 23rd of May 1874.* Richmond: Clemmitt and Jones, 1874.

Journals

"Archdeacon Russell Remains in Virginia." *The Southern Workman* 46, no. 8 (1917): 424.

Banks, Fred D. "The St. Paul's Farmers' Conference." *Southern Workman* 37, no. 10 (October 1908): 571.

"Black Intellectuals During the Harlem Renaissance." *The Historian* 60, no. 3 (Spring 1998): 487–505.

Bugg Jr., James L. "The French Huguenot Frontier Settlement in Manakin Town." *Virginia Magazine of History and Biography* 61, no. 4 (October 1953): 359–92.

"The Coming Episcopal Convention." *The Independent* 63, no. 3068 (1907): 703.

Eckenrode, Hamilton James. "The Political History of Virginia During Reconstruction." *Johns Hopkins University Studies in Historical and Political Science.* Series 22, nos. 6–8, 1904.

Evans, Maurice S. "International Conference on the Negro." *Journal of the African Society* 11 (1911–12): 416–29.

Funke, Loretta. "The Negro in Education." *The Journal of Negro History* 5, no. 1 (1920): 2.

"Man of the Month: An Archdeacon and Educator." *The Crisis* 14, no. 4 (August 1917): 189.

Russell, James S. "Communications." *The Journal of Negro History* 8, no. 3 (July 1923): 341–44.

"St. Paul School." *Southern Workman* 41, no. 9 (September 1912): 502.

Wood, John W. "The Missionary Story of the General Convention." *The Spirit of Missions: An Illustrated Monthly Review of Christian Missions* 78, no. 11 (November 1913): 769.

Work, Monroe N. "Some Negro Members of Reconstruction Conventions and Legislatures and of Congress." *The Journal of Negro History* 5, no. 1 (January 1920): 63.

Other Sources

Earnest, Joseph B., Jr. "The Religious Development of the Negro in Virginia." Ph.D. diss., University of Virginia, 1914.

Goodwin, W.A.R. "The Church's Missions in Christendom: A Speech Given on Race Problems in America." In vol. 6, section E, special issue, *Pan-Anglican Congress 1908* (1908): 123–25.

Heyrman, Christine Leigh. "The Church of England in Early America." Divining America, TeacherServe®. National Humanities Center. June 30, 2011. http://nationalhumanitiescenter.org/tserve/eighteen/ekeyinfo/chureng.htm.

Hinton, Albert. "3 Bishops, 40 Priests Among 3,000 at J.S. Russell Rites." *Norfolk Journal and Guide*, April 6, 1935.

Howard University Program Ceremony Bulletin. *The Inauguration of J. Stanley Durkee, A.M., Ph.D. As President of Howard University November 12, 1919 and the Readjustment and Reconstruction Congress, November 13, 1919.* Washington, D.C.: Howard University, 1919.

The Living Church Annual and Churchman's Almanac, 1918. Milwaukee: Young Churchman, 1918.

A Memorial to the Bishop and Convention of the Diocese of North Carolina: By the Colored Convocation Asking for a Missionary Jurisdiction for the Colored People — May 13–15, 1913. Tarboro: Diocese of North Carolina, 1913.

New York Times. "Mary Benson Leaves $609,781." August 13, 1919.

Russell, John Henderson. "The Free Negro in Virginia: 1619–1865." Ph.D. diss., Johns Hopkins University, 1913.

Russell, Ulysses W. "James Solomon Russell: Priest, Educator, Humanitarian." Master's thesis, Virginia State College, 1962.

Supreme Court of the United States. *James Holly vs. The Domestic and Foreign Missionary Society* [DFMS], No. 138 of October Term, 1900. In *The Supreme Court of the United States*, Record No. 17,523.

Thurman, Frances Ashton, "The History of St. Paul's College, Lawrenceville, Virginia, 1888 to 1959." Ph.D. diss., Howard University, 1979.

Virginia, Commonwealth of. *Virginia: A Guide to the Old Dominion*. American Guide Series. Compiled the Virginia Writers' Forum. Richmond: Virginia Conservation Commission; Federal Works Agency; Works Project Administration, 1940.

"A Wonderful Work Among the Plantation Negroes." *The Churchman* 39 (March 1, 1879): 18–23.

Index